RABINDRANATH TAGORE
I Won't Let You Go
SELECTED POEMS

NEW EXPAND~~ED~~   BY

KE~~TA~~   ⌡

BLOODAXE BOOKS

Copyright © Ketaki Kushari Dyson 1991, 2010

ISBN: 978 1 85224 898 7

First edition published 1991.
Second expanded edition published 2010 by
Bloodaxe Books Ltd,
Highgreen,
Tarset,
Northumberland NE48 1RP.

www.bloodaxebooks.com
For further information about Bloodaxe titles
please visit our website or write to
the above address for a catalogue.

Supported by
**ARTS COUNCIL
ENGLAND**

Printed in Great Britain by
Bell & Bain Limited, Glasgow, Scotland.

Dedicated to the tercentenary
of the city of Calcutta

Rabindranath Tagore in 1875.

Contents

12

Preface to the Second Edition

As I sit down to write a preface to this new edition of work first undertaken twenty years ago, I am thinking of Professor Nemai-sadhan Bose, at that time the Vice-Chancellor of Visvabharati, who had persuaded me to undertake the project. He is no longer with us. How he would have loved to hear that this book was receiving a new, enlarged edition! When he had first asked me to translate a selection of Tagore's poems into English, I had accepted the task more as a challenge than anything else, and not without a degree of trepidation. In the end doing the work proved to be a rewarding and absorbing experience. To select poems for translation I had to immerse myself in Tagore's poetic corpus for an extended period, and such sustained immersion in the work of a great poet is always a reward in itself. The process of transferring the poetry to the English language was both a pleasurable re-creative activity and an educative experience.

My remit, as I understood it, was to take Tagore's poetry to those who could not access him in the original language, but could read him in English, and make them see that he was a great poet. Over the years so many – both Westerners and non-Bengali-speaking Indians – have thanked me for revealing to them Tagore's great-ness as a poet that going by such feedback, a measure of success may indeed be claimed for the translation project envisioned and initiated by the late Professor Nemaisadhan Bose. Personally for me, it has led to further important work in Tagore studies and also in literary translation. I have also received invitations to semi-nars, conferences, and workshops, and requests to write on trans-lation issues and review works of translation. Besides many such articles in Bengali and English scattered in magazines, I have also prefixed prefaces to two other subsequent works of translation, explaining the rationale of my work methods.

In the 1950s the work of the great Bengali poet-translators of the post-Tagore era impacted on my generation. They were my inspiration in my first serious work of poetry translation, done in the mid-sixties, when I translated examples of Anglo-Saxon poetry into alliterative Bengali half-lines. The first fruits of those efforts were published with a preface in *Visvabharati Patrika* in 1971, and years later a little anthology of eleven pieces was published (*Anglo-Saxon Kabita*, Navana, Calcutta, 1987). My thinking on transla-tion issues has developed from those beginnings. Those who are interested to gain a quick overview of the conceptual framework within which I currently translate may look up a short article in English available on the Internet, based on a presentation I made at a conference at the University of Hyderabad in January 2009.[1] The Tagore translation project has indeed been fruitful in my overall literary life, generating opportunities for new work.

I would like to say a few words on the new translations incorporated in the present edition. The two poems from *Nabajatak* (1940) were published in a special issue of the *Visva-bharati Quarterly* commemorating Tagore's fiftieth death anniversary[2] and were translated at the request of Professor Shyamal Kumar Sarkar, who was the journal's editor at that time. The poem 'The Year 1400' from *Chitra* (1896) was translated for an event to celebrate the advent of the year 1400 according to the Bengali calendar. This event, jointly organised in 1993 by the Nehru Centre of the High Commission of India in London and the Tagore Centre of London, was held in the premises of the Nehru Centre, and I read out the poem on that occasion. It was subsequently published in the web magazine *Parabaas* (www.parabaas.com). The dramatic poem 'Dialogue between Karna and Kunti', from the collection *Kahini* (1900), was translated in the spring of 2000 at the request of Bithika Raha of London, who choreographed a dance performance to accompany the words. It was later published in the above-mentioned web magazine *Parabaas*. The background of this poem is elucidated in the Notes section.

The three poems from *Gitanjali* (1910) included in the poems section of this edition have been done specially for this edition. One Bengali critic had lamented the absence of any patriotic song in the first edition of this book, and I have always wished to make amends. Rummaging for suitable samples of patriotic sentiment in Tagore's word-hoard, I felt that I could do no better than translate three highly regarded poems from the Bengali *Gitanjali*, nos. 106, 107, and 108, but decided that they had to be presented as poems rather than as songs. Let me explain why.

No. 106 was set to music by Tagore, but only the first, second, and final stanzas were admitted to the 'Swadesh' or patriotic section of the definitive collection of his songs, the *Gitabitan*, and I did not wish to present this great poem in a truncated form. No. 108 was never set to music by Tagore himself, but another musician, with Tagore's permission, set it to music and recorded it. In that incarnation the song is familiar enough to Bengalis, and in my growing years I have heard it too, broadcast over the radio, but this lyric has never been included in the *Gitabitan* and is not technically a 'Tagore song', which is defined as a piece in which both the words and the melody are compositions of Tagore's. No. 107 is indeed a song and is included in the *Gitabitan*, but in the section marked as 'Puja' or 'worship', not under the banner of patriotism. This cluster of poems written in the first week of July 1910 may be regarded as companion pieces revealing some of the deepest layers of Tagore's thinking about his homeland. First he elaborates and praises what he regards as his country's greatest strength and most precious heritage: its embodiment of multi-racial, multicultural unity-in-diversity, offering a paradigm for the future development of all humanity.

No. 106 of *Gitanjali* contains, in a highly rhetorical and embellished form, that message of universal humanism – patriotic pride ∗ transcending itself and becoming an expression of transnational humanistic aspiration – that many international scholars of Tagore are now eager to claim and emphasise as one of the noblest intellectual heritages that Tagore has left behind for posterity. As we know, some years later, with the First World War revealing its horrors, Tagore would move away quite decisively from the European model of the nation-state, based on competition, aggression, and self-aggrandisement. He would reject everything that was divisive. Even in this mainly celebratory poem, no. 106 of *Gitanjali*, the perils of social division are not forgotten. The poem is followed by a searing acknowledgement of his country's caste-divided socio-economic structure, with its large underclass (no. 107), and a dire warning about the future if this state of affairs is not rectified (no. 108). Though a song-structure is plain in each poem, especially in an emphatic use of the refrain, these poems are not really in the same category as the more tender, God-yearning songs of *Gitanjali* which are clearly wrung from his personal bereavements, but are more in the nature of radical social discourses challenging orthodoxies. No. 107 resonates with no. 119 (not translated here), in which God is located where the manual workers are, labouring in the fields, digging roads, come sun, come rain.

We have to remember that these poems were written long before Gandhi started his struggle for the outcastes, calling them 'Harijans' ('God's people'). When Tagore was writing these poems, Gandhi was still in South Africa. It is in the modality of social discourse that such poems have been formative influences on the consciousness of Bengalis growing up in the twentieth century. They have acted as seminal texts, showing the poet-songmaker, the patriot,

15

and the angry prophet combined in the most creative way. Together with other works in his corpus, such as his drama *Chandalika* (1933), re-shaped as a dance-drama in 1938, emphatically rejecting untouchability and proclaiming the common humanity of all classes of society, such texts have left permanent marks on the intellectual and political life of Bengalis.

I should also mention here that in its theme and imagery no. 106 of *Gitanjali* bears a striking resemblance to a song written a year or so later and sung at the annual session of the Indian National Congress held in Calcutta over 26-28 December 1911. That song, 'Janaganamana-adhinayaka', sung in chorus on 27 December, the second day of the Congress session, was eventually selected to become independent India's national anthem.

This is an appropriate moment to remember Prasantakumar Pal, the biographer of Tagore, whose death in 2007 is a sad loss in the field of Tagore scholarship. We are indebted to him for the massive amount of documentary material that he gathered and brought to bear on Tagore's life, bringing the story of that life up to 1925-26 in nine densely packed, encyclopedic volumes. Pal connects the genesis of the three *Gitanjali* poems I have been discussing, nos. 106, 107, and 108, with a discussion Tagore had conducted, by means of correspondence, with an American lawyer interested in and sympathetic to India, named Myron H. Phelps. Trying to explain to Phelps the origins of the caste system, Tagore said that it had evolved in India through the process of history, in an attempt to accommodate the many different races that had met on Indian soil. Unlike the white races who had decimated the indigenous populations of America and Australia in order to establish their hegemony, the Aryans who came to India arranged society in a hierarchical order, according to colour and occupation. Later arrivals from other geographical regions of the world were absorbed and incorporated in the same way.

Tagore called this ordering a 'mechanical arrangement and juxtaposition, not cohesion and amalgamation', and commented that 'unfortunately, the principle[,] once accepted[,] grows deeper and deeper into the constitution of the race even after the stress of the original necessity ceases to exist'. He believed that acceptance of this arrangement had accustomed Indians 'for centuries not only to submit to every form of domination, but sometimes actually to venerate the power' that held them down. The foreign rule that then prevailed in India was the political consequence of the country's social malady, but it nevertheless had its positive side as a historical event, in that it had initiated a process of rejuvenation. 'The vivifying warmth from outside is gradually making us conscious of our own vitality and the newly awakened life is making its way slowly, but surely, even through the barriers of caste. [...] If at this stage vital help has come from the West even in the guise of an alien rule, India must submit – nay welcome it, for above all she must achieve her life's work.' And what was that 'life's work'? He passionately believed that it was India's destiny 'that East and West should find their meeting place in her ever hospitable bosom'. No. 106 of *Gitanjali* is the poetic articulation of this credo.[3] After the end of the First World War, Visvabharati was founded to embody this noble dream.

The section of song-lyrics in this edition has been significantly expanded, with seventeen new songs, fifteen of which have been raided from the larder of *Gitanjali*. There were only two songs from this collection in the previous edition, and I had felt for some time that the collection had been under-represented. I am delighted that I have now been able to rectify that shortcoming.

Several years back I had begun a sheaf of draft translations from *Gitanjali*, but having then put them aside in favour of some other writing commitment, had managed to forget about them completely. Finding the papers accidentally in a folder was like discovering a partially drawn map which presented me with a new challenge: the cartography cried out to be completed. I was spurred to finalise the drafts and soon came under the spell of the simple but mind-altering pieces, lyrics which could be described as psychedelic in the best, most positive sense. These inner dialogues between the poet's 'I' and 'Thou' are so compelling that they give us an insight into the nature of faith and the way it helps some people to survive the most gruelling ordeals. Overall, they are in the *bhakti* tradition, but within a more universal, more humanistic, Baul-influenced paradigm, not affiliated to any particular deity or mythology. They do not lean on any names like Krishna or Shiva, and in them faith and doubt, hope and sadness are in a continuous state of flux, ebbing and flowing in total psychological honesty.

They also gave me an insight into the manner in which such writings often crystallise into 'sacred texts' in human traditions. In the first place, the poet tries to put his fingers on an elusive dimension of human existence which is difficult to intellectualise, but contact with which is nevertheless intermittently (and deeply) felt. In leaving us delicately chiselled memoirs of those efforts and experiences, the poet creates cultural artefacts, touching which in turn mimics for us the original quest: we as readers can then hold on to such texts and cherish them as precious inscribed tablets. The beauty of Tagore's spiritual songs is that they are deeply moving, but not dogmatic. No one clutching them to his heart is likely to violate himself or others as a result of that attachment. Some of the songs are rich in humour and laughter as well.

The addition of several new songs from *Gitanjali* has meant a slight adjustment in the sequencing of the songs. The original ordering had been chronological. The present ordering is still mainly so, except that all the seventeen songs from *Gitanjali*, written over a four-year span, have been kept together for convenience and presented in the order intended by the poet, after which the chronological ordering of the remaining songs is resumed.

Special thanks are due to Dr Purnendu Bikash Sarkar of Gitabitan Archive, Calcutta, for checking and double-checking the dates of composition for the songs in this volume, using all the available sources. This help has been invaluable and is deeply appreciated.

The original Introduction has been left well alone, with one silent correction. That correction is in respect of Annapurna Turkhud's age and is due to the researches of Dr Ghulam Murshid of London, who has proved, by checking the document of Annapurna's marriage to Harold Littledale, that she was three, not six, years older than Rabindranath. One minor change in the wording of a poem had already been done in the 1996 reprinting of this book. The only significant change in the text of a poem in this edition is in the very first poem, 'The Suicide of a Star', where the star has changed its gender; the reason for my decision is provided in a new note on the poem. The poem 'Death-dream' has an additional note appended to the original note, in response to a view expressed by a critic. The additional poems and songs included in this edition have necessarily generated some additions in the critical apparatus.

When I prepared the first edition of this book, I had access to only four volumes of Prasantakumar Pal's multi-volume biography of Tagore. Since then five more volumes have seen the light of day. In the light of the new volumes, it has been possible to retrieve the A.D. dates of a few more poems and songs. It has also been possible to withdraw question marks after some places of composition. Editors have been ultra-conservative in the past, not accepting, it would seem, either the place or the date of composition of a piece unless explicitly given in Tagore's own hand on the manuscript. But where extensive biographical researches by scholars like Pal have helped to eliminate previous doubts, I have accepted their conclusions and withdrawn interrogation marks.

Another small point needs to be clarified. The printed volumes of Tagore's poetry tend to indicate Bolpur or Santiniketan beneath a piece in a somewhat indifferent manner. For poems written in the nineteenth century or the early twentieth century the name Bolpur is usually used. In a later period we notice that 'Bolpur' is being definitively replaced by 'Santiniketan'. Tagore's father had actually acquired the land near Bolpur in the early 1860s, and a legal document registering that acquisition indicates that already by March 1863 he had built a small house there, naming it Santiniketan ('the abode of peace').[4] A house, and some land around it: that is how the new place began. In spite of founding his school there in 1901, Tagore, in his manuscripts and letters, continued for many years to refer to the place simply as Bolpur.

In those days Santiniketan was naturally seen as an extension of Bolpur. For the most part, the nomenclature does not really matter, but because of the larger number of pieces from *Gitanjali* included in the present edition, the oscillation between the two names within the same collection became uncomfortable to my editorial eye. Bolpur, of course, is still the railway station where we get off to visit Santiniketan, and most of us take a cycle-rickshaw to continue the journey. It is just three kilometres or roughly a couple of miles from the station to the campus post office. But Bolpur has now become a bustling country town, with its own complex, inevitably ambiguous, set of attitudes towards its near neighbour. On the one hand, it is interested in making the most of the influx of tourists and all those who pass through it, and is conscious of its strategic position as the point of entry for those who arrive by rail for proceeding to Santiniketan. On the other hand, it is now proud of its own civic identity and does not wish to be regarded as a mere annexe to its internationally famous neighbour. It is embedded in local and regional politics, whereas Visvabharati is a university under the charge of the Central Government. There are inevitably frictions and tensions. Given these minutiae of the contemporary scenario, I did not wish to confuse readers by letting them imagine that while writing some of the *Gitanjali* poems in this locale, Tagore was somehow commuting between two adjoining spots in a random manner. Pal in his narrative mode in his biographical tomes leans to the name 'Santiniketan', though in some lists that he provides, following manuscript sources, 'Bolpur' is also used. Unable to resolve this anomaly in any other way, I have, in the context of *Gitanjali*, adopted a common-sense solution: for all the pieces from this collection written in this particular location I have hyphenated the two names, calling the place 'Bolpur-Santiniketan'. I have noticed that Pal does occasionally refer to the location exactly in this hyphenated way in the first volume of his biography.[5]

When working on the first edition, I had to consult the first and second volumes of Pal's biography of Tagore in their first editions, published by Bhurjapatra. The first volume of the book in my personal collection is still the Bhurjapatra edition. In 1989 when I was working in Santiniketan, the second volume had already become unavailable in the market, so all consultation had to be in the library, or perhaps someone, perhaps Pal himself, kindly lent me a copy – I have forgotten the exact circumstance. All nine volumes of the book are now published by Ananda, and the second volume in my possession is also the Ananda edition, bought on a subsequent visit. As a result, when compiling new notes for this edition, I have had no option but to consult the second volume in its second edition, though the older references to the same volume remained to the Bhurjapatra edition. I felt uncomfortable about this, as the pagination seems to have changed significantly between those two editions, so I tried to chase the references in order to provide additional references to the second volume in its second edition. I have tried my best in this respect, and apologise if by chance I have missed any instance where the reference to Pal's second volume is solely to its first edition.

Remembering all those who welcomed the first edition of this book and thinking also of all those who feel strongly that we should continue to widen Tagore's readership, let me make one concluding point. It takes time to educate a new reading public about a poet from a different linguistic-literary tradition, especially in a period when poetry, though continuing to be extremely important to those who write it, does not seem to be a fast-flowing current of mainstream cultural activity in many societies, and does not occupy a central place in education (as it certainly did in my youth). To win new readers for a poet when they do not know that poet's original language, the translations must of course have the pulse of poetry to attract them in the first place, but in the end reception is always a two-way process. Different languages give us different ways of relating to the world. In culture as in nature, it is in cherishing diversity that hopes for a healthy evolution lie, and not in any globalised monoculture that flippantly refuses to see any value in what others value. Readers of translated poetry must themselves be prepared to do some homework. They have to be curious about how others view and classify the world. They need to learn to tolerate the different, adjusting to slightly different angles of vision, and extend a courteous welcome to the unexpected.

When we Bengalis discovered the English poets in the nineteenth century, we eagerly claimed them as part of our common human heritage. Likewise in the twentieth century we claimed several poets from other European languages. Without a vibrant wish to know and greet others, and claim them as part of our extended family, a true expansion of our mental horizons cannot take place. Within India, there needs to be more learning of each other's languages and more direct translation between the country's many languages, without relying on a link language.

As I turn the pages of Tagore's works, I really wish I could have translated even more poems and songs – I see dozens and dozens of pieces I would have loved to translate – but life is short, and art is long, and a book of translated poetry has to be of a certain size to be vendible in a given market. If the right opportunity comes my way, maybe I shall translate some more Tagore pieces another time – who knows! – but I have no doubt that if humankind and poetry survive, many more poems and songs from Tagore's oceanic corpus will be translated in the years to come, and not just into English, but into many other languages of this wide world.

1. 'Translation: the magical bridge between cultures' [www.parabaas.com/translation/database/translations/essays/kkd_translation.html]. Interested readers may also look up various book reviews done by me in the same web magazine's translation section; my 'Translator's Prologue' to my play *Night's Sunlight*, translated from the Bengali by myself (Virgilio Libro, Kidlington, Oxon, 2000); my 'Translator's Testament' in my *Selected Poems of Buddhadeva Bose*, Oxford University Press, Delhi, 2003; and my article 'Prasanga: Anubad' in *Sahitya Parishat Patrika*, vol. 113, nos. 1-2, Baishakh-Ashwin 1413 (October 2006).

2. *The Visva-bharati Quarterly*, New Series, Volume 2, Numbers 1-4: May 1991 – April 1992.

3. Pal, *Rabijibani*, vol. 6, Ananda Publishers Private Limited, Calcutta, 1993, pp. 48-49. Tagore wrote to Phelps from Santiniketan on 4 January 1909; revised and polished, the letter was published in the August 1910 issue of the *Modern Review* under the title 'The Problem of India'.

4. Pal, *Rabijibani*, vol. 1, 1st edition (Bhurjapatra, Calcutta, 1982), pp. 50-52.

5. E.g., Pal, Rabijibani, vol. 1, 1st edition, p. 179.

[2010]

Acknowledgements

This translation project was initiated by Visvabharati University, Santiniketan, West Bengal, India. I would like to thank Nemai-sadhan Bose for having invited me to undertake this project during his vice-chancellorship of Visvabharati. A translation bursary from Southern Arts enabled me to begin the work in England; a Visiting Professorship attached to Rabindra Bhavana, Visvabharati, allowed me to concentrate on the work in Santiniketan for a period of three months; and a grant from the British Council enabled me to travel to India. It was a pleasure to be attached to Rabindra Bhavana not only because of the cooperation I received from the entire staff while I was working there, but also because everyone made me feel completely at home: I was like a member of a family. I would like to give my warmest thanks to Satyendra-nath Roy, Dwijadas Bandyopadhyay, Sanatkumar Bagchi, Supriya Ray, Indrani Das, Ashis Hajra, Nandakishor Mukhopadhyay, Sadha-na Majumdar, Sushobhan Adhikary, Shubhra Shil, Prasantakumar Pal, and Deviprasanna Chattopadhyay. Indrani Das gave a great deal of her time to help me to select suitable photographs for this book from Rabindra Bhavana's archival collection of photographs. I am grateful to Prasantakumar Bhanja and Indranil Bhattacharya of the Music Department for explaining certain musical terms to me; to Kashinath Bhattacharya, Ashiskumar Gupta, Pijushkanti Dan, and Badal Dutta of the Botany Department for preparing a list of relevant botanical names; and to Sankha Ghosh, Professor-Director of Rabindra Bhavana for a period until his return to Jadavpur University, and Amlan Datta, a former Vice-Chancellor of Visvabharati, for checking certain points and answering certain queries. Thanks are due to friends at other departments of Visvabharati who were encouraging and supportive, to Robert Sykes, formerly at the British Council, Calcutta, for his cooperation, and to Ashoke Sen of Calcutta for lending me various relevant publications.

As always, I am indebted to my husband Robert for "topping up" in every kind of support in the final months given to the preparation of this manuscript. I would like to thank Neil Astley of Bloodaxe Books on behalf of both myself and Visvabharati for the decision to publish this volume.

[1991]

List of Illustrations

23

*The earliest known photograph of Tagore, developed from
a group photograph taken in 1873.*

24

Introduction to the First Edition

Indian achievements are not an easy subject to introduce to a Western audience. A vague awareness of the Indian subcontinent as the homeland of an ancient civilisation is indeed diffused in the minds of the educated Western public, and a more active interest exists in limited circles, members of which are aware of India as a land of many races and languages, and as the nursery of some of the world's major religions. But these things are countered by ambivalent images projected by the media and popular publications: of a land of contrasts between riches and poverty, of palaces and slums, bazaars and beggars, elephants and rickshaws, holy men and sacred cows, a land whose main claim to importance is that it was the theatre of imperial British activities in the recent past, but which is now an ex-colonial nation struggling hard to "develop" itself, a member of that hapless 'Third World', the performance of which in any field of human activity is almost never to be taken seriously by the side of the West's own achievements, especially the achievements of that part of the West which likes to think of itself as 'the advanced industrial nations'. To an audience bombarded by such images, and possibly further confused by the rhetoric of this or that pundit who from time to time appropriates the sole right to "interpret" India to outsiders, how does one begin to suggest that India may have given the world one of the greatest poets of modern times, that he was, in fact, born in Calcutta, a city whose very name evokes the most negative associations in most Western minds? How does one establish an appropriate context in which such a figure may be introduced?

One fruitful approach to the subject is via a route which brings the West itself into the picture, a quick effort of "awareness raising", drawing attention to the nexus that has existed between India and the West in historical times, and to the important role that India has played over the centuries in a number of those developments, economic, social, political, intellectual, and artistic, that the West takes for granted in modern times.

Elements have been contributed by India to the development of European civilisation from the earliest times, through material goods, orally transmitted lore, translated texts, and religious and philosophical ideas brought over by merchants ever since the establishment of contact between Greece and India in the 4th century B.C. India very probably contributed to the doctrine of

25

divine incarnation on which the edifice of Christianity rests. The fables of the *Panchatantra* reached Europe through a chain of translations, reincarnating themselves in many European languages, including English, and the famous French versions of La Fontaine. The mathematics of Europe most certainly derived benefit from the decimal system of notation which the Arabs brought to Europe from India. The kitchens of Europe were enriched by pepper, ginger, sugar, and rice – all these words are of Indian origin – and the looms of India satisfied the Roman aristocracy's needs for muslin drapery. Lured by spices, textiles, precious stones, and other luxury items, European traders came to India by the overland route, and the contribution made by this commerce to the flowering of the Italian Renaissance could not have been insignificant. Then it was their anxiety to reach India by sea, avoiding the Middle East, that led not only to the discovery of the sea-route to the East via the Cape of Good Hope, but also to the European discovery of the New World. The manufacture of cotton fabrics established itself in Britain, first by learning from, then strangling, the equivalent industry in India. Not only did India provide some of the capital that enabled the Industrial Revolution to take off in Britain, but many of the basic patterns of the new British textile industries, from checks and floral prints to the tear-drop or Paisley motif, also came from India. Daily living was spiced up by curries and cleansed by the exotic habit of bathing the whole body and hair. The very word *shampoo*, now current in so many European languages, is of Indian origin...

The scene of many cultural confrontations since the earliest times, India became, in the eighteenth and nineteenth centuries, the ground of an East-West encounter on a grand scale, generating more than one movement which could be called a renaissance, the ripples of which are still travelling outwards today. The European Enlightenment's discovery of India's ancient history, languages, religious traditions, and cultural heritage in general, the discovery that there was such a thing as an Indo-European family of languages, led to the emergence of Europe's modern Oriental scholarship, the growth of comparative studies in philology, mythology, and religion, changing Europe's intellectual horizon for all times, directing eyes beyond the Judaeo-Christian framework and opening doors to the liberal thinking of modern times. Parallel to that, there was an Indian discovery of Western thought and learning, starting with the response of the Bengali intelligentsia to Western education. As a result of these two events working together, there was a notable intellectual ferment and cultural revival in India, beginning in Bengal and spreading to the rest of the subcontinent. Some of the movements and personalities associated with this re-awakening have had world-wide impact. Democratic self-government was supposed by many theorisers to be for white nations only, not for Asiatics who were used to 'Oriental despotism'; so when the Indian elite claimed it for their country, their daring and creative leap of aspiration became a model for non-white nations. The Indian struggle for independence from colonial rule gave the impetus and inspiration to the process of internal and external decolonisation in many other areas of the world. Gandhian influences have worked on prominent activists and movements of our times like Martin Luther King, the peace movement, and the Green movement. Less well-known, outside restricted specialist circles, is the contribution made to twentieth-century revolutionary thinking by that remarkable personality, M.N. Roy, who participated in revolutionary movements in India, Mexico, Germany, the USSR and China, founded the Communist Party of Mexico, worked alongside Lenin, and founded the radical humanist movement of India. It is also well worth remembering that during the period of British rule in India certain issues of social reform which were major battles in Britain were won in India with less struggle. For instance, the first women to graduate from Calcutta University did so in 1883, just five years after the permission to hold an official degree was given to women by London University, but decades before such permission was granted by either Oxford or Cambridge.[1] In archaeology, anthropology, geology, geodesy and surveying, zoology, botany, ornithology, and other disciplines, notable advances were made because of the opportunities for work that the Indian subcontinent presented in these areas.

It is against these rich, three-dimensional, historical realities, and not against a ragged, two-dimensional, hastily put together 'Third World' backdrop, that we should see the life and work of Rabindranath Tagore (1861-1941), India's greatest modern poet and the most brilliant creative genius of the Indian Renaissance. His life-span was roughly coeval with that of British imperial rule in India, his birth coming within three years of its formal commencement and his death just six years before its dissolution. He was born on 7 May 1861 at the Tagore family home in Jorasanko, Calcutta, into a rich and talented family that had already begun to make its mark on contemporary society. For the elite of undivided

The house at Jorasanko, Calcutta, where Tagore was born.

Bengal it was an exciting time, despite the British presence, and indeed partly because of the new things that were happening because of that very presence. The East India Company had been in power in Bengal for a hundred years. The British had just defused the challenge to their authority in India posed by the rebellion of 1857, eased the East India Company of its powers, and brought their Indian territories under the direct rule of the British crown. Calcutta was the centre of British power in India and the second most important city, after London, in the British Empire. The Tagores had become active participants in the intellectual and artistic reawakening which was rapidly gaining momentum and approaching its high noon.

The name Tagore is an anglicised version of Thakur, the *t* being hard, cerebral, and aspirated, and is actually a surname that was acquired by the family only accidentally, the real family surname having been Kushari. In the last decade of the seventeenth century, Rabindranath's ancestor Panchanan Kushari settled in Gobindapur, one of the three villages which went into the making of Calcutta, and earned his living by supplying provisions to the foreign ships which sailed up the Ganges. Being a brahmin, he was respectfully addressed by the locals as 'Panchanan Thakur', Thakur being something like 'Sir', and it was this honorific addition to the first name (just like 'Devi' for women) which was taken by the foreign merchants to be a surname and which stuck to the family.[2]

The foundations of the family's material prosperity were laid in the eighteenth century in the stewardship of European merchants, its rise going hand in hand with the rise of Calcutta as a commercial and political centre, the point from which the British were consolidating their power in the subcontinent. It was, as we have just seen, a brahmin family, but from a clan which had, at one stage of its history, in the fifteenth century, been forced to climb down some steps in the ladder of honour.[3] This demoted rank gave the Tagores a distance from mainstream brahmin orthodoxy and an inclination to try out new ideas.

The family acquired special prestige under the dynamic leadership of Rabindranath's grandfather, Dwarakanath Tagore (1794–1846), who acquired large landed estates, built up a substantial business empire, fraternised with the European community, and was generous in his public charities. A close friend of Rammohan Ray, one of the front-rank thinkers and activists of the Bengal Renaissance, Dwarakanath took an active interest in all the progressive causes of his time and was involved in the foundation and patronage of some of the major cultural and educational institutions of Calcutta, such as the Hindu College (which later became the Presidency College) and the Medical College. To break down the orthodox Hindu prejudice against the dissection of dead bodies, he would be personally present when medical students did their dissections. He became the first Indian member of the Asiatic Society of Bengal, which had been founded by the distinguished Orientalist Sir William Jones and which was responsible for the sponsorship of a great deal of scholarship in both the humanities and the sciences. Dwarakanath's life-style and views were unorthodox enough to alienate his wife, Digambari Devi, who in the end lived apart from him. He defied the ban which the Hindu orthodoxy of the time had imposed on sea-voyages, travelled to Europe twice, met Max Müller in Paris, and Queen Victoria and her court, and actually died in London. His business empire did not survive him, but he left enough landed estates for the comfortable survival of the next two generations.

Dwarakanath's eldest son, Debendranath (1817–1905), at first enjoyed the luxury in which he had been reared, but then came a reaction. He was devoted to his grandmother, at whose deathbed, as a young man, he had his first intense spiritual experience. He

Rabindranath Tagore in Brighton, 1878.

wrote about it in later life in his autobiography, which is a Bengali classic. He revived the reformed Hindu sect known as the Brahmo Samaj, which had been founded by Rammohan Ray, but he did not share Rammohan's keen interest in social reform. Compared to the views of other Indian radicals of the nineteenth century, Debendranath's views on matters like caste rules and the role of women were more orthodox. The greatest love of his life was the *Upanishads*, the discovery of which was yet another spiritual revelation in his life, also recorded in his autobiography. An interesting character with a somewhat British-Victorian flavour, he combined within himself a level-headed businessman, a puritan with a stern sense of duty, a patriarch who fathered fifteen children, and an authentic spiritual searcher. His sense of duty made him take on his dead father's business debts, though he had no legal obligation to do so, and pay everything off with scrupulous care over the years. The streak of austerity in his character might have been derived from his mother, who, as we have just seen, disapproved of her husband's modern ways and was estranged from him.

Records left of Debendranath's wife, Sarada Devi, portray her as a pious woman devoted to her husband and an astute matron in charge of her vast household. She cultivated the habit of reading religious works in Bengali. Rabindranath was her fourteenth child. The fifteenth child did not survive infancy, so Rabindranath was effectively his parents' youngest offspring.

Many members of the Tagore family are famous in their own right in the annals of Bengal. Dwijendranath, the eldest son of Debendranath and Sarada Devi, was an eccentric genius who interested himself in poetry, philosophy, mathematics, and music, among other things. Satyendranath, the second son, became the first Indian member of the Indian Civil Service and was a champion of female education. With his encouragement, his wife, Jnanadanandini Devi, became a smart and articulate woman. Indira Devi, the daughter of Satyendranath and Jnanadanandini, was given a sophisticated education, married the writer Pramatha Chaudhuri, and enjoyed a close friendship with her uncle Rabindranath. Jyotirindranath, the fifth son of Debendranath, was a talented painter, musician, and playwright; his wife, Kadambari Devi, who played a role in the artistic development of her brother-in-law Rabindranath, took a keen interest in contemporary Bengali writing, and in the literary, dramatic, and musical activities of the Tagore household. One of Rabindranath's sisters, Swarnakumari Devi, became the first woman writer of fiction in a modern Indian language. The

Tagores ran their own literary workshops and magazines, and wrote and produced their own plays, complete with music. A collateral branch of the family, descended from one of Debendranath's brothers, gave India two of her distinguished modern artists: Gaganendranath Tagore and Abanindranath Tagore.

The young Rabindranath stubbornly resisted the formal schooling that was available to boys of his social class in Calcutta. He would not settle in any school. Going to school in the morning, learning under pressure, being taught in the medium of English: all these things were irksome to him. His family saw to it that no matter what happened at school, he would be educated at home by tutors. As it happened, he received an incredibly comprehensive education at home, from tutors and under the supervision of his elder brothers, an education which was quite comparable to that purveyed by a British public school and which covered practically everything from languages, mathematics, drawing, and music, to the natural sciences, anatomy, and gymnastics.

At the age of seventeen Rabindranath accompanied his brother Satyendranath to England. He attended a school in Brighton, but it has proved impossible to establish the exact identity of the institution. At the age of eighteen he enrolled at University College, London, and for some three months enjoyed studying English literature under the guidance of an inspiring teacher named Henry Morley, an experience he never forgot. He also made excellent use of his foreign travels as any young gentleman of culture and leisure would. He observed the society around him, wrote home lively letters full of his observations and relevant comments, listened to Western music, took a lively interest in the young females around him, visited the British Museum, and listened to Gladstone and Bright speak on Irish Home Rule in the British Parliament. Apparently his 'outbursts of admiration for the fair sex in England caused a flutter among the elders at home', who deemed it would be unwise to let him live in London on his own, so when Satyendranath returned to India, his brother had to go back as well, early in 1880, without completing his course of study.[4] A second attempt to go to England for higher education in 1881 proved abortive at an early stage.

Fortunately, Rabindranath Tagore was one of those who go on educating themselves throughout their lives. He read widely. His enlightened and sympathetic brothers encouraged him to learn at his own pace and discover things for himself. His father taught him to love the *Upanishads*, aroused in him an interest in astronomy that was to last all his life, and allowed him to combine a literary career, which did not require degrees, with the management of the family estates. Rabindranath was well grounded in the Sanskrit classics, in Bengali literature and in English literature, and also familiar with a range of Continental European literature in translation. He could read some French, translated English and French lyrics in his youth, and made enough progress in German to read Heine and go through Goethe's *Faust*. In the end his own extended family and the state of cultural ferment all around him gave him the environment of a university and an arts centre rolled into one. It was in a cultural hothouse that his talents ripened. A man emerged, who had his father's spiritual direction and moral earnestness, his grandfather's spirit of enterprise and *joie de vivre*, and an exquisite artistic sensibility all his own.

❦

Rabindranath Tagore wrote poetry throughout his life, but he did an amazing number of other things as well. Those who read his poetry should have at least a rough idea of the fuller identity of the man. His long life is as densely packed with growth, activity, and self-renewal as a tropical rainforest, and his achievements are outstanding by any criterion. As a writer he was a restless experimenter and innovator, and enriched every genre. Besides poetry, he wrote songs (both the words and the melodies), short stories, novels, plays (in both prose and verse), essays on a wide range of topics including literary criticism, polemical writings, travelogues, memoirs, personal letters which were effectively belles lettres, and books for children. Apart from a few books containing lectures given abroad and personal letters to friends who did not read Bengali, the bulk of his voluminous literary output is in Bengali, and it is a monumental heritage for those who speak the language. Like the other languages of northern India, Bengali belongs to the Indo-European family of languages. A cousin to most modern European languages and sharing with them certain basic linguistic patterns and numerous cognate words, it is spoken by an estimated 170-175 million people in India and Bangladesh. When Tagore began his literary career, Bengali literature and the language in which it was written had together begun a joint leap into modernity, the most illustrious among his immediate predecessors being Michael Madhusudan Datta (1824-1873) in verse and Bankimchandra Chatterjee (1838-1894) in prose. By the time of Tagore's death in 1941 Bengali had become a supple modern language with a rich body of literature. Tagore's personal contribution to this development was immense. The Bengali that is written today owes him an enormous debt.

Throughout his life Tagore maintained a strong connection with the performance arts. He created his very own genre of dance drama, a unique mixture of dance, drama, and song. He not only wrote plays, but also directed and produced them, even acted in them. He not only composed some two thousand songs, but was also a fine tenor singer. He was not only a prolific poet, but could also read his poetry out to large audiences very effectively. Many of his contemporaries have attested that to hear him recite his own verses was akin to a musical experience. Leos Janáček had this experience in Prague and was so impressed and inspired that he wrote a choral work based on a Tagore poem, *The Wandering Madman* (1922). Another contemporary, Alexander Zemlinsky, based his *Lyric Symphony* (1923) on a set of Tagore poems.

In the seventh decade of his life Tagore started to draw and paint seriously. He has left a substantial output in this field and is acknowledged to be one of India's most important modern artists.

Tagore was a notable pioneer in education. A rebel against formal education in his youth, he tried to give shape to some of his own educational ideas in the school he founded in 1901 at Santiniketan near Bolpur (in the district of Birbhum, West Bengal). The importance he gave to creative self-expression in the development of young minds will be familiar to progressive schools everywhere nowadays, but it was a new and radical idea when he introduced it in his school. The welfare of children remained close to his heart to the end of his days. To his school he added a university, Visvabharati, formally instituted in 1921. He wanted this university to become an international meeting-place of minds, 'where the world becomes one nest', and invited scholars from both the East and the West to come and enrich its life. Under his patronage, the Santiniketan campus became a significant centre of Buddhist studies and a haven for artists and musicians. It was here that the art of *batik* printing, brought over from its Indonesian homeland, was naturalised in India.

Through his work in the family estates Tagore became familiar with the deep-rooted problems of the rural poor and initiated projects for community development at Shilaidaha and Potisar, the headquarters of the estates. At Potisar he started an agricultural bank, in which he later invested the money from his Nobel Prize, so that his school could have an annual income, while the peas-

Tagore with Leonard Elmhirst at Dartington, 1926.

ants could have loans at low rates of interest. He had his son Rathindranath trained in agricultural science at Illinois, and in the village of Surul, renamed Sriniketan, adjacent to Santiniketan, he started an Institute of Rural Reconstruction with the help of a Cornell-trained English agricultural expert, Leonard Elmhirst. The kind of work that was begun here has since then been repeated and elaborated in many programmes of self-help in India. For instance, Sriniketan pioneered the manufacture of hand-crafted leather purses and handbags, a cottage industry which has, since then, taken off elsewhere as well and now exports products to many parts of the world. It is not an exaggeration to say that the Santiniketan-Sriniketan complex became an important cultural institution in twentieth-century India. Tagore's friend Leonard Elmhirst went on to give shape to an educational institution of his own at Dartington Hall in Devon and has always acknowledged the inspiration he received from Tagore.

Though Tagore was not a systematic philosopher, he is of considerable contemporary relevance as a thinker, one of those far-seeing individuals whose ideas show us the way forward in the modern world and who are going to gain importance as time passes. Those who are interested in 'deep ecology' should find him a very congenial thinker. A 'Green' to his core long before the term was coined, he was what is nowadays called a holistic thinker, never forgetting the whole even when concentrating on the parts. His Upanishadic background made him constantly aware of the interconnectedness of all things in the cosmos. He saw human beings as part of the universe, not set apart from it, and knew that the human species must live in harmony with its natural environment. An outspoken critic of colonialism, he was at the same time in favour of international cooperation – genuine cooperation, not one country exploiting another in the name of cooperation. Always deeply appreciative of the solid achievements of the West, he criticised the West for its fragmented, mechanistic approach to reality, its scheme of values which overrated material power and underrated other human assets. Likewise, he was acutely aware of the limitations of merely traditionalist thinking in his own country. Although he went through a phase of looking back with nostalgia at India's past glories, he was never fatuous about it and quickly outgrew any attitude that was purely and ritualistically nostalgic. No one could be more aware of the elements in India's heritage that needed to be cherished and preserved, but at the same time he knew that many things had to be changed. Some of his most powerful satirical writings are directed against those who oppose necessary changes. He knew that political independence alone was not an adequate goal for his country, that the real task lay at grassroots level, of transforming and energising the rural masses through education and self-help programmes. He welcomed modernisation in many areas of life. For instance, he supported artificial contraception, which Gandhi opposed.

Tagore was a great champion of the individual. In his fictional work he often portrays the thinking, conscientious, lonely individual, alienated from the unthinking and dogmatical group and liable to be persecuted by it. The vulnerable individual is often the focus of his attention in poetry too, as in the poem 'The Boy' in this anthology. He was acutely aware of the oppression of women and looked forward to the coming of an epoch when men and women would be equal partners.

Tagore's thinking mind and the times in which he lived inevitably involved him in political gestures. At home, he wrote songs which protested against Curzon's partition of Bengal; returned his knighthood after the Amritsar massacre; spoke out against terrorism as a political strategy, to the displeasure of those who favoured it; criticised aspects of Gandhi's non-cooperation movement and engaged in dialogues and debates with him. These activities made him an all-India figure and won him the admiration of both Gandhi and Nehru. Abroad, he exposed the horrific dangers of competitive, aggressive nationalism in a series of lectures (*Nationalism*, 1917), to the annoyance of Britain, the USA, and Japan. He was fully aware of the pressing need to oppose fascism (see poem no. 18 of *Prantik* in this book) and died profoundly saddened by the way in which the world was hurtling towards another major war, but he never lost his faith in humanity. Some of his poems are known to have inspired conscientious objectors to war in Britain during the Second World War.[5] Tagore died before the full horrors of Nazism became common knowledge and before the partition of his native land.

The high quality of Tagore's achievements in a diversity of fields assures his pre-eminent position within the Bengali cultural tradition. In that context he is still very much alive, a focal point of lively debates and controversies. Fortunately for the Bengali literary scene, a generation of writers who regarded themselves as post-Tagoreans established themselves before Tagore's death, in the 1930s, so that there was no literary vacuum after his death. On the contrary, there were enough writers to take Bengali writing successfully forward from the point where he left it, and the two decades after his death were remarkably fruitful, despite the lacerations that Bengal underwent in 1947. Tagore was a pioneer in so many fields that he has become a natural point of reference. If people go away from him in search of something they cannot find in him, they tend to come back to him for something that they cannot easily find anywhere else. The extreme revolutionary left, as represented by the Naxalite movement of the late sixties and early seventies, did indeed reject him, as it rejected other leaders of the Indian Renaissance, but that extremism of attitude discredited itself. In the eastern wing of Bengal Tagore played a crucial role in the self-definition of the people after partition. After the region became a part of Pakistan, a propaganda war was launched to belittle Tagore by portraying him as belonging to Hindus only and not of any relevance to Muslims. This sectarian view was rejected by a regional elite who were becoming increasingly secularised, who derived inspiration from Tagore during their struggle for political independence from Pakistan, and who managed to rally the people round his memory as a symbol of their identity as Bengalis. This act of recognition was sealed by the adoption of one of his patriotic songs as the national anthem of the new state of Bangladesh. (The Indian national anthem is also a composition of Tagore's.)

But Tagore does not belong to Bengalis or Indians only. Many of the Bengali post-Tagoreans rebelled against him, finding him lacking in the ennui, grotesquerie, and sense of alienation of Western-style modernism. He was too whole, not cracked or fragmented enough, not in love with sickness or despair. For the thrills he could not provide, they went to Baudelaire or Rimbaud, Proust or Kafka, phases of Eliot or Brecht. But now a new generation of Westerners themselves have emerged, who turn with relief from the negative features of Western modernism to holistic perspectives, to qualities such as compassion and affirmation, nurturing and the making of connections, qualities for long despised as feminine, but now reinvested with value by the women's movement. To such an audience, Tagore's poetry should prove attractive. It is characterised by an impressive wholeness of attitude: a loving warmth, a compassionate humanity, a delicate sensuousness, an intense sense of kinship with nature, a burning awareness of the universe of which we are a part.

❦

Tagore in London in 1913 (shortly before the announcement of the Nobel Prize).

In the paragraphs above I have deliberately not included the Nobel Prize for Literature, awarded to Tagore in 1913, among his principal *achievements*. That award is a cultural institution of the Western world which has hardly any meaning in the context of Indian literature. An accidental concatenation of circumstances led to Tagore being given the award, more, one suspects, as a symbolic recognition of the reawakening of an old civilisation under the aegis of the British Empire than as anything else, for no other writer from the Indian subcontinent has been awarded this prize since that time. If some take this to mean that no other major author has appeared in that part of the world since 1913, they will be deceiving themselves. All it means is that because of the politics of culture the major writers in the modern languages of the sub-continent do not get translated for the Western markets and are "invisible" in the West. And in 1913 there were even protests in certain papers in the USA and Canada against the fact that an Asian, a non-white, a Hindu, a man whose name was difficult for Westerners to pronounce, should have been awarded the Nobel Prize for Literature![6]

Yet the Nobel Prize was definitely a landmark in Tagore's life. It made him internationally famous. He reached a world-wide audience, received invitations from many countries, travelled and lectured widely, acquired foreign friends, and thanks to his fame, met many other distinguished personalities of his time. There was a substantial widening of his artistic and political experiences. He saw the passion-play at Oberammergau, heard *La Traviata* at La Scala in Milan, saw the art of China and Japan as well as of modern Europe, watched the dance-dramas of Indonesia, witnessed the devastated state of Europe after the First World War (which saddened him) and the Communist efforts to uplift the masses in Russia (which stirred him profoundly). His foreign travels enriched and sharpened the elements of cosmopolitan humanism in his thinking and made him strongly anti-war. Seeing that he had gained a large audience, Tagore also tried, in the lectures he was invited to give, to use his influence for a good cause. There is a game that the West plays with men from the East: first, craving gurus, then criticising them for preaching like gurus. Tagore could not escape this fate, half seeing what was happening, yet reluctant to miss the opportunities for bridge-building that the encounters with foreigners afforded. It is true that he sometimes spoke like an angry prophet, but he was absolutely sincere. Angry prophets make us uncomfortable because they speak the truth and

At the house of William Rothenstein in London in 1912; seated (from left to right): Somendra Dev-Varman of Tripura, Rabindranath Tagore, his son Rathindranath; standing: D.N. Maitra, Rothenstein's young son, and Rothenstein.

disturb our complacency. Tagore's analyses of contemporary problems were radical and penetrating. His indictment of violence and commercial greed, his insistence that intelligent cooperation between nations was saner than the path of unbridled competition, are just as relevant today as they were in his lifetime, if not even more. The Nobel Prize is thus an event of some importance in his *vita*, not as an index of his literary merit, but because it invested his life with a new international dimension, and in that way helped him to modernise and radicalise himself at a faster rate.

An unfortunate side-effect of the Nobel Prize was the way in which Tagore's poetry was presented to the Western public after that event. The book that won him the prize, the English *Gitanjali* (1912), containing Tagore's own re-creations in poetic prose of verses taken from the Bengali *Gitanjali* (1910) and some other collections, was taken as a text in its own right and re-translated into other languages from the English. This Western *Gitanjali*, as it has been called, did indeed take the Western world by storm. The Dutch, French, and Spanish versions were particularly elegantly done. The English *Gitanjali* lent itself to good re-translation,

41

especially into other European languages. Its language was simple and unaffected, with a Biblical air, and its message had a universal appeal. But such a *tour de force* of re-creation could not necessarily be repeated. Tagore was not in a position to do it. Yet inadequate translations were hastily brought out, taken as texts in their own right, and re-translated into other languages as before. Some renderings were tolerable, but other poems were truncated and mutilated. To introduce an analogy from the food-processing industry of our times, the "dietary fibres" of the poems were often taken out and artificial sweeteners were added. Often the English versions were not translations at all, but rough paraphrases, abstracts. Tagore's reputation in the West was inevitably affected, especially in the English-speaking world.

Partly because re-translations may iron out the wrinkles of translations, and partly because of other complex cultural and political factors, Tagore's fortunes in other European languages did not necessarily follow a course parallel to that of his fortunes in English. He was, for instance, very popular between the wars in Germany; it is possible that many Germans, feeling humiliated and rejected after the First World War, turned to the consolations of his poetry with a passionate eagerness. Tagore also enjoyed a great vogue in the Spanish-speaking world, which included the Latin Americans. The Spanish re-translations were prepared by Zenobia Camprubí and her husband, the poet Juan Ramón Jiménez, who was probably influenced by Tagore in the concept of *'poesía desnuda'* or 'naked poetry' he put forward from 1916 onwards and also in other ways.[7] Tagore also enjoyed a great popularity in Mexico, and in Argentina, where he had a profound influence on Victoria Ocampo, and in Chile, where the young Gabriela Mistral and the young Pablo Neruda were influenced by him. Yet, as new translations failed to appear, an ambivalence crept into the attitude of the Latin Americans too, as is evinced by Jorge Luis Borges' flippant comment that Tagore was, 'above all, a hoaxer of good faith, or, if you prefer, a Swedish invention'.[8]

Tagore has been called his own worst enemy in allowing his inadequate English translations to see the light of day, yet it would be quite naïve of us to blame him entirely for the process in which he became caught. It is doubtful if the reputation of *any* poet could survive for very long outside his own home territory if that reputation had to depend on the poet's own capacity to translate himself into a second language. If Shakespeare's reputation had depended upon his capacity to translate himself into French

Tagore with Rani Mahalanobis (to his right), daughter-in-law Pratıma Devi (to Rani's right), and others in Italy, 1926.

or Latin, he might have had a tough time becoming famous! Shakespeare has been very lucky in that the language in which he wrote was subsequently disseminated throughout the world by the British Empire and large numbers of people all over the world are able to read him in the original language. The extraordinary demand made on Tagore, that he translate himself into English for the sake of publication in the West, was possible only in the colonial context. He was a busy man, busy writing new things and doing new things all the time. He was badly advised and badly taken care of by those who took charge of his publicity in the English-speaking world. They did not look after his real and long-term interests. One English edition which has been available for a long time does not even mention that the contents are translations, and there is no name of any translator given anywhere in the book. No wonder that recently I met an academic from Britain visiting Tagore's university at Santiniketan, who thought that Tagore actually wrote his poems in English.

Other factors entered into the decline of Tagore's reputation in the English-speaking world. Changing fashions in the Anglo-American literary scene, Tagore's repudiation of the knighthood after the Amritsar massacre, his open condemnation of the cult of nationalism, his popularity in inter-war Germany: all took their toll. The English-speaking literary world was rapidly becoming a world dominated by fashions rather than guided by abiding intellectual curiosities. If a reputation fell, it would be quickly trodden over in the pursuit for the next craze. It was not fashionable to delve deeply to find out what might have gone wrong. English translations of selections of his poems were done from time to time by Bengalis, usually for the Indian market outside Bengal, but occasionally for publication outside India as well, but these did not help to put Tagore back on the map. Looking at the phenomenon from a historical perspective, it would be correct to say that the root cause of the decline was the fact that there was no one in the English-speaking world competent enough to translate this great poet from the original language. The days of the Empire did not favour the emergence of such individuals.

When the British were still establishing themselves in India under the aegis of the East India Company in the latter half of the eighteenth century, they were marked by a relative lack of arrogance. Intellectually they were shaped primarily by the Enlightenment, which meant that they were curious about India's social, political, and religious institutions. This attitude was reinforced by their own expatriate social lives, their enjoyment of spiced dishes, hookah-smoking, nautches, Urdu ghazals, and Indian mistresses. The great surge of British Orientalist researches relating to India took place in the closing decades of the eighteenth century and the early years of the nineteenth. Its landmarks were the foundation of the Asiatic Society of Bengal in Calcutta in 1784, the regular publications of which, the *Asiatick Researches*, were widely read in Europe and ushered in a new era of scholarship, the first English translations of classic Sanskrit texts, and the foundation of the College of Fort William in Calcutta in 1800 for the training of British civil servants who would be acculturated to India and fluent in Indian languages.[9]

But as the British gained political confidence in India, these positive attitudes were gradually replaced by attitudes which were negative towards India and therefore less favourable to Indian studies. Waves of Christian fundamentalism in the shape of the Evangelical revival and of secular radicalism in the form of Utilitarianism gathered strength in Britain and hit India. To men moulded by such movements at home the Company's Indian territories seemed a stage ready for action. The Evangelicals wanted India to be opened up for missionary enterprise; the Utilitarians wanted to see India westernised by means of effective legislation and strong centralised administration; other radicals wanted India changed by means of English education. One of the most powerful of the anglicisers was T.B. Macaulay, whose 1835 minute on education, notorious in Indian history, swept aside the modern Indian languages as rude dialects and all Oriental literature as intrinsically inferior to Western literature, maintaining that 'a single shelf of a good European library was worth the whole native literature of India and Arabia', that 'all the historical information which has been collected from all the books written in the Sanskrit language is less valuable than what may be found in the most paltry abridgements used at preparatory schools in England'. He proposed that a class of anglicised Indians should be trained to be interpreters between the British and the Indian masses, 'a class of persons, Indian in blood and colour, but English in taste, in opinions, in morals, and in intellect'.[10] This new climate of ideas encouraged the Indian elite to acquire English to the best of their abilities and discouraged the British from learning Indian languages in any depth. It was the British understanding of the modern Indian languages that suffered most from this change. The foundations for the study of ancient India had already been laid, and in 1837 James Prinsep deciphered the rock edicts of the emperor Ashoka, the key to the rediscovery of Buddhist India. A few British scholars would continue to study Sanskrit and Pali, but the modern languages of India, in which exciting new developments were beginning to take place, *which were becoming the space in which the Indian Renaissance was taking shape*, were neglected. This re-awakening happened because the Indian elite welcomed the new influences without throwing their own traditions overboard. They managed to create a space for themselves in which they could express themselves, experiment with new things and still be themselves. The British could not take this space away from them or interfere with it.

No wonder, then, that no literary personality emerged in either Britain or in the British community of imperial India who could tackle the translation of Tagore's poetry, despite the very long commercial and political connection between the two countries. Britain's cultural attitude rubbed itself onto the rest of the Empire and the English-speaking world. A competent translator could have hardly emerged in Canada or the USA when Britain, with all her ties with India, could not produce such a person.

Generally speaking, this legacy of the Empire is still the prevailing situation in the cultural interchanges between the English-speaking world and the world of the modern South Asian languages. If translations from the latter have to be done, it is the Asians themselves who have to do it. It is they who have to be the mediators and bridge-builders. The English-speaking literati are much more comfortable with those South Asian authors who produce literary works in the English language. It is assumed that these texts require no mediation, and they have been quickly and conveniently appropriated into the new academic category of 'Commonwealth Literature', bypassing the bulk of modern literature in the subcontinent, which continues to be written in the South Asian languages and is invisible in the English-speaking world. A new leviathan called 'Third World Literature' is also beginning to appear in discussions, and certain authors of Indian origin who write only in English are being co-opted by the West as representatives of the Indian segment of this mammoth category. Do anything, in short, except face the challenge, the intellectual effort, of acquiring new tongues and penetrating new universes! This latest tendency to co-opt certain authors who write in English to represent Indian literature is essentially a form of cultural neo-colonialism, a continuation of Macaulay's old reliance on 'a class of persons, Indian in blood and colour, but English in taste, in opinions, in morals, and in intellect'.

However, at long last, there are some signs of change. The first serious literary translator from Bengali to emerge in Britain is William Radice, whose translations of selected poems from Tagore appeared in 1985, and of his stories in 1991, both from Penguin. (Before him, E.J. Thompson, an Englishman who was a contemporary of Tagore, had learned some Bengali and written about Tagore, and done some translations also; Radice attempts an analysis of Thompson's achievements and limitations in the preface to his own book of translations of the poems.) I am aware that translators from Bengali have emerged in the USA and Australia. Continental Europeans are also realising that they must translate directly from the Indian languages and not just re-translate from English translations.

❧

These translations have therefore been undertaken in the belief that Tagore's poetry (as indeed his other work) deserves to be rescued from the morass of misadventures and cultural politics in which it became bogged down, and looked at with fresh eyes, without any negative pre-judgments derived from colonial times.

Tagore writing, Santiniketan.

My aim has been to put together a substantial selection which can give readers an idea of the quality of his poetry, showing them what a varied and exciting poet he is, how relevant to our times, and where there may be sufficient "inter-resonance" between the poems to produce a cumulative effect, conveying something of his total personality, his recurrent and obsessive images, and something, too, of his craftsmanship.

This could not be done by means of academic decisions on what would be a "representative" selection. It was more appropriate to let my creative, artistic decisions as a translator determine the choice. In other words, I would go through the corpus, turn the pages, look at a poem, and ask myself: 'Would this come out well in English? Can I do it? Is there a chemistry, a match, between this poem and my capabilities as a translator?' So the poems have chosen me as much as I have chosen them. And my file of translations has grown. It was not possible to include something from every book of poems published by Tagore, but I hope that the poems chosen for this selection will give the reader some idea of the range and depth of his poetry. The translations follow the texts and arrangement of the West Bengal Government's Tagore

Tagore in January 1940, a year and a half before his death.

Centenary edition of Tagore's collected works (1961). I also consulted the earlier Visvabharati edition of the collected works on many occasions, whenever I had any doubts about the interpretation of a particular line or phrase or about any punctuation, and especially for compiling the notes, but nowhere have I noticed any significant discrepancies. The books from which the poems are taken are arranged chronologically, as in the collected works; even when two books have been published in the same year, we know which comes first because the month of publication is known. The sequence of poems from a particular book corresponds to Tagore's own intentions.

A note on one of the translations may be of interest to readers. During my student days at Oxford in the early sixties, friends sometimes urged me to translate Tagore. Looking back, I think their curiosity might have been provoked by media references to the centenary of his birth in 1961. I did translate a few things, one of which, through the assiduity of an enterprising friend, eventually found its way to the Dublin magazine *Poetry Ireland*, where it saw the light of day in 1964. 'The Victorious Woman', included in this anthology, is a revised version of that early effort. Richly descriptive and sonorous, it had been an ambitious choice for those days. I am sure I had been unconsciously goaded to show off the pedigree of my native tongue, for two of the most irksome questions that I was frequently asked were: first, whether, seeing that I was studying English literature and spoke English with reasonable fluency, I had not really always spoken English at home in my childhood, and secondly, whether Bengali could as yet be called a language, properly speaking, or was it not still in the stage of a dialect. (Dialects had not acquired class in those days. And Macaulay's ghost was tenacious.)

I have also ventured to include some songs, all taken from *Gitabitan*, the standard collection of Tagore's songs, which is also included in the collected works. The songs have been arranged chronologically, following the chronology given in a standard work of reference,[11] which has been kindly re-checked by Professor Sankha Ghosh. Some of the songs also occur in other books, verse-collections or plays. Such information will be found at the end of each song. Thus those who may wonder why I have not translated anything from the famous *Gitanjali* will find their answer in the section of songs: two songs from the Bengali *Gitanjali* (1910) have in fact been translated. Songs have also come, via *Gitabitan*, from *Gitimalya* (1914) and *Gitali* (1914). But I must

49

emphasise that Tagore's songs have very strong independent lives as songs. That is how most Bengalis approach *Gitabitan* – as an anthology in its own right, in which each piece happens to be a song. All the songs have therefore been translated from *Gitabitan*, as individual songs and discrete pieces. Each song has been treated as a text in its own right.

I am aware of the opinion expressed by Radice in his *Selected Poems* of Tagore that songs cannot be translated. In so far as this means the obvious, that a song is made up of its words and its melody, and the melody cannot be translated, one necessarily agrees, but granting that the translation of all poetic material is a difficult and delicate task, the translation of the lyric of a song is no more difficult than that of a poem which has not been set to music. Indeed, because of its structure, the lyric of a song may be much easier to translate than a complex poem. A rigid division between poems and songs cannot be maintained, certainly not in the Indian context, where a considerable overlap between the two modalities has traditionally been taken for granted by artists as well as audiences. The *bhajans* of Mirabai are both poems and songs. The Baishnab lyrics from the "medieval" period of Bengali literature are both poems and songs. It is clear from Tagore's own use of words that he often thought of the roles of the poet and the singer/songmaker as interchangeable, and surely this is true of many other cultures as well, much of folk poetry being also folk song, and vice versa.

I have always been attracted to songs in different languages, and I believe that like poems, they can be marvellous introductions to a new language and genuine aids to language-learning, making it a pleasurable experience, a fact which does not seem to be much appreciated by modern language teachers in British schools. Being simple-structured poems, songs exhibit the "works" of the language like a device in a crystal jar. I remember the pleasure I used to get as a young girl from the 78 r.p.m. records of French songs my father used to borrow from the Alliance Française de Calcutta, and in later life I learned to follow Spanish by comparing the Spanish texts of songs with their English translations on the sleeves of records. Indian children who are not born to Hindi or Urdu learn them from Bombay film songs, and all over the world youngsters today pick up lines of English from pop songs. I have also enjoyed translating songs from other languages into Bengali, for instance, Shakespeare's 'When icicles hang by the wall' and the folk songs of the Judaeo-Spanish

Ladino tradition, and the results have been appreciated. These experiences have given me the confidence to attempt the translation of a few of Tagore's songs, without which, to my mind, a selection such as this would not be complete, because it is through his songs that Tagore speaks, *as a poet*, to his widest audience in Bengali, and no Bengali party is really ever complete until some Tagore songs have been sung. I have kept the songs together in one section so that readers do not forget that the originals do have melodies and are meant to be sung, but I hope my renderings have also captured something of their swing and lilt.

Capturing the form and the content together when one is trying to translate poetry into poetry (and not into prose) is admittedly the hardest task. By allowing my selection to proceed along the free-flowing route outlined above, I have spared myself unnecessary struggles with structures that refuse reincarnation. Some poems are simply untranslatable. There is no need to wrestle with these when one is trying to introduce the poet to a new audience, because there is a whole range of excellent poems which can, with a little sensitive effort, be given an English form. Given the structure of a poem in the original language, the aim is to create a parallel or corresponding poetic structure in the language into which one is translating, using the various sonic devices available in the latter. The two structures will not be 'equal in all respects' like the congruent triangles we cut out of paper in school geometry lessons, but there should be a certain resemblance or correspondence between the two. It is an act of approximation, a dance of interpretation, making good use of the area of overlap between the two languages in meanings, sounds, moods, suggestions, and so forth. A good rule of thumb in practice is to adjust to the natural rhythm and cadence of the language into which one is translating by means of many micro-decisions, while *stretching* the capacity of that language by allowing it to mirror slightly alien patterns of thought. The meandering free verse or prose poetry of Tagore's later years is naturally fun to recreate, but I have also attempted a fair number of poems with much tighter structures. The language of Tagore's poetry is exceptionally rich and musical; I hope I have succeeded in conveying something of these qualities in the translations.

A fact of which readers should be aware is that Bengali does not distinguish between masculine and feminine forms in its third person pronouns, between *he* and *she*, between *him* and *her*, between *his* and *her*. Naturally, most of the time the context tells

51

us quite unambiguously how to interpret the signs, but sometimes no such help is available. Nor does Bengali have gender-markers in verbs, as some other Indian languages do. In Tagore's lyric poetry and songs one encounters certain instances of gender-ambiguity which make one suspect that he has in fact used the "unisex" third person pronoun in a deliberate manner to create an atmosphere of refined poetic ambiguity. It is as if he is asking us to forget the *he* and *she* and to concentrate on the essence of the human situation. It is a great pity that this androgyny, which contributes substantially to the subtlety of the original pieces in which it occurs, cannot be captured in translation. A translator has no option but to reach out for either a *he* or a *she*. I have tried to do my best, using my instincts as a Bengali and looking carefully for cultural clues in the inner landscape of each text. But what this means in effect is tuning oneself to respond to certain conventional cues, ignoring the rich possibilities of an unconventional interpretation. And as soon as a choice is made, which can sometimes be alarmingly automatic (so powerful is the hold of gender-stereotypes on our minds), the possibility of the alternative interpretation is blocked and the androgynous power of the original inevitably destroyed. This is an intractable problem. No matter how carefully we proceed, taking all kinds of other factors into account, such as connections a particular text may have with other texts, the fact remains that an ambiguity within a particular text is still an ambiguity within that particular text. It is embedded there, was perhaps consciously put there by the poet, and is an integral part of the poetic gestalt of *that text*. A poetic ambiguity destroyed is a poetic ambiguity destroyed, and there is really no way in which one can compensate for it. Perhaps some readers will enjoy the intellectual exercise of spotting for themselves the pieces where this specific form of ambiguity occurs in the originals.

In the transliteration of Bengali names and words I have adopted a working compromise. Without considerable modification, the Roman script is not suitable for the representation of most Indian languages, because it simply does not have enough characters to cope with the needs of these languages. To mention just a few problems, it cannot readily distinguish between the short *a* and the long *a*, it cannot aspirate except by the addition of a whole character (*h*), and it cannot distinguish between dentals and cerebrals. Thus Bengali has a separate character for each of the following: dental *t* and *d*, cerebral *t* and *d*, and an aspirated version of each of these, eight characters in all. If we use the resources of the

Roman script in the way as it is used in English, we have just *t*, *d*, *th*, *dh*, and no way to distinguish between the dentals and cerebrals at all, a distinction which is vital to Bengali and other Indian languages. To counteract these and other problems, an elaborate system with many additional diacritical marks has been developed by Sanskritists for the romanisation of Sanskrit. This system, however, is not really very appropriate for Bengali, where orthography and pronunciation are not in the same accord as in Sanskrit, and apart from the inconvenience that non-specialists do not know how to interpret its signals, the system constantly gives rise to distorted ideas about the pronunciation of Bengali names and words. One could develop a new system altogether, which would do more justice to the sound of Bengali, but it would leave us with the following problem. A certain convention about the romanisation of Indian names and words has already grown up over the years, not the complicated system used by Sanskritists, but for general use, without diacritical marks, but still rather spelling-oriented. Introducing a new system for Bengali all of a sudden would be a source of confusion, disorienting readers, both Westerners and non-Bengali Indians, who have become familiar with certain transliterations. Drastic changes in the spellings of names of authors or book-titles would present problems of recognition in bibliography. So unless Bengali studies came into vogue in English in a big way, a new system would be a pointless exercise. I have therefore adopted the system in general use as the basis of my transliterations, adding slight tilts, wherever I have felt it to be necessary, to the real Bengali sound-values. This means that there are inconsistencies in the way I have done things, but I reckon it is the lesser evil. I have tended to leave certain conventional spellings well alone, to avoid problems of recognition, but have felt freer to adapt to Bengali pronunciation in other cases, such as the names of trees and flowers within poems. I have also refrained from italicising such names in the poems, to avoid giving them a false exotic air. They are not aliens in the contexts of the poems, so should not stand out when one is reading the poems. The place where they should stand out is the Glossary. I would like to point out to readers the Bengali pronunciation of two important names: Rabindranath is pronounced 'Robindronath', with the *d* soft, as in French and Spanish, and Santiniketan is pronounced 'Shantiniketon', with the *t* soft, as in French and Spanish.

Wherever possible, I have tried to supply, immediately after each piece, the place and date of composition. Tagore sometimes recorded his dates according to the Bengali calendar, and in such cases exact conversions to the Western calendar can be done by consulting old almanacs or reference works that collate calendars. One such work collating several calendars in very fine print was shown to me at the Rabindra Bhavana; I took one look at it and realised that I could not trust myself to recover the right dates from it. I could have pestered others to help me and then worried about *their* accuracy as well. In the end I decided that I would not turn a translation project into a full-scale research project. Some relevant dates in Anno Domini could be retrieved from the meticulous volumes of Prasantakumar Pal's new biography of Tagore which have come out so far. Where this was not possible, I have given the Bengali date and an approximation in A.D. The months and seasons of the Bengali calendar are as follows:

1. Baishakh, summer (mid-April to mid-May).
2. Jyaishtha, summer (mid-May to mid-June).
3. Ashadh, monsoon (mid-June to mid-July).
4. Srabon, monsoon (mid-July to mid-August).
5. Bhadra, post-rains (mid-August to mid-September).
6. Ashwin, post-rains (mid-September to mid-October).
7. Kartik, autumn (mid-October to mid-November).
8. Agrahayan, autumn (mid-November to mid-December).
9. Poush, winter (mid-December to mid-January).
10. Magh, winter (mid-January to mid-February).
11. Phalgun, spring (mid-February to mid-March).
12. Chaitra, spring (mid-March to mid-April).

From Baishakh to Agrahayan, one adds 593 to the Bengali year to get the A.D; in the case of Poush one would have to add 593 or 594, depending on the date; from Magh to Chaitra one adds 594 to get the A.D. Except a few borderline dates in the month of Poush, retrieving the Western year presents no problem. In many dates the corresponding Western months can be easily given; where the date falls in a borderland, at least the season can be given. If a poem was written on 26 Ashadh 1335, I know at once by the above method that it was written in July and in 1335+593 = 1928 A.D. If a poem was written on 13 Agrahayan 1322, I can at least point to autumn 1915. That is what I have done.

It is, in any case, a good idea for readers to get used to the names of the Bengali months and to the six seasons of the year, because they are very important to the poetry. Tagore refers to them constantly. The Tropic of Cancer runs right through the middle of

Bengal, so one should not expect the seasons to behave exactly as in the northern latitudes. They have a different pattern and slightly different connotations and associations for poetry. Summer burns: it is not the season when one sits out in the garden. (Winter may be more appropriate for that.) If one is far away from one's loved one, he or she is missed more if it is the rainy season. The rains heighten the longing. The first month when the monsoon is supposed to be retreating can still have a lot of rain and be hot and humid, but the second month of the post-rains is usually pleasant and temperate with blue skies. There is fog in autumn and winter, but never any snow except in the northernmost Himalayan part of Bengal. Spring is more voluptuous than in the temperate zone. In agriculture there is, naturally, more than one growing season.

In the two sections entitled Notes and Glossary I have provided as much of a critical apparatus as is appropriate in an edition like this. Both sections should be consulted, because it was easier to give some kinds of information in the Notes, while it was easier to enter other items in the Glossary. Cross-references from one section to the other are also provided where appropriate. Readers are urged to consult this critical apparatus for anything that may seem opaque at first sight. Plant-names with which readers are likely to be familiar have not been included in the Glossary, except where a tree's product may be known, but not the tree, and where it is necessary to have some idea about the tree to appreciate the poetry fully. Providing information on the tropical flora was a major task of annotation for me, and investigating the botanical identities of the names was certainly very educative. I am very grateful to those who helped me to chase the mutating names, prepared a list of current names for me, and wrote down for me on a piece of paper the magic name *Index Kewensis*. The *Index Kewensis* with its many volumes of supplements is a fascinating book, an index to human tenacity, a textbook of magic, with "found poems" on every page. Unfortunately the *Index* by itself cannot enable the lay person to navigate in the troubled waters of botanical taxonomy. Decisions to modify old names are taken at conferences or announced in journals. And as in every subject, there are sometimes differences of opinion amongst experts. I have done my best in such difficult circumstances and have decided to postpone becoming a professional botanist (and a professional reader of collated calendars) until my next incarnation.

Clearly, as with poetry from any part of the world, the more detailed knowledge one has of the physical and cultural habitat of these poems – the geography, the seasons, the landscape, the flora and fauna, the architecture, the clothes, the "manners and customs of the people" which the old travellers always like to talk about, the religious and philosophical concepts, the mythological allusions and so on – the more one will enter into the poetry. Some of this kind of knowledge had some dissemination in this country during the period of imperial connection, and some of the words I have had to gloss can indeed be found in the *Shorter Oxford English Dictionary* or the celebrated *Hobson-Jobson*,[12] but these days no part of that body of knowledge can be taken for granted, while the clichés about India in the media are likely to be a hindrance rather than a help. I must emphasise, however, that there is nothing esoteric or inaccessible in these poems, nothing that cannot be understood with a little work.

It is not so much the mythological references or religious or philosophical concepts that present problems in the study of literature from a different land, for such things can, after all, be looked up in a work of reference if one is really curious, but those details about the environment which one is most unlikely to find explained in any book and which can be illuminated by direct experience alone. I remember the effort of imagination I required as a child growing up in the Bengali countryside, reading a Bengali translation of some Western book, to appreciate the description of a young woman walking over a frozen river. I had never seen snow or a frozen river. But I was even more intrigued to find a man described as poor because he had no hat on his head and no shoes on his feet. I could appreciate that a man who had nothing to eat was poor, but hatlessness or shoelessness did not seem such terrible mishaps at all. I was myself hatless and frequently shoeless as I wandered around, and certainly did not consider myself to be a sorry sight on account of that. I remember my father explaining to me that in a very cold climate those conditions would be much more uncomfortable and could even make one ill.

Because of its natural habitat, Bengali poetry is poetry of 'the warm South', and its images may therefore have a slightly different feel from those of the poetry of northern climates, especially when, as in the English poetry of our times, literary influences from the Mediterranean region have waned and the northernness has been deliberately accentuated.

Tagore's images often refer to an item of clothing like a loose wrap which is worn on the upper part of the body by men. He often refers to the end of the sari, the part that goes over the shoulder and hangs from there, or is brought round to the front again and tucked into the waist. This is an important part of the sari, perhaps heavily embroidered if it is an expensive one, but a part with which many jobs can be done if the sari is homely. Then it is like a Western woman's apron. The busy housewife may mop her wet hands on it or dust something with it; a young girl can gather fruit or flowers in it; a child can cling to it. It is also the mobile and unpredictable part of a woman's attire, which can slip or get blown in the wind. Note that Tagore may also refer simply to a cloth rather than to a sari, because that is exactly what a sari or its masculine equivalent, a dhoti, is – a piece of cloth.

Tagore refers a great deal to the horizon; this is because most of the Bengali country is flat, and the green fringe of a wooded horizon encircles the flat landscape. He talks about the moon with a great deal of ardour; when above the horizon, the moon looks very big, and a full moon on a clear night is quite something to see, like a golden platter which one could almost touch if one could stretch one's hand just a little further. He often describes the moon very precisely with reference to the stage of the lunar cycle in which it is; this shows a strong connection with the country and with those days when almanacs were consulted every day. An urban poet of today is less likely to describe the moon quite in that way.

In landscapes the important formative influences on Tagore were environments where nature was in close proximity to humanity. Tagore's attitude to nature was shaped essentially by peasants' India. The villas overlooking the Ganges in Chandernagore in western Bengal, where he spent holidays with Jyotirindranath and Kadambari Devi, the bungalow in Ghazipur by the Ganges, in the heart of the northern Indian Gangetic plain, where he spent some time with his young wife and growing family, the riverine landscape of rural eastern Bengal, now in Bangladesh, where, as a young man in charge of the family's landed estates, with their head-quarters in Shilaidaha, Potisar, and Shahjadpur, he went up and down the rivers by boat, often living in houseboats, and the drier plain of Birbhum in western Bengal, where he founded his school, university, and centre for rural reconstruction, and where he finally made his home: all have left their mark on him and were areas where working humanity mingled with the natural environment.

During his river voyages in eastern Bengal, Tagore moved through densely populated and highly cultivated areas. A description of one such district may be regarded as fairly representative:

'a vast alluvial plain, dotted with villages and clusters of trees, intersected by several fine rivers, with numerous channels, backwaters, minor streams, and swamps'.[13] These areas also afforded him marvellous opportunities to observe the rural people, the fruits of which can be seen in both his poems and short stories.

Santiniketan was located in a drier country, but a "greening" process was started under the patronage of Tagore and his son, which gradually converted the place into a garden. The later poems are dotted with references to the trees and flowers of Santiniketan. In this area he had opportunities to observe the Santhals, a tribal people who made a large contribution to the rural workforce.

If it is true that a part of the function of poetry is to remind us, magically, what our relationship to the earth is,[14] then Tagore's poetry fulfils that role most admirably. Directly and indirectly he reminds us constantly of our bond with the earth, and nature is for him both a direct and proper subject and a perennial fountainhead of imagery. That is why, of course, I had to wrestle with all those names of plants. In this he is solidly rooted in the Indian poetic tradition.

The passion with which Tagore addresses the earth as a mother, in whose womb he once was and whose milk he has drunk, may strike the Western reader with its cultural difference. It was born of the close connection between the earth and the peasantry in his milieu, reinforced by a religious tradition which had not repudiated goddesses. The earth, by definition, is no remote, abstract goddess in heaven. She is the here and the now, the cradle where we are all necessarily rocked, and is as vulnerable as a human mother.

> Ah, mother,
> pauperised, afflicted, tearful, tarnished earth,
> after so many days at last today my heart
> stirs with weeping for your sake, alas!
> ('Farewell to Heaven')

It is sobering to realise that these powerful lines, which are likely to rouse sympathetic vibrations in contemporary ears, were written in 1895, the urgency in the poet's voice deriving at least in part from his perception of the colonial exploitation of his motherland.

The earth is a mother who is often powerless, unable, in years of drought, to feed her hungry children. Her hands hold not 'infinite riches' but 'unfinished pleasures'. She is a mother who clings to all her offspring, saying 'I won't let you go' to the tiniest blade of grass that springs from her womb, and she is as powerless to prevent their departure as Tagore's young daughter is to prevent her father's going away to his place of work. In these respects she is analogous to

Annapurna Turkhud, teacher of spoken English to the adolescent poet (prior to his first voyage to England) and inspirer of some of his early poems.

Kadambari Devi.

Tagore in the leading role of Valmiki in his musical play Valmiki-pratibha, *1881.*

Rabindranath and Jyotirindranath composing at the keyboard.

the 'mater dolorosa' of the Christian tradition.

But the Hindu universe is not unlike David Bohm's 'implicate order', where everything is enfolded into everything and the whole is enfolded into every part.[15] Accordingly, Tagore is just as much aware of the vast universe and its stars as he is of the planet earth and its flora, and readers should be prepared for the vulnerable, girlish earth–mother's apotheosis and radiant supremacy. She is

the earth, she is all Nature, she is the cosmic maya whose ulti-
mate authority we cannot escape.

> Ah, greater than great,
> you are above, showing your billions of stars,
> your moons, planets! Should you suddenly frown
> hideously, and lift your thunder-fist,
> where would I be, so puny, such a weakling?
> So, she-devil, let me decoy you to be a mother!
>
> ('Hope Against Hope')

> Your creation's path you've spread with a magical net
> of tricks, enchantress...
>
> (No. 15 of *Shesh Lekha*)

These poetic utterances spring from a tradition which is not
unused to addressing and worshipping God as Mother. I am not
anthropologist enough to make a definitive statement on this, but
the Bengali Hindus could be among the last "sophisticated" people
left on earth whose tradition endorses such an attitude at the high-
est level. In Christianity, the madonna represents the point where
the Church has had to yield to the old goddesses, and she has
effectively performed the function of a divine mother, but theology
has formally denied her full status, holding her to be the Mother
of God, but not God Herself. In the calendar of the Bengali
Hindus, however, the most important annual festival is that of
Durga, who is worshipped as a Supreme Mother. This small but
significant difference gives a certain tilt to their culture, introduc-
ing a tension between a social reality which is largely patriarchal
and a cosmic principle which is perceived as feminine, which in
turn puts its unique mark on their art and poetry.

Tagore does, of course, address a paternal God as well, and it
was mainly a group of poems in that mode through the medium
of the English *Gitanjali* that won him the acclaim of the West.
Many religious and philosophical strands went into the making of
Tagore's world, and he absorbed the different influences and min-
gled them in the characteristically eclectic Hindu fashion. Such
strands include the Upanishadic concept of the seamless unity of
the universe, the Baishnab view of the world as the play between
Krishna and Radha, the Shaiva image of the cosmos as Shiva's
dance, and the images of the Sufi-influenced Baul sect of Bengal,
on which a note has been provided in the Notes section. None of
these influences is mutually exclusive, and while acknowledging
this rich and complex tapestry of ideas, it is at the same time
essential to remember that the poetry itself is without labels.

Tagore with his young wife Mrinalini Devi shortly after their wedding, 1883.

Tagore's poems and songs do not belong to any closed cult; they record an authentic spiritual autobiography which can be shared by others. It is an open-ended poetic corpus that oscillates in a human fashion between a faith that sustains the spirit in times of crisis, or fills it with energy and joy in times of happiness, and a deep questioning that can find no enduring answers. It is relig-ious, not in a sectarian sense, but in the deepest sense. Tagore moves with effortless ease from the literal to the symbolic, from the part to the whole, from a tiny detail to the cosmos. This movement is natural to the Indian mind, and Tagore displays it magnificently. I would like to emphasise that I have chosen poems as poems, not because they exemplify this or that attitude.

❧

Tagore was somewhat lonely as a young boy, being the last surviv-ing child of a mother exhausted by fifteen pregnancies. Under the care of family servants, he was often on his own for long hours, daydreaming and amusing himself as best as he could. This initial loneliness did leave a permanent mark on him. When he lost his mother at the age of fourteen, quite a bit of mothering came to him from his sister-in-law Kadambari Devi, the wife of his brother Jyoti-rindranath. Kadambari had entered the Tagore household as a daugh-ter-in-law at the tender age of nine, when Rabindranath was seven, and the two had grown up together like siblings. As I have said, she took a keen interest in contemporary Bengali writing, and took an active part in the family's cultural activities. She was an impor-tant formative influence on the budding poet.

The adolescent Rabindranath is known to have been stirred by an accomplished young Maratha woman three years older than himself, named Annapurna Turkhud. Vivacious, sophisticated, and fluent in several languages, Annapurna (also known as Anna or Annabai) was the daughter of Atmaram Pandurang Turkhud, an eminent Bombay doctor with remarkably progressive views, and had completed her education in Britain. Rabindranath stayed with the family prior to his first voyage to Britain and had lessons in spoken English from Annapurna. There is evidence that the two were attracted to each other, though Rabindranath was very shy. He gave her the nickname of Nalini, which she afterwards used as a pen-name when she wrote, and she inspired some of his early poetic effusions. She married a Briton named Harold Littledale and died at Edinburgh at an early age in 1891.[16] Tagore never forgot her and reminisced about her in his old age.

Flutters were also caused in Rabindranath's heart by the friendly daughters of the Scott family, with whom he stayed in London during his first visit to Britain. Of the three sisters, he seems to have been particularly friendly with the second and the third. The third Miss Scott sang and played on the piano, and taught him English and Irish songs. Possibly it was she who expressed a wish to learn Bengali and had lessons from him. It is likely to have been his goodbye to these sisters which was recalled in a tenderly romantic poem in *Sandhyasangit* entitled 'Dui Din' (Two Days). I was tempted to translate this poem, but in the end did not attempt it.

After his return from England in 1880 the young Rabindranath enjoyed a period when his creative spirit received notable stimulation from the friendship and company of his sister-in-law Kadambari Devi. He then accepted a marriage that his family arranged for him. The choice was limited, because a girl had to be found from the brahmin sub-caste of demoted rank to which the Tagores belonged: other brahmin families would not give their daughters to the Tagores. The girl chosen was Bhabatarini, the daughter of Benimadhab Raychaudhuri from a village in the district of Jessore, a minor official who worked for the Tagore family. The marriage took place on 9 December 1883, when the bride was approximately three months away from her tenth birthday. After the marriage, her old-fashioned name was changed to Mrinalini.

In April 1884, four months after Rabindranath's wedding, Kadambari Devi, still two-and-a-half months away from her twenty-fifth birthday, committed suicide. She is thought to have taken opium and did not die immediately. For two days doctors battled to save her life, but failed. She died on either 20 or 21 April, just a few days before Rabindranath's twenty-third birthday. The postmortem examination was conducted in the Jorasanko house and the Tagore family paid money to stop the news of her suicide from appearing in the newspapers.[17]

Silence was maintained by the family and clues were destroyed in such a way that it is nearly impossible to get at the real story behind the tragedy. Beneath the brilliant surface of the family life of the Tagores there were hidden tensions, some caused directly by the uneven process of modernisation which such families were undergoing. Young men were being given all the psycho-sexual stimuli of a vigorous arts education and were being exposed to romantic Western literature with its assumptions of free mixing between the sexes, but were nevertheless being paired off, while at the height of their sexual development, with immature child-

Mrinalini Devi in her days as a mature matron.

brides. All a young man could do in such a situation would be to wait for his bride to reach puberty so that the marriage could be consummated and in the meantime continue to flirt with the wife of an older brother, who might be a young woman closer to him in age. The young women were also being encouraged to educate and develop themselves up to a point, and the pursuit of literature and music would nurture romantic egos in them as well. Kadambari was artistic, sensitive, and childless. She had married at the age of nine. Jyotirindranath was ten years older than her and is known to have liked the company of his older brother Satyendranath's wife, the smart Jnanadanandini Devi. There are rumours that Kadambari found letters from another woman, perhaps an actress, in the pocket of a tunic of her husband which she was sending to the laundry. There are also rumours that she had made a previous unsuccessful attempt to kill herself. Such rumours cannot be authenticated, though clearly some hurt, some loneliness must have been gnawing her. She had suffered from some prolonged illness in the latter half of 1883, shortly after the arrangement of the match for Rabindranath, in which she participated along with others. In a chapter of one of my Bengali books I have tried to present a retrospective analysis, in the light of the psychiatric insights of our times, of the kind of depression that might have driven Kadambari to suicide.[18]

Jyotirindranath never married again. Rabindranath's long story 'Nashtanid' (The Broken Nest) portrays a situation which was probably modelled on the triangular relationship between Jyotirindranath, Kadambari, and himself. There is no suicide. The story was adapted by the director Satyajit Ray for his successful film *Charulata*. It seems highly likely that Kadambari's suicide was one of those events which provoked Tagore to explore the situation of women within the traditional Hindu family in several stories.

Tagore's writings show that he suffered horribly at first, undergoing an inner orphaning, but then began to recover, thanks to his youth and the normal healing processes of nature. At the hour of his devastating grief he could not have received much support from his ten-year-old child-bride, with whom his marriage would not as yet have been consummated, but she reached puberty soon enough and the first child arrived when Rabindranath was twenty-five-and-a-half and his wife not quite thirteen.

Some have wondered how a young man like Rabindranath, who was both wildly romantic in his temperament and rebellious in his social ideas, as evinced by his adolescent writings, could have accepted an arranged marriage with a child-bride, but these contradictions were part of the times and *mores*. His father wished him to get married, and he did not go against that wish, doing just what his other brothers had done before him. As long as the patriarch Debendranath was alive, Rabindranath's actual social behaviour remained fairly conservative. He even hurried the wed-

Tagore's favourite niece, Indira Devi.

The proud father: Tagore with his two eldest children, Bela and Rathi, in 1890.

Four of Tagore's five children (left to right): Shomi, Rani, Bela (seated) and Mira.

dings of his own first two daughters so that his father could see
his granddaughters wedded before he died. But it is interesting to
note that *after* his father's death he arranged his son Rathindra-
nath's marriage with Pratima Devi, who was a young widowed
girl from a collateral branch of the Tagore family. This was the
first instance of widow remarriage in the Tagore family. And

Tagore with daughter-in-law Pratima Devi in Persia, 1932.

Rathindranath was strenuously exhorted by his father to allow Pratima to develop herself fully as a person.[19]

As a bride, then, Mrinalini Devi was not essentially all that different from other daughters-in-law who had joined the Tagore family as children. She had already received some primary education in her village, and the Tagore family sent her to school and gave her a reasonable education. She learned English as well as Sanskrit, and is known to have read the original *Ramayana* with a teacher in order to prepare, at her husband's insistence, an abridged Bengali version suitable for the use of children. This seems like one of her husband's educational experiments, a part of his plans for the education of both his wife and his children. The unfinished manuscript has not survived, but her son Rathindranath has recorded that he and his siblings used to read it with great eagerness.[20] She also appeared on stage once in one of her husband's plays. Her face, on the photographs that have come down to us, looks a little homely, but is not unattractive, and by all accounts she seems to have given her husband the quiet nest he needed to mature as a writer. Gentle, affectionate, and devoted to her husband and children, she is known to have been a good cook and an expert manager of household affairs. She supported her husband's efforts to found a school at Santiniketan and parted with nearly all her jewellery to finance the venture. The few letters from Rabindranath to her which have survived, written during temporary stretches of separation, show how solid the foundation of mutual respect and tenderness between the two was, and how anxious he was to remove her and their children from the politics of the extended family and bring them over to a spot where he could share with them the delights and responsibilities of living as a nuclear family. She bore him five children. There can be no doubt that the serene splendour of much of Tagore's poetry written while Mrinalini was alive and active owes something to the stability she gave him.

Tagore was forty-one-and-a-half when Mrinalini, still a few months away from her twenty-ninth birthday, died of an undiagnosed illness on 23 November 1902. He nursed her himself, but could not save her. Rathindranath speculated in later life that his mother might have died of appendicitis, a condition not very well understood in those days.[21] There is every reason to think that Mrinalini would have developed her personality further had fate permitted her to be at her husband's side for a longer period.

In 1903, nine months after her mother's death, Tagore's second daughter, Renuka (Rani), died of tuberculosis. Again, Tagore tried desperately to save her, but could not. In 1907, Tagore's younger son Shamindranath (Shomi) fell a victim to cholera while on holiday in Bihar. These shattering griefs deepened the religious strain in Tagore's temperament, consolidating a profoundly religious phase in his development. Basically, it was poems from this phase which won him acclaim in the West. With the death of his firstborn child and eldest daughter, Madhurilata (Bela), in 1918, also from tuberculosis, only two of Tagore's five children were left alive.

Tagore never remarried and nurtured a core of loneliness within him for the rest of his life. His poems suggest that the wound left in his mind by Kadambari's death had to some extent healed over when the death of his young wife opened it again. Both deaths left him with a sense of guilt and remorse. Kadambari's death shook him profoundly, making him suddenly realise how lonely and unhappy she must have been, much more than he had realised. Clearly he had not done enough to help her. Nor had he been able to tell her how much he owed her, as a young man and a young poet. It was then too late to make amends. Mrinalini's death left him feeling guilty too, because he felt he had not shown enough appreciation, while she had been alive, of her quiet devotion and sacrifices for his sake. The two deaths merged into one profound sense of loss, creating the composite ghost of a dead beloved which began to haunt his poetry and songs, investing many of them with a mood of bitter-sweet nostalgia and unconsummated longing. As readers will see, Tagore's poetry is full of the "unfinished business" of grieving. He often evokes the image of a woman who has gone away, leaving him with the pain of an incomplete communication, of things left unsaid.

Tagore's need for a feminine touch in his daily life as well as his deeper artistic need to be inspired by a woman remained with him, to be filled, from time to time, more or less, by various women of the family and later by other attractive women who clustered round him, drawn by his personality and fame. From an early period, from before Mrinalini's death, his niece Indira Devi, the daughter of Satyendranath and Jnanadanandini, was very close to him. Just a couple of months older than Mrinalini, Indira was the recipient of some of Tagore's most brilliant letters (*Chhinna-patrabali*, 1960). After the death of his daughter Bela, Tagore found comfort in the company of the young Ranu Adhikari, later the noted arts patron of Calcutta, Lady Ranu Mookerjee. She inspired the character of Nandini in the play *Raktakarabi* (1926) and was the recipient of the letters of *Bhanusimher Patrabali* (1930).

ABOVE: *Tagore outside the villa Miralrío, San Isidro, Argentina, 1924.*
BELOW: *Tagore with Victoria Ocampo in Argentina, 1924.*

In 1924 in Argentina Tagore met Victoria Ocampo (1890-1979), a young Argentine woman who was an ardent admirer of his works, and who later became a distinguished woman of letters and the founder and director of *Sur*, which has been called the most important literary magazine to emerge from Latin America in the present century, and of the publishing house of the same name. For two months Tagore and his honorary secretary and travelling companion Leonard Elmhirst were her personal guests. Tagore was stirred by this encounter, and a triangular friendship sprang up between himself, Victoria, and Leonard Elmhirst. Victoria was the dedicatee of *Purabi* (1925) and continued to be a distant Muse for Tagore in the last years of his life, playing a role also in his development as a visual artist. Tagore cherished hopes that she might visit him at Santiniketan, but although they met once more, in France in 1930, when she managed to organise his first art exhibition, she never made it to India. References in Tagore's later poetry to the pain of separation and the enigmatic image of a woman who had failed him in some way may be linked to this experience.[22]

In 1926, disappointed in his hopes of meeting Victoria in Europe, Tagore took consolation in the company of the attractive Nirmalkumari (Rani) Mahalanobis. Mrs Mahalanobis and her husband were Tagore's travelling companions for the major part of his European travels in 1926, and she was the recipient of the letters of *Pathe o Pather Prante* (1938). Tagore also received substantial companionship from Rathindranath's wife Pratima Devi, who was encouraged to develop her artistic talents and was a very supportive daughter-in-law to him in his later years. And there were other women from whom he received emotional support in his long life as a widower, as well as other bereavements of those close to him, besides the ones I have enumerated.

After a life of incessant creative activity, Tagore died, at the age of eighty years and three months, on 7 August 1941, in the family house in Calcutta where he had been born. The quality and quantity of his achievements seem all the more astonishing when placed against the amount of grief he had to cope with in his personal life. Much of his poetry is necessarily about love and suffering, about how one copes with loss, and can be called *passional* in the radical sense. Yet he is at the same time one of the most affirmative and celebrative poets of all times. I hope readers of this volume will see for themselves that he was neither 'a hoaxer of good faith' nor 'a Swedish invention', but a genuine poet who still speaks to us.

NOTES

1. Ghulam Murshid, *Reluctant Debutante: Response of Bengali Women to Modernization, 1849-1905* (Sahitya Samsad, Rajshahi University, 2nd impression, 1983), pp. 49-50.

2. Krishna Kripalani, *Rabindranath Tagore: A Biography* (Visvabharati, Calcutta, 2nd edition, 1980), p. 16.

3. Kripalani, pp. 14-15.

4. Kripalani, p. 89.

5. Vera Brittain, 'Tagore's Relations with England', *A Centenary Volume, Rabindranath Tagore, 1861-1961* (Sahitya Akademi, New Delhi, 1961), p. 118.

6. Kripalani, p. 235.

7. Tagore's influence on Jiménez is discussed in Sisirkumar Das & Shyama-prasad Gangopadhyay, *Sasvata Mauchak: Rabindranath o Spain* (Papyrus, Calcutta, 1987).

8. For more information, see my book *In Your Blossoming Flower-Garden: Rabindranath Tagore and Victoria Ocampo* (Sahitya Akademi, New Delhi, 1988), pp. 65-66 and 347; further references are provided in the notes. Borges' comment can be found in Jean de Milleret, *Entretiens avec Jorge Luis Borges* (Editions Pierre Belfond, Paris, 1967), p. 240. Victoria Ocampo showed how absurd the comment was in her article 'Fe de erratas (*Entrevistas Borges-Milleret*)', *Testimonios*, vol. 9 (Sur, Buenos Aires, 1975), pp. 240-47.

9. See my book *A Various Universe: The Journals and Memoirs of British Men and Women in the Indian Subcontinent, 1765-1856* (Oxford University Press, New Delhi, 1978), pp. 19-26, where further references can be found.

10. Quoted in Michael Edwardes, *British India, 1772-1947* (Sidgwick & Jackson, London, 1967), pp. 122-27.

11. Prabhatkumar Mukhopadhyay (editor), *Gitabitan: Kalanukramik Suchi* (vol. 1, Santiniketan, 1969; vol. 2, Tagore Research Institute, Calcutta, 1978).

12. Henry Yule & A.C. Burnell, *Hobson-Jobson: A Glossary of Colloquial Anglo-Indian Words and Phrases, and of Kindred Terms, Etymological, Historical, Geographical and Discursive*, first published in 1886; new edition, edited by William Crooke, 1903 (Routledge & Kegan Paul, London, 1969).

13. W.W. Hunter, *A Statistical Account of Bengal* (London, 1877), quoted in Ghulam Murshid, *Rabindravisve Purbabanga Purbabange Rabindracharcha* (Bangla Academy, Dhaka, 1981), p. 45.

14. Kim Taplin, *Tongues in Trees: Studies in Literature and Ecology* (Green Books, Bideford, Devon, 1989), p. 20.

15. The idea is developed in several of David Bohm's books, including *Wholeness and the Implicate Order*, first published in 1980, known to me in a paperback edition (Ark Paperbacks, Routledge, London, 1988).

16. Prasantakumar Pal, *Rabijibani*, vol. 2 (Bhurjapatra, Calcutta, 1984), pp. 41-43, or vol. 2, 2nd edition, Ananda, Calcutta, 1990, pp. 11-14, 29-32.

17. Pal, op. cit., vol. 2, 1st edition, pp. 268-72, or 2nd edition, pp. 204-07.

18. Ketaki Kushari Dyson, *Rabindranath o Victoria Ocampor Sandhane* (Navana, Calcutta, 1985), pp. 318-36.

19. Rabindranath Tagore's letter to his son Rathindranath, 19 Baishakh 1317, *Chithipatra*, vol. 2 (Visvabharati, 1942), pp. 9-10.

20. Rathindranath Tagore, *On the Edges of Time*, 2nd edition (Visva-bharati, Calcutta, 1981), p. 21.

21. Rathindranath Tagore, *Pitrismriti* (Jijnasa, Calcutta, 2nd edition, 1387), p. 81.

22. For further details, see my study *In Your Blossoming Flower-Garden*.

[1991]

I WON'T LET YOU GO

The Suicide of a Star

From a luminous shore into an ocean of darkness
   leaped a star
   like a madwoman.
They stared at her, the innumerable stars,
     astonished
that the speck of light, their erstwhile neighbour, could
   vanish in an instant.
     She's gone
   to the bottom of that ocean
   where lie the corpses of
   hundreds of dead stars,
   whom anguish of mind has driven to suicide
   and the eternal extinction of light.

   O why? What was the matter with her?
   Not once did anyone ask
   why she abandoned her life!
     But I know what she would have said in reply
   had anyone posed the question.
     I know what burned her
   as long as she was alive.
   It was the torment of laughter,
     nothing else!
A burning lump of coal, to hide its dark heart,
   maintains a continuous laughter.
   The more it laughs, the more it burns.

So, even so did laughter's
     fierce fire
burn, burn her without end.
That's why today she's run off in sheer despair
from a brilliant solitude full of stars
to the starless solitude of darkness.

   Why, stars, why do you
mock her and laugh like that?

You've not been harmed.
You shine as you did before.
　· She'd never meant
　(she wasn't that arrogant)
to darken you by quenching herself.

Drowned! A star has drowned
　　in the ocean of darkness –
　　in the deep midnight
　　in the abysmal sky.
Heart, my heart, do you wish
to sleep beside that dead star
　　in that ocean of darkness
　　in this deep midnight
　　in that abysmal sky?

[Calcutta, 1880?]

Invocation to Sorrow

　　Come, sorrow, come,
　I've spread a seat for you.
Pull, rip out each blood-vessel from my heart,
place your thirsty lips on each split vein
and suck from my bloodstream drop by drop.
With a mother's affection I shall nurture you.
My heart's treasure, come you to my heart.

Within my heart's nest cosily you may sleep.
　Ah, how heavy you are!
A few of my veins may burst,
　but what do I care?
With a mother's affection I shall carry you
　even on my feeble breast.
　Sitting alone at home,
　in a continuous drone
I shall sing lullabies in your ears,
　until your weary eyes
　are lulled to sleep.

My breath, drawn from my innermost recesses,
   will fan your tired forehead;
      you'll sleep in peace.

      Come, sorrow, come.
   My heart's full of such longing!
   Press your hands on your mouth,
   fall tumbling on my heart's ground.
Like an orphaned child cry loudly within me once
   till it echoes in all my heart.
In my heart of hearts there's a musical instrument
      that's broken.
   Pick it up with your hands,
   play it with all your strength,
   like a madman strum it twang twang.
   Instrument and strings –
   if they break, let them.
   Never mind, pick it up,
   play it with all your strength,
   like a madman strum it twang twang.
   Bruised by sharp sounds,
   all the echoes, troubled,
   will cry out in chorus
         in pain.
      Come, sorrow, please come.

      Oh, how lonely this heart is!
      Just do this, nothing else:
   come close, lift my heart's face,
      set your eyes on it
         and gaze.
      This homeless heart
      wants a companion –
         that's all.
   You, sorrow, come, keep it company.
   You may not wish to speak;
   just sit without words
   day and night by my heart's side.
   When you want to play,
   you can play with it,
   for my heart does need a playmate.

Come, sorrow, treasure of my heart.
Right here I've spread your seat.
   Whatever little blood
   is left in my heart of hearts,
all of that you may drain if you wish.

[Calcutta, autumn 1880 (Kartik 1287)?]

ॐ

FROM *Prabhatsangit* (1883)

Endless Death

Loaded with millions and millions of minute deaths,
   this globe careers in the sky.
   Death laughs and plays around it.
   A death-track is this earth.
   It's a world of death.

Should only the present be called life –
   just an instant, a wink?
On its back sits the dead weight of the past –
   who knows where that ends?
I've been dead as many years as I've lived
   and every moment I'm dying.
Living deaths, we live in death's own house,
   ignorant of its meaning.

Life: is it then a name for a handful of deaths –
   an aggregate of dyings?
Then a moment's a cluster of a hundred trivial deaths –
   so much fuss over a naming!
As death grows, so will life:
   minute by minute we shall ascend the sky
   to the very dwelling of starlight.

As death grows, we shall walk far:
   life's scope will expand.
Within life's vastness stars and planets will
   frolic here and there.
My life will rise, traversing so many skies,
   cover moons and suns,
gain new kingdoms as the ages pass,
   netting the latest stars.

   Oh, when will that day come
   when I may ascend that skyey path
   and tie with my death's filament
   one world and another!
   Our death-mesh we shall spread
   and enclose the world,
   entirely encircle
   this endless sea of sky.

Victory, victory to death!
   Endless death is our lot.
   Death will never die.
Little children of this century, we
   seek your protection, death!
Come to us, take us in your arms,
   give us your breast-milk
   and all the nurturing we need.
We are filled with joy as we behold
   death's endless carnival.
Someone has invited us to this grand
   and noisy party!

Child, don't you know who calls you lovingly?
   Why this fear?
Death's just another name for what you call life,
   not an alien at all.
   Why then, come and embrace her!
   Come and hold her hand!

[Calcutta? 1882?]

84

FROM *Kadi o Komal* (1886)

Breasts

No.2

Truly, we have the sacred Sumeru here,
that golden mountain, dalliance-land of gods.
The high breasts of this virtuous lady light
with rays of heaven the earth, man's mortal lot.
From there the infant sun rises at dawn
and there in the evening, exhausted, he sinks.
At night a deity's irises keep watch
on two secluded unpolluted peaks.
A nectar-flow from love's perennial source
wets the thirsty lips of the universe.
Sustenance without end for a weakly world
for ever wakes on a serenely sleeping earth.
Man, the child of gods, has a motherland
which is on this very earth, but kisses heaven.

[1885?]

The Kiss

Lips' language to lips' ears.
Two drinking each other's heart, it seems.
Two roving loves who have left home,
pilgrims to the confluence of lips.
Two waves rise by the law of love
to break and die on two sets of lips.
Two wild desires craving each other
meet at last at the body's limits.
Love's writing a song in dainty letters,
layers of kiss-calligraphy on lips.
Plucking flowers from two sets of lips
perhaps to thread them into a chain later.
This sweet union of lips
is the red marriage-bed of a pair of smiles.

[1885?]

Desire

A fast damp wind blows sharply from the east,
sweeping dark-blue clouds on the sunrise-path.
Far off, on the Ganga – not a boat! – the sand drifts.
I sit and wonder: who's where today!

Withered leaves are blown on empty paths.
From a distance comes the woodland's mad commotion.
The morning birds are silent. Their nests shake.
I think continually: where is she today?

Ah, how long she was near me, and I said nothing!
And the days went by, one after another.
Laughter and jokes, throwing words at each other:
within them lurked the heart's intended hints.

If I could have her by me today, I feel
I could tell her all I wanted to say.
Clouds would cast dark shadows across my words
and the wind would lend its wildness to my breath.

From afar it would gather – the stillness before a storm.
Clouds, woods, riverbanks – all would merge into one.
Her loose hair would cascade over her face
and her eyes would hold back the dewy drops.

Speeches most solemn, covering life and death,
inner longing, like the forest's uproar,
vital throbbing – from here to hereafter,
hymns of grandeur, high effusive hopes,

huge sadness-shadows, deep absence-pangs,
restless desires, locked up, heart-concealed,
half-formed whispers, not for elaboration,
would fill the solitude like clouds heaped on clouds.

As at the end of day, in midnight's mansion
the universe displays its planets and stars,
so in my heart, freed from laughter and jests,
she would perceive infinity's outburst.

The noise, the games, the merriment would be below;
the spirit's tranquil sky would soar above.
In light you see but the gambolling of a moment;
in darkness alone am I myself without end.

How small I was when she left me and went away!
How small that farewell, spoken with trivial words!
I neither showed her imagination's true realm,
nor made her sit in my soul's dark solitude.

If in such privacy, stillness, grand ambience
two minds could spend an eternal night together –
in the sky no laughter, no sound, no sense of direction,
just four loving eyes waking like four stars!

No weariness, no satiety, no road-blocks:
life expanding from one world to the next!
From the strings of twin spirits in full unison
a duet would rise to the throne of the limitless.

[Ghazipur, 1 May 1888]

Death-dream

The night after full moon. Early in the evening
the pale moon rose in a corner of the sky.
The small boat, quivering, sped with a billowing sail,
as on time's stream glides
an idle thought in a mind half-awake.

One bank, high and jagged, cast a shadow.
The other sloped and merged
with white sand, looking the same in moonlight.
Below the banks in lazy languor flowed
Ganga – slim, sluggish in Baishakh.

The wind blew from the east, my home's direction,
like the sighing of distant relatives who missed me.
Before my waking eyes sometimes the moon,
sometimes a loved face drifted.
One half of me was wistful, the other half elated.

Dense orchards of mango appeared on the north bank.
They looked unreal, like remembered groves.
Bank, tree, hut, path – sketched on moonlight's scroll –
and sky, reflected in water,
like the image of a far-off magical world.

Eyes shut, dream-immersed, I imagined
a swan gliding along the boundless sky:
upheaval of large white wings in moonlight,
myself stretched on its back, on a downy ride.
Sleep crept on me like a pleasurable death.

There were no hours, nor night-watchmen to call them.
Night without end, disconnected from day.
In the hushed, deserted world only the waves,
the murmuring waters softly lapped my ears –
sea of sleep dream-ruffled.

Ages passed – I couldn't count how many.
Like a lamp without oil, the universe began to flutter.
A giant shadow swallowed the firmament,
and with head bowed, the universal night
began the countdown to death: three, two, one...

The moon began to wane, to disappear.
The liquid murmur faded, fell silent.
All the stars, unflinching, like ghosts' eyes
without mercy fixed themselves on me,
the only creature in the entire heavens.

Through that long night the billions of stars
slowly went out, one after another.
I opened my eyes wide, but received no light.
Ice-hard, death-chill, that darkness
couldn't pierce my irises.

Numbed, then, the bird-wings started to droop.
The long neck plunged. The swan began to descend.
For ten thousand years the deafening sound of a fall
struck my ear-drums. The horrendous
gaping night split into two.

Suddenly all the memories of my life
woke for a moment, and in a flash sped
ahead of me, crashing to a thousand pieces.
The hottest chase I gave them, but couldn't retrieve
a particle from that debacle, alas.

Nowhere could I rest this body of mine,
wholly wearied by my own iron weight.
I wanted to cry, but found neither breath nor voice,
my throat choked by darkness:
solely within me it was happening – the cosmic collapse.

The fierce velocity made me long and thin
like the shrill whistle of a swift hurricane.
Sharp as an arrow, as fine as a needle's tip,
piercing infinite time's breast I went,
my body and mind merged, reduced to a line.

Gradually the limits of time dissolved.
An instant and eternity became one.
The ocean of empty space shrank to a point
of the deepest, the most ultimate blackness.
I was swallowed by that ocean of a point.

The dark lost its darkness. There was none called 'I',
yet in a curious way it seemed there was.
Awareness, gagged, blind beneath unawareness,
waited for someone or something, like a life-breath
lingering eternally after death.

I opened my eyes. Ganga flowed as before,
and my boat was speeding westward to its mooring.
Faint lamps flickered in cottages on the bank,
and above, the moon was as honey-faced as ever.
The earth kept her vigil, creatures asleep on her lap.

[Ghazipur, 28 April 1888]

The Amatory Conversation of a Young Bengali Couple

The Wedding Night

GROOM. Life to life   when first united
      brings a peerless pleasure.
  Forget all else!   With lifted eyes
      let's just gaze at each other.
  Heart to heart   in shy confusion
      in one spot joined together,
  drugged by the same   fascination, let's
      suck honey from the same flower.
  I'm but ashes,   'cause since I was born
      I've simply been on fire;
  but your ocean   of love is boundless;
      burning, I've come for water.
  Just say this once,   'I too am yours
      and truly desire none other.'
  What? Sweetheart?   Wherefore do you rise?
BRIDE.   I want to sleep with my Nan. [*She cries.*]

A Few Days Later

GROOM. Sweetest love,   forlorn in a corner,
      wherefore all this weeping?
  Has the morning lost   its morning star?
      Are these its dewdrops peeping?
  Has the spring gone?   And is that why
      the forest goddess is wailing?
  Is wild memory   sitting on the grave
      of buried hope, complaining?
  Or is a meteor   missing its home,
      the blue sky, which it's mourning?
  Why these tears?
BRIDE.   For my pussy-cat
  left at home, I'm crying.

In the Back Garden

GROOM. Lighting up this space   beneath a tree,
      what are you doing in the forest greensward?

Look at these locks   brushing your soft cheeks!
    Aren't they wily? Aren't they wayward?
Look at this stream   curling at your feet:
    as it flows, it seems to weep.
All day long   you're listening to its song:
    tell me, isn't it lulling you to sleep?
Fallen flowers   heaped on your cloth-end,
    sad and neglected: what a shame!
Remembering someone's   face, did you
    make mistakes as you tried to thread 'em?
The breeze that blows,   swaying your ear-rings,
    of whom does it whisper in your ears?
The busy bees   with their specious buzzing –
    whose name do they murmur? Can you hear?
Your eyes are smiling,   your memories happy
    in this deliciously private grove.
What are you doing   in this arbour, this alcove?

BRIDE.   Sitting and eating some juicy jujubes.
GROOM.   I've come to you   to tell you all
    that's pent up in my wretched mind.
Weary of its own   weight, this heart
    can nowhere any comfort find.
My mind's a-flutter   with *je ne sais quoi*
    in this honeyed springtime.
Recklessly   does the wind entreat
    the malati buds to open.
Ah, those eyes –   they look toward me –
    a message of hope is being expressed!
And that heart bursts,   a love escapes,
    half-nervous, half-embarrassed.
Day and night   my soul is awake
    only for your sake;
wants to give its all   in your service,
    from you its commands to take.
My life, my youth –   everything I'll risk,
    plunder the world to fetch you a gift.
Sweetheart, tell me –   what can I fix?

BRIDE.   Get me more jujubes, – say, another six.
GROOM.   Well then, friend,   let me depart
    with a life vacant, despondent.
Might you shed   but one tear-drop
    for me when I am absent?

The spring breeze   with its magic breath
        may well set your heart on fire
and resurrect   within your breast
        slumbering desires.
Doleful girl   in this lonely woodland,
        what will you do, my darling?
How will you spend   your time when I'm gone?
BRIDE.   I'll arrange a dolls' wedding.

[Ghazipur, 6 July 1888]

❦

FROM *Sonar Tari* (1894)

I Won't Let You Go

The carriage stands at the door. It is midday.
The autumn sun is gradually gathering strength.
The noon wind blows the dust on the deserted
village path. Beneath a cool peepul
an ancient, weary beggar-woman sleeps
on a tattered cloth. All is hushed and still
and shines brilliantly – like a sun-lit night.
Only in my home there's neither siesta nor rest.

Ashwin's gone. The Puja vacation's ended.
I've to return to the far-off place where I work.
Servants, busybodies, shout and fuss
with ropes and strings, tying packages sprawled
in this room and that, all over the house.
The lady of the house, her heart heavy as a stone,
her eyes moist, nevertheless has no time
to shed tears, no, not a minute: she has
too much to organise, rushes about,
extremely busy, and though there already is
too much baggage, she reckons it's not enough.
'Look,' I say, 'what on earth shall I do with these –

so many stewpots, jugs, bowls, casseroles,
bedclothes, bottles, boxes? Let me take
a few and leave the rest behind.'

              Nobody pays
the slightest attention to what I say. 'You might
suddenly feel the need for this or that
and where then would you find it far from home?
Golden moong beans, long-grain rice, betel leaves,
areca-nuts; in that bowl, covered, a few blocks
of date-palm molasses; firm ripe coconuts;
two containers of fine mustard oil;
dried mango, mango-cakes; milk – two seers –
and in these jars and bottles your medicines.
Some sweet goodies I've left inside this bowl.
For goodness's sake, do eat them, don't forget them.'
I realise it would be useless to argue with her.
There it is, my luggage, piled high as a mountain.
I look at the clock, then look back at the face
of my beloved, and gently say, 'Bye then.'
Quickly she turns her face away, head bent,
and pulls the end of her sari over her eyes
to hide her tears, for tears are inauspicious.

By the front door sits my daughter, four years old,
low in spirits, who, on any other day,
would have had her bath well completed by now,
and with two mouthfuls of lunch would have succumbed
to drowsiness in her eyelids, but who, today,
neglected by her mother, has neither bathed
nor lunched yet. Like a shadow she has
kept close to me all morning, observing
the fuss of the packing, silent, wide-eyed.
Weary now, and sunk in some thought of hers,
she sits by the front door quietly, without a word.
'Goodbye then, poppet,' when I say,
she simply replies, sad-eyed, her face grave:
'I won't let you go.' That is all.
She sits where she is, makes not the slightest attempt
to either hold my arm or close the door,
but only with her heart's right, given by love,
proclaims her stand: 'I won't let you go.'

Yet in the end the time comes when, alas,
she has to let me go.

       Foolish girl, my
daughter, who gave you the strength
to make such a statement, so bold, so self-assured –
'I won't let you go'? Whom will you,
in this universe, with two little hands
hold back, proud girl, and against whom fight,
with that tiny weary body of yours by the door,
that stock of love in your heart your only arms?
Nervously, shyly, urged by our pain within,
we can but express our innermost desire,
just say, 'I do not wish
to let you go.' But who can
say such a thing as 'I won't let you go'!
Hearing such a proud assertion of love
from your little mouth, the world, with a mischievous smile,
dragged me from you, and you, quite defeated,
sat by the door like a picture, tears in your eyes.
All I could do was mop my own eyes and leave.

On either side of the road as I move on
fields of autumn, bent by the weight of their crops,
bask in the sun; trees, indifferent to others,
stand on either side, staring all day
at their own shadows. Full, autumnal,
Ganga flows rapidly. In the blue heavens
white cloudlets lie like delicate new-born calves,
fully satisfied with their mother's milk
and blissfully asleep. I sigh,
looking at the earth, stretching to the horizon,
weary of the passing epochs, bare in the brilliant sun.

In what a profound sadness are sky and earth
immersed! The further I go,
the more I hear the same piteous note:
'I won't let you go!' From the earth's edge
to the outermost limits of the blue heavens rings
this perennial cry, without beginning, without end:
'I won't let you go! I won't let you go!' That's what
they all say – 'I won't let you go!' Mother earth,

94

holding the littlest grass-stalk to her breast,
says with all her power: 'I won't let you go!'
And in a lamp about to go out, someone seems
to pull the dying flame from darkness's grasp,
saying a hundred times, 'Ah, I won't let you go!'
From heaven to earth in this infinite universe
this is the oldest statement, the deepest cry –
'I won't let you go!' And yet, alas,
we have to let go of everything, and they go.
Thus it has been since time without beginning.
In creation's torrent, carrier of deluging seas,
they all rush past with fierce velocity,
eyes burning, eager arms outstretched,
moaning, calling – 'Won't, won't let you go!' –
filling the shores of the cosmos with their clamour.
'Won't, won't let you go,' declares the rear wave
to the front wave, but none listens
or responds.

      From all directions today
that sad heart-rending wail reaches my ears,
ringing without pause, and in my daughter's voice:
a cry of the cosmos quite as importunate
as a child's. Since time began
all it gets it loses. Yet its grasp
of things hasn't slackened, and in the pride
of undiminished love, like my daughter of four,
ceaselessly it sends out this cry: 'I won't let you go!'
Face wan, tears streaming,
its pride is shattered each hour, every minute.
Yet such is love, it never concedes defeat
and in a choked voice rebelliously repeats:
'I won't let you go!' Each time it loses,
each time it blurts, 'How can what I
love be ever alienated from me?
Is there anything in this whole universe
as full of yearning, as superlative,
as mighty, as boundless as my desire?'
So saying, it arrogantly proclaims:
'I won't let you go', only to see at once
its cherished treasure blown away by a breath
like trivial dry dust, whereupon

eyes overflowing, like a tree uprooted,
it collapses on the ground, pride crushed, head bent.
Yet this remains love's plea:
'I won't let the Creator break His promise to me.
A great pledge, sealed and signed, to me was given,
a charter of rights in perpetuity.'
Thus, though thin and frail, and face to face
with almighty death, it says, swollen with pride,
'Death, you don't exist!' What cheek!
Death sits, smiling. And that eternal love,
so death-tormented, for ever in a flutter
with restless anxiety, has quite overpowered
this infinite universe, like the dampness of tears
suffusing sad eyes. A weary hope against hope
has drawn a mist of dejection over the whole
universe. Yes, I think I see
two hapless imploring arms lie quietly,
encircling the world, in a vain attempt
to bind it in its embrace, like a still reflection
lying in a flowing stream – some illusion
of a cloud charged with raindrops and tears.

Wherefore today I can hear
so much yearning in the rustling of the trees,
as the noonday's hot wind, idly unmindful, plays
meaningless games with dry leaves, and as the day wanes,
lengthening the shadows under the peepul trees.
The cosmos is a field where the infinite's flute
plays a pastoral lament. And she sits and listens,
earth, her hair down, and it fills her with longing,
there, in the far cornfields, by Ganga's borders,
a golden cloth-end, sunlight-yellow, drawn
over her breast. Her eyes are still,
fixed on the far blue sky, and she says nothing.
Yes, I've seen her pale face,
no different from the face of my daughter of four,
so quiet, so hurt, and nearly lost in the door-edge.

[Calcutta, 29 October 1892]

Earth

Earth, take me back,
your lap-child back to your lap
in the shelter of your sari's voluminous end.
Mother made of earth, may I
live diffused in your soil; spread
myself in every direction like spring's joy;
burst this breast-cage, shatter this stone-closed
narrow wall, this blind dismal jail
of self; swing, hum, shake,
flop, radiate, disperse,
shudder, be startled by
sudden lights and thrills,
flow through the whole globe –
edge to edge, north to south,
east to west; burgeon
with secret sap in moss, lichen, grass,
branch, bark, leaf; touch
with rippling fingers cornfields bent with the weight
of golden ears; privily fill
new blossoms with colour, aroma, nectar;
fill too, with blue, waters of vast seas,
and dance to ceaseless waves on quiet beaches;
hurrah language from wave to wave everywhere;
lay myself like a white scarf on mountain-tops,
in lofty regions of solitude, lands of hushed
unsullied snow.

　　　　The desire that unawares to me
has long been welling in me like a secret spring,
now, having brimmed the heart, wants to get out
in a flow that will be free, generous, bold,
uncontrolled – in order to bedew you.
How shall I crack this heart, how unfetter
that anguished wish, send it in a million streams
to all lands and directions!
Therefore, simply sitting at home,
I'm always greedily devouring travelogues,
tales of those whom curiosity has driven
to roam in strange places. And with them
I girdle you in my imagination's meshes.

Far lands difficult of access,
endless savannahs with neither trees nor tracks,
theatres of dire thirst, where the glare
from burning sand-heaps pierces eyes like needles,
beds of dust to the horizon upon which
earth, flushed with fever, lies and pants,
breath inflamed, throat parched, body on fire,
ruthless, taciturn, all alone.
Many a time sitting at home by my window,
looking out, I've imagined scenes far away:
say, a blue lake, hushed, secluded,
clear as crystal, circled by sierras,
cloudlets clinging to the peaks like suckling infants;
snow-lines, visible above the mountains' blue,
block our sight, like row upon row
of immobile barricades mushroomed through heaven,
sentries posted at yoga-immersed
matted-hair Shiva's hermitage.
In my mind I've roamed
on far-off polar beaches where earth's vowed
eternal virginity in chill attire,
bereft of jewels, desires, company;
where at long night's end, day returns,
but without sound or music; and night comes,
with none to sleep, stays steadfastly awake
in the endless sky, like a mother whose sleep's been murdered,
whose bed is empty, whose child is dead.
The more I study the names of new countries
and their varied accounts, the more my mind
rushes forward, wanting to touch all; say, by a sea,
between small blue hills there lies a hamlet where
fishing-nets lie on the beach, drying in the sun,
a boat hovers on the waters, a sail stirs,
a fisherman fishes, and through a steep ravine
a narrow stream winds its way, twists and turns.
How I wish I could
embrace with my arms, press to my heart that nest
of human habitation, cosily ensconced
in the lap of hills and resonant with the waves!
Whatever exists anywhere I wish to make mine,
melt myself into a river's current,
to village after village on either bank

offer myself as water to quench men's thirst,
sing my murmuring song both day and night;
become a chain of lofty mountains stretching
from the sea where the sun rises to the sea where it sets,
rim to rim, a cincture to the earth,
noble in my mystery, which none may fathom,
and on my hard stone lap, where the chill wind sharply blows,
secretly cradle, rear to manhood new
unknown nations. Deep is my desire
in country after country to identify
myself with all men; to be born
as an Arab child in the desert, fearless and free,
raised on camel's milk; to explore
cold stone mansions, Buddhist monasteries
on Tibet's plateau; to drink grape-wine
as a Persian in a rose-garden; to ride
horses as an intrepid Tartar; to be polite
and vigorous as a Japanese; to toil
with dedication as in the ancient Chinese land;
to experience existence in all homes.
Oh, to be a naked barbarian, sturdy, robust, fierce,
neither to duties nor to prohibitions geared,
bound by nothing – neither customs, nor scruples, nor doubts,
nor a sense of mine and thine, nor the fever of thought;
one whose life-flow always rushes unchecked,
colliding with what's in front, bearing clouts
without a whimper, never looking back –
stung by conscience or in vain remorse –
nor regarding the future with false hopes,
but on the wave-peaks of the here and the now
dancing and moving on in thrilled delight!
Yes, that life's unruly, but I still love it,
and how often have I wished I could submit
to that vitality's storm, hurtling like a light-weight
boat in full sail!

      The forest's ferocious tiger
easily bears his own enormous heft
by his immense strength. His body, vivid and bright
like thunder within which fire lurks, beneath
forests which are like clouds, with a mighty roar
as deep as thunder springs suddenly upon his prey

with lightning's speed. Effortless is that greatness,
violence-keen that joy, that proud triumph:
even such things I wish to savour once!
I would, if I could, drink again and again
the manifold wines of joy that overflow
all the goblets that this cosmos holds.

Beautiful earth, as I have looked upon you,
how often has my spirit leapt into song
with huge happiness! How I have craved
to get a firm grip on your ocean-girdled waist
and keep it pressed to my breast;
to spread myself in every direction, as pervasive
and boundless as the morning sun; to dance
all day long upon forests, upon mountains,
on the undulations of trembling leaves; to kiss
every flower that buds; to embrace
all the tender densely growing greenswards;
to oscillate as on a swing of delight
on every wave; and quietly at night
with hushed footsteps to come as cosmic sleep,
stroking the eyes of all your birds and beasts
with my own fingers, entering every bed,
nest, home, cave, den that there is, spreading myself
like a gigantic sari-end upon
all that exists, cloaking it
with the gentlest darkness!

       My earth, you are
so many years old; with me mixed in your clay,
unwearied in the limitless firmament,
you have orbited the sun; and for nights and days
spanning millennia within me your grass has grown,
flowers in clusters have opened,
so many trees have shed their leaves, buds, fruits,
odoriferous pollen! Hence in the present time,
maybe one day, sitting alone with a drifting mind
on Padma's bank, gazing with charmed eyes,
with all my limbs and awareness I can sense
how grass-seeds sprout with shivers within your soil,
how, inside you, streams of vital fluids
circulate night and day, how flower-buds

appear with blind ecstatic delight,
shielded by lovely calyces, how in the morning sun
grass-blades, climbers, trees, shrubs rejoice,
with a concealed thrill and almost foolish elation,
like infants wearied by suckling at mothers' breasts,
fully satisfied, smiling at pleasant dreams.
Likewise some day when post-rains sunrays
fall on fields of ripened golden crops,
rows of coconut palms quiver in the breeze,
shimmer in the sun, there rises within me such
an immense yearning, as if in remembrance
of bygone days when my sentience was dispersed
everywhere – in land, water, leaves,
the sky's azure. And the entire world
seems to send me a hundred inarticulate calls,
like the familiar hubbub of manifold
gladsome games played by my perennial
companions, a happy commingled murmur
issuing from a vast, varied nursery.
Take me back
once more to that refuge, remove that hurt
of separation that throbs from time to time
within my mind, when in the evening's rays
I look at a big meadow, as cows return
from far pastures, kicking dust from field-paths,
smoke curls from tree-encircled hamlets
up to the evening sky, far off the moon
appears slowly, slowly like a weary farer,
and on the deserted sandbank by the river
I feel so lonely, such an alien,
like an exile, and with arms outstretched
I rush out to receive the entire outer world
within myself: sky, earth, river-nestled
heaps of sleeping calm white moonlight. But I can't
touch anything and just stare at an emptiness
in utter despondence. Take me back
to the centre of that wholeness, whence continually
life germinates in a hundred thousand ways,
sends out shoots and buds, whence songs burst
in a million melodies, dances emanate
in countless gestures, where the mind flows
in torrents of ideas and emotions, where every hole

belongs to a flute that plays, and where you stand,
black mythic cow of plenty, being milked
from a thousand angles by plants, birds, beasts,
numberless thirsty creatures, the juice of joy
raining in so many ways and all the directions
echoing to that murmuring music. I wish
to taste that various, universal bliss
in one moment, all elements together,
united with all. And will not your groves
be even greener, mingled with my gladness?
Will not a few new trembling rays invade
the morning sunshine? Surely my ecstasy
will dye both earth and sky with the heart's pigments,
gazing at which, within a poet's mind
poems shall rise, lovers' eyes shall fill
with emotion's intoxication, and from bird-beaks
sudden songs shall spring. O earth,
all your limbs are dyed with the happiness
of so many thousands!
Floods of creatures have again and again
enveloped you with their lives, gone and returned,
mixing their hearts' affection with your humus,
writing so many scripts, spreading in so many directions
such yearning eager embraces! With them I shall
mingle all my love with diligent care,
dye your sari's end with vivid colours.
Yes, I shall
deck you with my all. And will not
some enchanted ear on a river-bank
hear my song in the water's murmur? Will not
some earth-dweller rise from sleep, perceive
my song in the dawn-light? A hundred years hence
will not my spirit quiver in this lovely forest's
layers of leaves? In home after home
hundreds of men and women will for long
play their games of domesticity, and will not
something of myself remain in their loves?
Tell me, will I not
descend as laughter on their faces or as lush
youth on all their limbs? Will I not be
their sudden pleasure on a spring day or a young
keen bud of love sprouting in a nook

of their minds? Could you, motherland,
abandon me altogether? Could the tough
earthen cord that has endured for ages
suddenly be severed? Might I have to leave
the soft lap that has cradled me a million years?
Rather, from all sides won't they pull me to them:
all these trees, shrubs, mountains, rivers, glens,
this deep blue sky that belongs to eternity,
this generous breeze that wafts such vitality,
light that wakes, the knitted social lives
within which all creatures live enmeshed?
Yes, I'll circle you; I shall dwell among
your own kinsfolk; as birds, beasts, worms,
trees, shrubs, creepers you'll call me again and again,
draw me to your warm throbbing bosom;
age after age, life after life you'll press
your breasts to my mouth, assuage the million
hungers of my lives with the dripping ambrosial milk
of a million delights, emptying yourself
and making me drink with your deepest tenderness.
Then shall I, a young man, earth's grown up son,
travel the world, traverse continents,
venture far, far among constellations
along inaccessible tracks. But as yet
I've not had enough; thirst for your nectar-milk
still clings to my mouth; your face
still brings lovely dreams before my eyes;
nothing of you have I finished yet;
all is mysterious, and my steady gaze
hasn't yet plumbed the depth of its own amazement.
Like a child I still cling to your bosom,
my eyes on your face. Mother, hold me, please,
within the firmest embrace of your arms.
Make me your own, one who belongs to your breast:
that secret source from where the fountain rises –
of your vast vitality and varied delights –
do take me there. Don't keep me away.

[11 November 1893]

On the Doctrine of Maya

Joyless country, in tattered decrepitude dressed,
burdened by your own sagacity, you think
that God's deception has been caught red-handed
by your too-clever discriminating gaze.
With a wit as sharp as a needle of kush-grass,
unemployed, you sit at home night and day,
convinced that this earth, this universe,
planets and stars in the firmament are fakes.
Birds and beasts, creatures of many species,
bereft of fear, have breathed here for ages.
To them this created world is a mother's lap,
but you, old dotard, have faith in nothing! And this
cosmic concourse, fairground of millions, billions
of living things is to you child's play.

[Simla? November 1893?]

Play

Well, maybe it's play, but one which we must join
with everyone, in a happy hullabaloo!
What would be the point of leaving it all and sitting
silently in a dark corner of the self?
Know that you are but a child in this vast world,
in the cradle of infinite time, in the sky's playground:
you think you know it all, but you know nothing!
Pick it up – with faith, humility, love –
that grand toy – coloured, musical, scented –
which your mother's given you. Well, maybe it's dust!
So what? Isn't it dust beyond compare?
Prematurely senile, don't mope, sitting alone:
you won't be an adult till you join the merry-go-round!

[Simla? November 1893?]

104

On Her Powerlessness

Where I've found myself, there I belong,
a needy offspring of this indigent earth.
The burden of pains and pleasures I've had since birth
I've decided to accept as my sheer good luck.
My earthen mother, green and all-enduring,
I know your hands don't hold infinite riches.
You want to feed all hungry mouths, but alas,
so often you can't; and 'What, what can we eat?' –
your children cry, their faces pale and withered.
Mother, I know your hands hold unfinished pleasures:
whatever you shape and give us breaks into pieces.
Death, omnivorous, pokes his fingers in every pie
and all our hopes you can never satisfy,
but that's no reason to forsake your warm breast!

[Simla? November 1893?]

❦

FROM *Chitra* (1896)

Farewell to Heaven

Now fades the garland of mandars round my neck,
o great Indra, and the radiant mark is quenched
on my sullied forehead. My piety's strength
wanes. And gods, goddesses, today I must
say goodbye to heaven. Gladly have I spent
many millennia in the kingdom of the gods
as one of the immortals, and had hoped to see
at this parting-hour a hint of tears
in heaven's eyes. But heartless, void of grief,
indifferent, this happy celestial land

just looks on. The passing of millennia
is not a blink to its eyes; not even the hurt
a branch of the peepul-tree feels, when from its edge
the driest leaf falls, can be felt by heaven, when
hundreds of us, like burnt-out refugee stars,
are dislodged, to descend, in an instant,
even from the region of the gods down to the earth's
unending stream of births and deaths. And should
such hurt have been felt, should the merest trace
of separation's shadow have fallen across heaven,
then would its eternal brilliance have been veiled
with soft dewy vapours as on earth; Nandan-garden
would have murmured sighs; Mandakini,
lapping its banks, would have, in liquid voice,
sung sad tales; at the day's end
evening would have come, walked like a hermitess
to the horizon, beyond lone fields; still nights
would have played the chanting crickets' ascetic chorus
under the assembled stars; in the hall of the gods
at times dancing Menaka's golden anklets
would have missed a beat; leaning on Urbashi's breast,
her golden vina, strings roughly pressed,
would have at times, as if unawares to her,
burst into sudden bars of tragic music.
Lines of idle tears might then have appeared
on the dry eyes of the gods; by her husband's side,
throned on the same seat, Shachi might have suddenly looked
into Indra's eyes, as if seeking water for her thirst.
And the wind might have wafted towards heaven
sudden gusts of the earth's long-drawn sighs,
shaking petals off the Nandan branches.

Stay laughing, heaven. Gods, keep drinking your nectar.
Heaven is indeed your very own place of bliss,
where we are aliens. Earth – she is no heaven,
but she's a motherland; that's why her eyes
stream with tears, if after a few days
anyone leaves her even for a few hours.
The humble, the meek, the most incompetent,
sinners and sick men – all she would hold tight
in an eager embrace, fasten to her soft breast,
such is the pleasure a mother gets from the touch

of her children's dusty bodies. So let there flow
nectar in heaven, and on earth let love,
for ever mixed with pains and pleasures, stream,
keeping earth's heaven-spots evergreen with tears.

Nymph, may the pain of love never diminish
the shine of your bright eyes. I bid you goodbye.
You desire nobody, nor grieve for any.
Should my love be born in the poorest home on earth,
by the side of a river, at the edge of a village, in a hut
half-hidden in the shade of a peepul, she might
carefully save for me her ambrosial store
within her breast. When she's a child,
she will in the mornings sit on the river-bank,
fashion images of Shiva with the riverside clay
and pray to have me as her bridegroom. When evening falls,
she'll light a lamp and let it float on the waters,
and alone on the ghat, her breast trembling with fear,
she'll figure her fortunes with total concentration.
One day, at an auspicious hour,
her eyes lowered, she will walk into my home,
draped in red silk, sandal tracery on forehead,
to the playing of festive flutes. Then will she be,
in days of rejoicing and in days of affliction,
with good-omen bangles and propitious vermilion dot
below her parted hair, the presiding goddess
of my home, the full moon's orb
by the bedside of the world's tumultuous ocean.
Sometimes, gods, I shall remember this heaven
like a far-off dream, when half-way through the night
waking suddenly from sleep, I'll see the moon
flooding the white bed, and my love fast asleep,
slack arm lying loosely, sari dishevelled,
shyness forgotten, until roused by my soft
amorous kisses, she will, startled, fold me
fast in her arms, twine around my chest,
as the south wind wafts flower-scents, and wide awake,
a koel calls from a distant branch.

Ah, mother,
pauperised, afflicted, tearful, tarnished earth,
after so many days at last today my heart

stirs with weeping for your sake, alas!
As soon as the sadness of farewell filled these eyes,
which had been dry before, the celestial world
vanished who knows where like an idle dream
or a shadow-picture. And your blue sky, your light,
your populous human habitations, long lines
of sandy beaches by the seas, white snow-streaks
on blue mountain-heads, quiet dawns
between avenues of trees, face-lowered evenings
on deserted river-banks: all, all fell down
onto a tear-drop, reflections within
a mirror's depth.

           Ah, sonless mother,
the torrent of tears you shed at our last adieu,
which, welling from your eyes, overflowed
and anointed your maternal breasts, has now
evaporated. Yet in my mind I know
when I return once more to your homestead,
instantly you'll hold me within your arms,
to the sound of auspicious conch-shells, and you'll welcome
me as one long known to you, to love's shade
in your home, familiar world of affections,
filled with pains, pleasures, fears, and children.
From the next day, I know, you'll be at my bedside,
ever vigilant, with a trembling heart,
panic inside you, sad gaze upturned
to the gods above, and pensive, wondering when
you might lose him, whom you had regained.

[Shilaidaha, or approaching it on boat? 9 December 1895]

The Victorious Woman

When into the waters of Lake Achchhod the lady
stepped down for bathing, then was the young spring
straying all over the world, in fits of trembling
like first love, hairs standing on end
every now and then. Then was the wind

idly prattling on a bed of leaves,
where the shade was the densest; noon's radiance
was aswooned on the forest's lap; a pair of pigeons,
perched on a still and peaceful champak branch,
were, in an interval between close beak-kissings,
rapt, in their privacy, in ecstatic cooing.

On the bank, beneath a white stone, her deep-blue cloth
lay forlorn in a corner, from glory dropped,
uncared-for, the lovely body's warm scent
still clinging to it, like a last flicker of breath
in a fainted body whose term has come to an end.
The girdle lay, discarded from her waist,
silent in rejection's hurt, the anklets too,
the breast-cloth in disorder upon the ground,
fallen from the twin heavens on the hard stone.
The golden mirror gazed into emptiness,
recalling a face. Arranged on a golden plate –
sandal-and-saffron paste; ravished and abashed,
two red lotuses; beautiful, unwithered,
a garland of white oleanders; a washed white cloth,
light, translucent, like a sky lit by the full moon.
Brimful and blue the waters, still and unruffled,
deep and rapturous, stretched from bank to bank,
a mass of embraces overflowing the breast.
At the lake's edge, in the bokul's dense shade,
sitting on a white stone-slab, the lovely woman,
breast-deep in water, her trembling reflection
spread in the transparent liquid, drew to her breast
the white she-swan that had been reared with care
and fondled her, folding her delicate wings
in her bare arms, placing her long neck
on her own shoulder, speaking again and again
affection's ravings, brushing her soft cheek,
drunk with touching, on the swan's feathery back.

From the four directions sweet melodies were rising
in water, land, and sky; someone was framing
a winsome story in shadow and sunshine,
in the forest's slumber and the leaves' susurrus,
in the many tremors and throbs of the spring day,
in breath and swelling, language, hint, and hum,

in flashes and wonders: as though the sunray-strings
of the sky's vina, plucked by a celestial girl's
champak-fingers, were pouring lamentations
in bursts of music, piercing the quiet
with their keen anguish, while without a sound
the limp bokuls kept falling from their tree
in the seclusion, and ceaselessly sang
the indefatigable koel, whose vain calls
travelled the forests as echoes – single-minded,
blind to all else. Not far in the shade
a streamlet came to meet the edge of the lake
ringing her ruby-spangled bells in dance
to a murmurous mingling; on the grass-swathed bank
a crane slept, lulled by the water's gentle lapping
in the noon air, his long slender neck
gracefully curved and tucked under his back
between grey wings. Meanwhile in the sky
a flock of swans pursued their hurried flight
to Kailas, where the snows had melted,
leaving behind them distant, favourite haunts –
rivers and beaches. Weighted with woodland smells,
sometimes the weary wind had warm impulses
and flung itself with deep, long-drawn sighs
into the charmed lake's bosom, its cool arm-embraces.

Eager and curious, the Love-god, friend of Spring,
was sitting concealed at the foot of the bokul tree,
on fallen flowers, carelessly leaning on the trunk,
his feet stretched out on the layer of new grass before him.
The edge of his yellow wrap trailed on the ground;
a chain of malatis hung from his curly hair
to his white neck. Smiling with sidelong glance,
in fun he observed the alluring young woman's
bathing-dalliance. Avid and impatient,
his restless fingers awaited the right time
to aim his floral arrow at her pure, soft breast.
A million bees were flitting from flower to flower,
murmuring; a rapt-eyed deer
from time to time gave little, gentle licks
to his mate asleep in the shade. The touch of spring
had filled the forest with languor and desire.

Leaving hurt, piqued ripples in the water's edge,
with wet footprints, one by one, marking the steps,
the beautiful woman came up to the bank:
her heavy hair came undone and cascaded down her back.
In all her limbs the surging waves of youth
were held immured by the magic formula of grace,
still and hypnotised. And on their peaks
fell the midday's sunshine, – on forehead, lips,
thighs, waist, breast-tips,
arms, – gleaming on all the lines
of that dripping body, as round her gathered,
together in one place, air's entire sphere
and the infinite sky, bent in humble zeal,
kissing her whole body, like a diligent servant
wiping off, with a warm towel, all the wetness.
Her shadow cast at her lac-dye-reddened feet
lay prostrate like a cloth that had slipped down.
Hushed with amazement, the woods stayed ever so still.

Then rose the Love-god, leaving the bokul's base,
a soft smile on his face.
                    Coming before her,
suddenly he came to a halt. At her face
for a moment he looked with a steady, transfixed gaze,
and at the next, kneeling on the ground,
speechless with wonder, his head bowed down,
at her feet laid his offerings of adoration,
his flower-bow and all his flower-arrows,
emptying his quiver.
                    At Love after his disarmament
the beauty looked benignly, with a serene countenance.

[14 January 1896]

The Year 1400

                    A hundred years from today
who are you, sitting, reading a poem of mine,
                    under curiosity's sway –
          a hundred years from today?

111

Not the least portion
of this young spring's morning bliss,
            neither blossom nor birdsong,
                  nor any of its scarlet splashes
            can I drench in passion
                  and despatch to your hands
                  a hundred years hence!

Yet do this, please: unlatch your south-faced door,
                  just sit at your window for once;
basking in fantasy, eyes on the far horizon,
                  figure out if you can:
            how one day a hundred years back
roving delights in a free fall from a heavenly region
                  had touched all that there was –
the infant Phalgun day, utterly free,
                  was frenzied, all agog,
while borne on brisk wings, the south wind
                  pollen-scent-brushed
had suddenly arrived and in a flash dyed the earth
                  with all youth's hues
                  a hundred years before your day.

There lived then a poet, ebullient of spirit,
                  his heart steeped in song,
who wanted to open his words like so many flowers
                  with so much passion
            one day a hundred years back.

            A hundred years from today
                  who is the new poet
whose songs flow through your homes?
                  To him I convey
            this springtime's gladsome greetings.
May my vernal song find its echo for a moment
                  in your spring day
in the throbbing of your hearts, in the buzzing of your bees,
                  in the rustling of your leaves
                  a hundred years from today!

[13 February 1896 (2 Phalgun 1302)]

112

FROM *Chaitali* (1896)

Renunciation

Said a man fed up with the world in the depth of night,
'I'll leave home tonight for the sake of the God I adore.
Who's it that keeps me ensnared within this house?'
'I,' said God, but it didn't enter his ears.
Clasping their sleeping infant to her breast,
his wife lay happily asleep on a side of the bed.
'Who are you all, maya's masks?' he asked.
'They are myself,' said God, but no one heard.
'Lord, where are you?' said the man, leaving his bed.
'Right here,' was the answer, but still the fellow was deaf.
The child cried in his sleep and clung to his mother.
'Return,' said God, but the man didn't hear the order.
Then at last God sighed. 'Alas,' said He,
'where's my devotee going, leaving me?'

[Shilaidaha? 26 March 1896]

An Ordinary Person

A stick under his arm, a pack on his head,
at dusk a villager goes home along the river.
If after a hundred centuries somehow –
by some magic – from the past's kingdom of death
this peasant could be resurrected, again made flesh,
with this stick under his arm and surprise in his eyes,
then would crowds besiege him on all sides,
everyone snatching every word from his lips.
His joys and sorrows, attachments and loves,
his neighbours, his own household,
his fields, cattle, methods of farming: all
they would take in greedily and still it wouldn't be enough.
His life-story, today so ordinary,
will, in those days, seem charged with poetry.

[Potisar? 29 March 1896]

113

The Ferry

A ferry-boat crosses and re-crosses the river.
Some go home, some go away from home.
Two villages on two banks know each other.
From dawn to dusk the folks go to and fro.
Elsewhere so many strifes, disasters happen;
histories are made, unmade, re-written.
Foaming upon cascades of spilt blood,
crowns of gold like bubbles swell and burst.
Civilisation's latest hungers, thirsts
throw up so many toxins, honeyed draughts.
Here on two banks two villages stare at each other,
to the big wide world their names quite unknown.
Daily the ferry-boat plies upon the waters,
with some going home, some going away from home.

[Potisar? 30 March 1896]

The Worker

Not a sign of my servant in the morning.
The door wide open.   No water for my bath.
        The rascal had absconded last night.
I hadn't the faintest idea   where my clean clothes were
        or where my breakfast was.
The clock ticked away.   I sat in a bad mood.
        I would tell him off, I would!
At last he appeared,   saluted as usual.
        With his palms together, he stood.
'Go away!' I said   in a fit of rage,
        'I don't want to see your face!'
Like an idiot, for a minute,   as if robbed of speech,
        he stared at my face, then said
in a voice choked with emotion,   'Sir, at midnight
        last night my little girl died.'
So saying, in a hurry,   with his duster on his shoulder
        alone he went to do his jobs,

114

and as on any other day   scrubbed, scoured, polished,
        left not a chore unfinished.

[Potisar? 30 March 1896]

Big Sister

They dig by the river for bricklaying –
labourers from the west country. Their little girl
keeps scampering to the ghat. Such scrubbing and scouring
of pots and pans and dishes! Comes running
a hundred times a day, brass bangles jangling
clang clang against the brass plates she cleans.
So busy all day! Her little brother,
bald, mud-daubed, not a stitch on his limbs,
follows her like a pet, patiently sits
on the high bank, as Big Sister commands.
Plates against her left side, a full pitcher on her head,
the girl goes back, the child's hand in her right hand.
A surrogate of her mother,
bent under her work-load, such a wee Big Sister!

[Potisar? 2 April 1896]

The Mediatrix

And one day I saw the same naked boy
sitting on the ground, legs stretched on the dust.
Big Sister at the ghat sat scrubbing a pot
with clay, turning and turning it.
A soft-haired kid was grazing near by,
gently nibbling the grass of the river-bank.
Suddenly the kid drew near, and looking at the lad's face,
gave a few bleats.
Startled, the boy trembled and burst into tears.
Big Sister left her pot, came running down.

115

Her brother on one side, the goat on the other,
she consoled both, giving them equal attention.
Sister to both children, animal and human,
mediatrix, she knit them in mutual knowledge.

[Potisar? 2 April 1896]

On the Nature of Love

The night is black and the forest has no end;
a million people thread it in a million ways.
We have trysts to keep in the darkness, but where
or with whom – of that we are unaware.
But we have this faith – that a lifetime's bliss
will appear any minute, with a smile upon its lips.
Scents, touches, sounds, snatches of songs
brush us, pass us, give us delightful shocks.
Then peradventure there's a flash of lightning:
whomever I see that instant I fall in love with.
I call that person and cry: 'This life is blest!
For your sake such miles have I traversed!'
All those others who came close and moved off
in the darkness – I don't know if they exist or not.

[En route to Shahjadpur by boat? 3 April 1896]

Putu

It was a long-drawn Chaitra noon;
the earth was thirsty, burnt by the day.
Suddenly I heard someone calling
somewhere outside, 'Puturani, come!'
The river-bank's deserted in the midday,
so the voice of affection made me curious.
Closing my book, I slowly got up,
opened the door a little and looked outside.

116

A huge buffalo, covered in mud,
tender-eyed, was standing on the bank.
A young man was in the water, calling her
to give her a bath, 'Puturani, come!'
When I saw the young man and his Puturani,
gentle tears mingled with my smiles.

[En route to Shahjadpur by boat? 4 April 1896]

The Companion

And I remember yet another day.
One afternoon I saw a gypsy girl
sitting on the green grass at a meadow's edge,
just by herself, doing her hair in a plait.
Her pet puppy came behind her, took
the movement of the hair to be some sport,
and jumping high and barking loudly, began
to bite the moving plait again and again.
The girl shook her neck and told him off,
which only increased the puppy's playful mood.
She gave him a little rap with her forefinger;
he took it for more play, got more excited.
Laughing then, she got up, drew him to her breast
and smothered him with cuddles.

[En route to Shahjadpur by boat? 4 April 1896]

A Scene of Affection

He would be about twenty, with a wasted body
reduced to skin and bones through many years' illness.
Looking at his vacant face – not a smile on it –
you would think he was wholly incapable
of sucking out the least pleasure from this world
even with all his body and mind and soul.

117

His mother carries him like a child –
his long thin withered barely throbbing body –
and without hope, yet patient, with a sad face, without words,
daily she brings him by the side of the road.
Trains come and go; people rush; just in case
the commotion revives the moribund's interest
in the world, and he looks at it a little –
with such meagre hope does his mother bring him.

[En route to Shahjadpur by boat? 5 April 1896]

Against Meditative Knowledge

Those who wish to sit, shut their eyes,
and meditate to know if the world's true or lies,
may do so. It's their choice. But I meanwhile
with hungry eyes that can't be satisfied
shall take a look at the world in broad daylight.

[Shahjadpur? 8 April 1896]

True Meditation

The more I love you and see you in your greatness,
the more, dearest, I see you in true light.
The more I lower you, the less I seem to know you,
sometimes losing you, sometimes keeping you in sight.
This spring day, with my mind enlightened,
I see a vision I've never seen before:
this world's vanished; there's nothing at all;
before me only a vast ocean unfolds.
There's neither day nor night, no minutes or hours;
the cataclysmic waters are controlled;
in the midst of it all, with all your petals unfurled,
you hover, sole lotus, and stay afloat.
The king of the cosmos sits for ever, impassioned,
and beholds in you his own self's reflection.

[Shahjadpur? 9 April 1896]

118

Drought

In olden days, I've heard, gods in love
with mortal women used to descend from heaven.
Those days are gone. It's Baishakh, the dry season,
a day of burnt out fields and shrunken streams.
A peasant's daughter, piteously suppliant,
begs again and again, 'Come, rain, come!'
Her eyes grieving, restless, and expectant,
from time to time she casts a look at the sky.
But no rain falls. The wind, deaf to her cries,
rushes past, dispersing all the clouds,
and the sun has licked all moisture from the sky
with its tongue of fire. Alas, these degenerate days
the gods are senile. And women can only appeal
to mortal men.

[Shahjadpur? 13 April 1896]

Hope Against Hope

'Mother! Mother!' I call to you in terror
in order that my wretched cries might make you
behave like a mother.
Perchance you will, as tigresses are known to do,
abjure all violence and lick this human child.
Well might you hide your claws and press to my mouth
your swollen teats, allow me to doze and rest,
nestled against your striped-as-a-picture breast.
Such is my hope! Ah, greater than great,
you are above, showing your billions of stars,
your moons, planets! Should you suddenly frown
hideously, and lift your thunder-fist,
where would I be, so puny, such a weakling?
So, she-devil, let me decoy you to be a mother!

[Shahjadpur? 13 April 1896]

Give Us Deeds, Not Words

Said the wasp to the bee, 'This is such a tiny hive!
and you are so proud of such a small achievement!'
'Why, then, brother,' was the bee's reply,
'let's see you make a smaller hive for a change!'

Relationship of Convenience

Said the beggar's bowl to the rich man's money-bag,
'We're related by marriage; let's not forget that.'
The bag said, 'Should what I have be transferred to you,
all relationship you would forget too.'

Kinship Analysed

Said the paraffin lantern to the earthen lamp,
'Call me brother, and I shall have you flanned.'
Up rose the moon in the sky soon thereafter.
Quickly the lantern said, 'Hallo, Big Brother!'

Too Good

Good-Enough said to Even-Better,
'In which heaven do you show your lustre?'
'Alas,' cried Even-Better, 'I live in the impotent
jealousy of the insolent and incompetent.'

Positive Proof

Thunder says, 'As long as I'm far away,
they refer to my roar as the rumble of clouds,
and my brilliance is attributed to lightning,
but when I fall on heads, they say: thunder indeed!'

ॐ

FROM *Katha* (1900)

The Repayment
(Adapted from a Buddhist story)

'Theft from the royal treasury! Catch the thief!
Or else, Police Chief, you'll come to grief—
there won't be a head on your body!' Terrified
of royal wrath, policemen scoured streets
and houses in search of the thief. Outside the city
in a ruined temple lay Bajrasen,
a foreigner there, a merchant from Taxila,
who had come to Benares to sell horses,
and having been robbed of all, made destitute,
was sadly returning to his native land.
On him they pounced, arresting him as the thief,
binding his hands and feet in iron chains,
dragging him to prison.

        At that very instant
Shyama, queen of the city beauties, sat
at her window in a mood of indolent fun,
spending her time watching the flow of the street,
the dreamlike procession of people. Suddenly
she shivered and cried, 'Alas! Who's this?
So tall, handsomer than great Indra himself,
being dragged to prison like a common thief
in harsh chains! Quick, my friend!

Go to the Police Chief, mention my name
and say I would speak to him. Could he come
just once with the prisoner to my humble home? –
It would be a favour.' Such was the attraction
of Shyama's name that the Police Chief, impatient,
thrilled to be invited, quickly came,
behind him, in chains, Bajrasen, head bowed,
cheeks shame-red. Said the Chief with a smile,
'Untimely comes such an unsolicited favour
toward this undeserving person. I'm on my way
to do the king's business. So, my Lovely, permit me.'
Suddenly Bajrasen lifted his head and said,
'Beauty, what sport, what perverse humour is this
that makes you call me from the street into your house
to humiliate this innocent foreigner's hurt
of humiliation?' But Shyama said, 'Alas,
foreign traveller, this is no sport at all!
All the jewels I carry on my person
I could give up to take your chains on myself,
and this insult to you, believe me, insults
me to my inmost core.' As she said so,
her eyes, their lashes wet, seemed to want
to wipe off all the insult from the limbs
of the foreigner. And she begged the Chief,
'Take all I have and in return set free
the prisoner.' But the Chief replied,
'Beauty, it's a request I may not grant.
To satisfy you there's beyond my power.
The royal treasury's robbed, and royal wrath
won't be appeased till blood-price is paid.'
Holding the policeman's hands, poor Shyama pleaded
pathetically, 'Keep the prisoner alive
just for two days – this is my humble plea.'
'All right, then, I'll do just that,' said he.

At the end of the second night, a lamp in her hand,
the woman opened the prison doors and entered
the cell where Bajrasen lay in iron chains,
waiting for death's dawn, silently repeating
to himself his God's name. At her eyes' signal
a guard came quickly, freed him from his chains.
The prisoner, his eyes surprise-whelmed,

gazed at that fair face, soft, open as a lotus,
amazingly lovely, and in a choked voice said,
'After the horrors of a grotesque nightmare-night
who are you, appearing in my prison-cell
like the white dawn, the morning star in your hand,
life to the dying, liberation incarnate,
merciful Lakshmi in this merciless city!'

'Me merciful!' The woman laughed so loudly
that the grim prison woke again with shudders
of renewed terror. She laughed and laughed
till her bizarre lunatic laughter burst
into a hundred mournful tear-streams, and she said,
'Many are the stones that pave the city's streets,
but none as hard as Shyama, who's hard indeed!'
So saying, she firmly grasped his hand
and took Bajrasen outside the prison gates.
Day was breaking then on Baruna's banks
above the east woods. A boat was ghat-tied.
'Come, foreigner, come,' said the belle,
standing on the boat, 'listen, my love,
only remember what I'm saying now –
that I'm floating with you on the same stream,
bursting all bonds, o lord of my life and death,
my heart's sovereign!' She untied the boat.
On either side in the woodlands the birds
merrily sang their festive songs. Uplifting
his lady-love's face with both hands, filling his breast,
Bajrasen begged, 'Love, tell me, please,
with what riches you have set me free.
Foreign woman, let me know in full
how big a debt this poor miserable man
owes to you.' Tightening her embrace,
the beauty said, 'We won't talk of that now.'

A brisk breeze and a fierce current made
the boat sail away. Above, a blazing sun
ascended to the zenith. Village wives
went home in wet drapery after their bathes,
carrying bell-metal pitchers of Ganga-water.
The morning market closed; the hubbub stopped
on either side of the river; village paths

emptied. Below a banyan was a stone ghat;
to it the boat was tied so bath and lunch
could be had. On the drowsy banyan branches
shade-immersed birds' nests were songless.
Only the indolent insects buzzed and buzzed.
When the noon wind, stealer of ripe-corn-odours,
blew off Shyama's drapery from her head,
suddenly then, tormented, oppressed
by the fullness of his passion, voice near-muffled,
Bajrasen whispered thus in her ears,
'In eternal chains you've bound me, freeing me from
transient chains. But you must inform me
how such a feat, so difficult, was achieved.
Love, if I but knew what you did for me,
with my life, I vow, I would repay you.'
Drawing the end of her drapery over her face,
the beauty said, 'Let's not talk of that yet.'

Far away, folding its golden sails,
daylight's boat went quietly to the ghat
of the sunset-mountain, and by a grove on the bank
Shyama's boat was moored in the evening breeze.
The moon – fourth day of waxing – had nearly set;
a faint light glimmered in long lines upon
the calm unruffled waters; the darkness massed
at tree-bases vibrated with crickets
like vina-strings. Blowing off the lamp,
below the boat's window in the southern breeze
Shyama sat, her face deep-sigh-tense,
and leaned on the young man's shoulder. Her tresses
unbound, fragrant, fell without restraint,
covering the foreigner's breast with soft cascades
of darkness, like a net of the deepest sleep.
'Dearest,' murmured Shyama in whispered tones,
'what I did for you was hard enough,
hard indeed, but even harder it is
to tell you about it now. I must be brief.
Listen to it once and then wipe the story
off your mind. –
                    A young teenager,
his name Uttiya, was nearly driven mad
by his hopeless passion for me. At my request

he pleaded guilty to the charge held against you
and gave his own life. And this is my pride –
that the greatest sin of my life I have committed
for your sake, o most-excellent of all!'

The slim moon set. The speechless woodland,
the sleep of hundreds of birds upon its head,
stood still. Slowly, ever so slowly
the lover's arms around the lady's waist
slackened, and a harsh distance settled
silently between the two. Bajrasen
stared before him, mute, stiff, as rigid
as a stone image, and her head on his feet,
Shyama, released from the embrace, collapsed
like a torn climber. The massed riparian darkness
slowly thickened on the ink-black river-waters.

Suddenly, clasping the young man's knees with force
within her arms, the tormented woman cried
in a dry voice, free from tears, 'Liege, forgive!
May that scourge, the punishment for my sin,
be that fiercer at the Creator's hand,
but may you forgive what I have done for your sake!'
Looking at her, but moving his legs away,
Bajrasen burst out, 'Why? What need had you
to save this life of mine? Now until death
bought at your sin-price, a sharer in a great sin,
this life's a disgrace, thanks to you, shameful woman!
Fie on my breath that stands indebted to you!
Fie on my eyes that blink in each moment that passes!'
So saying, he rose with assertive force,
left the boat, went ashore, wandered aimlessly
in the sylvan darkness. There his feet
trampled the dry leaves, each step startling the forest.
In the stuffy airless underwood, thickly packed
with strong vegetal odours, trunks of trees
raised their twisted branches everywhere,
assuming so many grotesque, frightening shapes
in the darkness. All exits were blocked.
The creeper-manacled forest spread its hands
like mute forbiddings. Utterly exhausted,
the wanderer slumped to the ground. Like a ghost

someone stood behind him. She had come
on his heels in the darkness a long way,
following him without words, with bleeding feet.
Clenching both his fists, the wanderer shrieked,
'Won't you leave me yet?' At that the woman
rushed with lightning-speed and fell upon him,
covering all his body with the flood-waves
of her embraces, tresses, dishevelled drapes,
sniffs, kisses, caresses, deep breaths,
her voice emotion-choked, almost muffled,
repeating, 'I won't leave you! No, I won't!'
'Liege,' she begged, 'for your sake I sinned.
Punish me yourself, hurt my inmost being.
Pass it on me – your sentence, my reward.'
The sylvan gloom, bereft of planets and stars,
blindly experienced something – a nightmare.
Hundreds of thousands of tree-roots all around
shuddered with terror, buried underground.
One last pitiful plea could once be heard,
in a choked, strangled voice; the next minute
a body fell on the ground with a heavy thud.

When Bajrasen came away from the forest,
the temple's trident-peak on Ganga's bank
was the colour of lightning in the dawn's first rays.
On deserted sandy beaches along the river
heedless of all things, he spent the livelong day
like a madman. The fiery midday sun
lashed him all over with its burning thong.
Pitcher-on-waist village wives, seeing his state,
said with compassion, 'Who are you, homeless waif?
Come to us.' But he did not respond.
Thirst split his chest, yet he did not touch
a drop of water from the river before him.
At the day's end, with his body, fevered, burnt,
he ran and went aboard the empty boat,
even as an insect, seeing fire, runs
with ardent zeal. And there upon the bed
he saw an anklet lying. A hundred times
he pressed it to his breast. Its tinkling sound
pierced his heart like an arrow with a hundred tips.

In a corner lay
her blue drape, which he gathered to a heap,
then pressed his face against it, lying down,
drinking in with insatiable passion
the delicate odour of her body with his breath.
The moon – fifth day of waxing – about to set,
had slipped to the crown of the saptaparna tree,
dipping into branches. With his arms outstretched,
Bajrasen, looking at the forest, began to call,
'Come, come, my love!' Whereupon
on the sandy beach, against the deep-black woods,
appeared a shadowy figure, like a ghost.
'Come, come, love!' 'My love, I'm here!'
Shyama fell at his feet. 'Forgive me, please!
Alas, from my body my tough life couldn't be released
by your merciful hands.' For just a minute
Bajrasen set his eyes upon her face,
stretched out his arms, as if for an embrace,
then, startled, pushed her away from himself,
roaring, 'Why, why did you come back?'
He took the anklet, flung it from his breast,
and from his feet kicked the blue drape off
as if it was live coal. Even the bed
was like a bed of fire beneath his feet
and burned him. He then closed his eyes,
averted his face, said, 'Go, go back.
Leave me, go away!' The woman, for a minute,
stayed quiet, her head bowed, then kneeled
upon the ground and saluted his feet.
She then got off the boat, stepped on the bank,
softly walked towards the dark woodland,
as when sleep is sundered, a moment's miraculous dream
merges into night's obscurity.

[Shilaidaha? 9 October 1899]

The Realisation of Value
(Adapted from a Buddhist story)

On a bitter night of Aghran,　　bitten by the cruel frost,
　　all the lotuses had died,
save one in the garden-pond　　of Sudas the florist,
　　which had somehow survived.
He picked it up to sell it,　　went to the palace-gate,
　　asked to see the king himself,
when a traveller came by　　and so delighted was he
　　by the flower that he immediately said,
'I would like to buy　　your out-of-season lotus;
　　how much are you asking for it?
The godlike Buddha's　　in this city today:
　　at his feet I'd put it as a gift.'
Said the florist, 'I hope　　to get a masha of gold,'
　　and the traveller was ready to pay it,
when with much pomp　　and worship-offerings
　　the king came out through the gate.
King Prasenajit,　　chanting holy hymns,
　　was going to pay the Buddha a visit,
saw the out-of-season flower,　　asked, 'How much?
　　I want to buy it for the Lord's feet.'
'King,' said the florist,　　'with a masha of gold
　　this gentleman's buying it already.'
'But I'll pay ten!'　　the monarch exclaimed,
　　and the traveller said, 'I'll pay twenty!'
'It's mine!' cried each,　　wouldn't concede defeat,
　　and the price – it simply rocketed.
'How much more might I get　　if I gave it to him
　　for whose sake they tussle!' thought the florist.
'Excuse me,' he cried,　　his palms pressed together,
　　'I don't want to sell this flower!'
So saying he ran　　to the spot where the Buddha
　　was seated, lighting up a bower.
Calm and composed,　　he sat lotus-fashion,
　　an immaculate image of bliss.
His eyes dripped peace,　　and a light of compassion
　　glimmered on his smiling lips.
Sudas – he stared　　with a steadfast gaze.
　　No, not a word could he speak!

Then he slumped on the earth   and placed his lotus
        there on the Lord's lotus-feet.
Showering nectar,   the Buddha asked, smiling,
        'Son, what is it you need?'
Sudas, full of longing,   said, 'Lord, nothing else,
        just a trace of the dust of your feet!'

[Shilaidaha? 12 October 1899]

❦

FROM *Kahini* (1900)

Dialogue between Karna and Kunti

KARNA. On sacred Jahnavi's shore I say my prayers
        to the evening sun. Karna is my name,
        son of Adhirath the charioteer, and Radha is my mother.
        That's who I am. Lady, who are you?

KUNTI. Child, in the first dawn of your life
        it was I who introduced you to this wide world.
        That's me, and today I've cast aside
        all embarrassment, to tell you who I am.

KARNA. Respected lady, the light of your lowered eyes
        melts my heart, as the sun's rays melt
        mountain snows. Your voice
        pierces my ears as a voice from a previous birth
        and stirs strange pain. Tell me then,
        by what mystery's chain is my birth linked
        to you, unknown woman?

KUNTI.   Oh, be patient,
        child, for a moment! Let the sun-god first
        slide to his rest, and let evening's darkness
        thicken round us. – Now let me tell you, warrior,
        I am Kunti.

129

KARNA.   You are Kunti! The mother of Arjun!

KUNTI.   Arjun's mother indeed! But son,
         don't hate me for that. How I still recall
         the day of the tournament when you, a young bachelor,
         slowly entered the arena in Hastina-city
         as the newly rising sun enters the margin
         of the eastern sky, still pricked out with stars!
         Of all the women watching from behind a screen
         who was she, bereft of speech, of luck,
         who felt within her tortured breast the pangs
         of hungering love, a thousand she-snake fangs?
         Whose eyes covered your limbs with blessing's kisses?
         It was Arjun's mother! When Kripa advanced
         and smiling, asked you to announce your father's name,
         saying, 'He who is not of a royal family born
         has no right to challenge Arjun at all,' –
         then you, speechless, red with shame, face lowered,
         just stood there, and she whose bosom your gleam
         of embarrassment burnt like fire: who was that
         unlucky woman? Arjun's mother it was!
         Blessed is that lad Durjodhan, who thereupon
         at once crowned you prince of Anga. Yes, I praise him!
         And as you were crowned, the tears streamed from my eyes
         to rush towards you, to overflow your head,
         when, making his way into the arena,
         in entered Adhirath the charioteer, beside himself
         with joy, and you, too, in your royal gear
         in the midst of the curious crowds milling around
         bowed your only-just-anointed head, and saluted
         the feet of the old charioteer, calling him Father.
         Cruelly, contemptuously they smiled –
         the friends of the Pandabs; and right at that instant
         she who blessed you as a hero, O you jewel amongst heroes,
         I am that woman, the mother of Arjun.

KARNA.   I salute you, noble lady. A royal mother you are:
         so why are you here alone? This is a field of battle,
         and I am the commander of the Kaurab army.

KUNTI.   Son, I've come to beg a favour of you –
         Don't turn me away empty-handed.

KARNA.   A favour? From me!

Barring my manhood, and what dharma requires,
the rest will be at your feet if you so desire.

KUNTI. I have come to take you away.

KARNA.   And where will you take me?

KUNTI. To my thirsty bosom – to my maternal lap.

KARNA. A lucky woman you are, blessed with five sons,
and I am just a petty princeling, without pedigree –
where would you find room for me?

KUNTI.   Right at the top!
I would place you above all my other sons,
for you are the eldest.

KARNA.   By what right
would I enter that sanctum? Tell me how
from those already cheated of empire
I could possibly take a portion of that wealth,
a mother's love, which is fully theirs.
A mother's heart cannot be gambled away
nor be defeated by force. It's a divine gift.

KUNTI.   O my son,
with a divine right indeed you had one day
come to this lap – and by that same right
return again, with glory; don't worry at all –
take your own place amongst all your brothers,
on my maternal lap.

KARNA.   As if in a dream
I hear your voice, honoured lady. Look, darkness has
engulfed the entire horizon, swallowed the four quarters,
and the river has fallen silent. You have whisked me off
to some enchanted world, some forgotten home,
to the very dawn of awareness. Your words
like age-old truths touch my fascinated heart.
It's as if my own inchoate infancy,
the very obscurity of my mother's womb
was encircling me today. O royal mother,
loving woman, – be this real, or a dream, –
come place your right hand on my brow, my chin
for just a moment. Indeed I had heard
that I had been abandoned by my natural mother.

131

How often in the depth of night I've had this dream:
that slowly, softly my mother had come to see me,
and I've felt so bleak, and beseeched her in tears,
'Mother, remove your veil, let me see your face,' –
and at once the figure has vanished, tearing apart
my greedy thirsty dream. That very dream –
has it come today in the guise of the Pandab mother
this evening, on the battlefield, by the Bhagirathi?
Behold, lady, on the other bank, in the Pandab camp
the lights come on, and on this bank, not far,
in the Kaurab stables a hundred thousand horses
stamp their hooves. Tomorrow morning
the great battle begins. Why tonight
did I have to hear from Arjun's mother's throat
my own mother's voice? Why did my name
ring in her mouth with such exquisite music –
so much so that suddenly my heart
rushes towards the five Pandabs, calling them 'brothers'?

KUNTI. Then come on, son, come along with me.

KARNA. Yes, Mother, I'll go with you. I won't ask questions –
without a doubt, without a worry, I'll go.
Lady, you are my mother! And your call
has awakened my soul – no longer can I hear
the drums of battle, victory's conch-shells.
The violence of war, a hero's fame, triumph and defeat –
all seem false. Take me. Where should I go?

KUNTI.   There, on the other bank,
where the lamps burn in the still tents
on the pale sands.

KARNA.   And there a motherless son
shall find his mother for ever! There the pole star
shall wake all night in your lovely generous
eyes. Lady, one more time
say I am your son.

KUNTI.   My son!

KARNA.   Then why
did you discard me so ingloriously –
no family honour, no mother's eyes to watch me –
to the mercy of this blind, unknown world? Why did you

let me float away on the current of contempt
so irreversibly, banishing me from my brothers?
You put a distance between Arjun and me,
whence from childhood a subtle invisible bond
of bitter enmity pulls us to each other
in an irresistible attraction. –
                              Mother, you have no answer?
I sense your embarrassment piercing these dark layers
and touching all my limbs without any words,
closing my eyes. Let it be then –
you don't have to explain why you cast me aside.
A mother's love is God's first gift on this earth;
why that sacred jewel you had to snatch
from your own child is a question you may choose
not to answer! But tell me then:
why have you come to take me back again?

KUNTI. Child, let your reprimands
like a hundred thunderclaps rend this heart of mine
into a hundred pieces. That I'd cast you aside
is a curse that hounds me, which is why
my heart is childless even with five dear sons,
why it is *you* that my arms go seeking in this world,
flapping and flailing. It is for that deprived child
that my heart lights a lamp, and by burning itself
pays its homage to the Maker of this universe.
Today I count myself fortunate
that I have managed to see you. When your mouth
hadn't yet uttered a word, I did commit
a horrendous crime. Son, with that same mouth
forgive your bad mother. Let that forgiveness burn
fiercer than any rebukes within my breast,
reduce my sins to ashes and make me pure!

KARNA. O Mother, give – give me the dust of your feet,
and take my tears!

KUNTI.   Son, I did not come
simply in the happy hope of clutching you to my breast,
but to take you back where you by right belong.
You are not a charioteer's son, but of royal birth –
so cast aside the insults that have been your lot
and come where they all are – your five brothers.

133

KARNA. But Mother, I *am* a charioteer's son,
and Radha's my mother – glory greater than that
I have none. Let the Pandabs be Pandabs, the Kaurabs
Kaurabs – I envy nobody.

KUNTI.   With the puissance of your arms
recover the kingdom that's your own, my son.
Judhisthir will cool you, moving a white fan;
Bhim will hold up your umbrella; Arjun the hero
will drive your chariot; Dhaumya the priest
will chant Vedic mantras; and you, vanquisher of foes,
will live with your kinsmen, sole ruler in your kingdom,
sitting on your jewelled throne, sharing power with none.

KARNA. Throne, indeed! To one who's just refused the maternal bond
are you offering, Mother, assurances of a kingdom?
The riches from which you once disinherited me
cannot be returned – it's beyond your powers.
When I was born, Mother, from me you tore
mother, brothers, royal family – all at one go.
If today I cheat my foster-mother, her of charioteer caste,
and boldly address as my own mother a royal materfamilias,
if I snap the ties that bind me to the lord
of the Kuru clan, and lust after a royal throne,
then fie on me!

KUNTI.   Blessed are you, my son, for you are
truly heroic. Alas, Dharma, how stern your justice is!
Who knew, alas, that day
when I forsook a tiny, helpless child,
that from somewhere he would gain a hero's powers,
return one day along a darkened path,
and with his own cruel hands hurl weapons at those
who are his brothers, born of the same mother!
What a curse this is!

KARNA.   Mother, don't be afraid.
Let me predict: it's the Pandabs who will win.
On the panel of this night's gloom I can clearly read
before my eyes the dire results of war:
legible in starlight. This quiet, unruffled hour
from the infinite sky a music drifts to my ears:
of effort without victory, sweat of work without hope –
I can see the end, full of peace and emptiness.

134

The side that is going to lose –
please don't ask me to desert that side.
Let Pandu's children win, and become kings,
let me stay with the losers, those whose hopes will be dashed.
The night of my birth you left me upon the earth:
nameless, homeless. In the same way today
be ruthless, Mother, and just abandon me:
leave me to my defeat, infamous, lustreless.
Only this blessing grant me before you leave:
may greed for victory, for fame, or for a kingdom
never deflect me from a hero's path and salvation.

[26 February 1900]

❦

FROM *Kalpana* (1900)

A Stressful Time

Though the evening's coming with slow and languid steps,
    all music's come to a halt, as if at a cue,
in the endless sky there's none else to fly with you,
    and weariness is descending on your breast,
though a great sense of dread throbs unspoken,
    and all around you the horizon is draped,
        yet bird, o my bird,
            already blind, don't fold your wings yet.

No, this is no susurrus of a forest,
    but the sea swelling with a slumber-snoring thunder.
No, this is no grove of kunda flowers,
    but crests of foam heaving with fluid palaver.
Where's that shore, dense with blossoms and leaves?
    Where's that nest, branch that offers shelter?
        Yet bird, o my bird,
            already blind, don't fold your wings yet.

Ahead of you still stretches a long, long night;
   the sun has gone to sleep behind a mountain.
The universe – it seems to hold its breath,
   sitting quietly, counting the passing hours.
And now on the dim horizon a thin curved moon,
   swimming against obscurity, appears.
     Bird, o my bird,
       already blind, don't fold your wings yet.

Above you the stars have spread their fingers,
   as in a mime, with a meaning in their gaze.
Below you death – deep, leaping, restless –
   snarls at you in a hundred thousand waves.
But on a far shore some are pleading with you.
   'Come, come': their wailing prayer says.
     So bird, o my bird,
       already blind, don't fold your wings yet.

Ah, there's no fear, no bonds of love's illusion;
   there's no hope, for hope is mere deceit.
There's no speech, no useless lamentation,
   neither home nor flower-strewn nuptial sheet.
You've only your wings, and painted in deepest black,
   this vast firmament where dawn's direction's lost.
     Then bird, o my bird,
       already blind, don't fold your wings yet.

[Calcutta, 27 April 1897]

Dream

A long, long way away
in a dream-world, in the city of Ujjain,
by River Shipra I once went to find
my first love
from a previous life of mine.

Lodhra-pollen on her face,
dalliance-lotus in her hand,

kunda-buds perched on her ears,
kurubaks pinned to her hair;
on her slim body
a red cloth waist-knot-bound;
ankle-bells making a
faint ringing sound.
On a spring day
I wandered far,
figuring out my way.

In the Shiva-temple
in solemn tones just then
the evening service
began to resound.
Above the empty
shopping arcades gleamed
on darkened buildings
the last of the evening sun.

At last I reached
by a narrow winding road
my love's house,
secluded and remote.

Conch-shell and wheel were
painted on her door.
On either side stood a
young kadamba tree –
growing like sons.
A carved lion,
majestic and proud,
sat above the white
columns of the gate.

All her pet doves
returned to their dovecot.
Her peacock slept,
perched on a golden rod.
At such a time
a lighted lamp in her hand,
slowly, slowly
my Malavika came down.

She appeared outside the door,
above the stairs,
like a goddess of evening
holding the evening star.
Her saffron-scented limbs
and incensed hair
shed all over me
gusts of their restless breath.
Her drapery, slightly slipped,
by chance revealed
tracery of sandal
painted on her left breast.

Like a statue she stood
in that quiet evening
when the humming city was mute.

Seeing me, my love
slowly, ever so slowly
put her lamp down,
came before me,
put her hand in mine,
and without words
asked with her tender eyes,
'Hope you're well, my friend?'

I looked at her face,
tried to speak,
but found no words.
That language was lost to us:
we tried so hard
to recall each other's name,
but couldn't remember.

We thought so hard
as we gazed at each other,
and the tears streamed from
our unflickering eyes.

We thought so hard
by that door
beneath a tree!

And I don't know when
under what pretext
her soft hand slid into my
right hand like a bird
of evening seeking its nest,
and slowly her face
like a drooping lotus
came to rest on my breast.

Keen with yearning,
they mingled quietly –
her breath and my breath.

Night's darkness swallowed
the city of Ujjain.
The wild wind blew out
the lamp left by the door.
In the Shiva-temple
on River Shipra's bank
the evening service
came to an abrupt end.

[Bolpur, 22 May 1897]

FROM *Kshanika* (1900)

What the Scriptures Say

After fifty thou'lt walk to the forest,
    so our scriptures say.
But we say a forest retreat
    is better in the youthful days.

Bokuls flowering in their plenty,
    koels killing themselves with singing,
nature's arbours, leaves and creepers,
    the merrier for hiding, seeking!
Moonlight falling on champak branches –
    for whom was such a sight created?
Those who appreciate such beauties
    are definitely your under-fifties.

Inside the house, the boring rows,
    all the lips alive with gossip,
nosy neighbours prying, poking.
    Privacy? You must be joking!
Time's so short. It's all devoured
    by do-gooders who come to visit,
sitting down for hours and hours
    discussing their holy topics.
No wonder then that hapless youths
    are always on the lookout for verdant groves.
They know full well liberation's
    never to be had indoors.

We are modern young men,
    smart, born to disobey.
Manu's codes need amending.
    There'll be new laws under our sway.
Let old men stay at home,
    pile their rupees and pices,
manage the property affairs,
    seek the legal advices.
Let youths pick almanac-dates
    and in Phalgun walk to the forest.
There let them work hard
    all through the night without rest.

After fifty thou'lt walk to the forest,
    so our scriptures say.
But we think a forest retreat
    is better in the younger days.

140

Straightforward

Eye runs to eye,
    heart runs to heart;
in the story of two creatures
    that's all there is to that.
On moonlit Chaitra evenings
when the henna perfumes the air,
you sit with flowers on your lap
    while my flute's by my feet somewhere.
    This love between us two
        is a straightforward affair.

Your sari, springtime-yellow,
    drugs me, clings to my eyes;
the jasmine chain you weave me
    like a song of praise on me lies.
A little giving, a little keeping,
a little showing, a little hiding,
a little smile, a touch of shyness:
    that's our mutual understanding.
    This love between us two
        is a straightforward affair.

No profound mystery resides
    in the couplings of springtime.
No truth beyond cognition
    sticks like a thorn in our minds.
No shadow creeps behind
this bliss of yours and mine.
No quest, staring at each other,
    unknown depths to find.
    Our couplings in springtime
        are straightforward affairs.

We do not dive into language
    for what's beyond expression,
nor beg the sky to give us what's
    beyond our expectation.
What little we give, what little we get –
that's all we have, no more to net.

We do not hang on to happiness
  and have a tug-of-war.
    Our couplings in springtime
      are straightforward affairs.

Oh, we had heard on the sea of love
  there was no navigation,
that infinite hunger, infinite thirst
  were the price of passion,
that love's music was a strain
on instruments and snapped their strings,
that love's grove was a labyrinth
  with crooked culs-de-sac!
    But this our union, love,
      is a straightforward affair!

❦

FROM *Naibedya* (1901)

No. 88

This I must admit: how one becomes two
is something I haven't understood at all.
How anything ever happens or one becomes what one is,
how anything stays in a certain way, what we mean
by words like *body, soul, mind:* I don't fathom,
but I shall always observe the universe
quietly, without words.

          How can I
even for an instant understand the beginning, the end,
the meaning, the theory – of something outside of which
I can never go? Only this I know –
that this thing is beautiful, great, terrifying,
various, unknowable, my mind's ravisher.

This I know, that knowing nothing, unawares,
the current of the cosmos's awareness flows towards you.

No. 89

Unknown to me is the moment when I passed
through life's lion-carved gateway into this world's
magnificent mansion. What power was it
that opened me in this immense mystery's lap
like a bud in a vast forest in the middle of the night?

Yet when, in the morning, I lifted my head high,
opened my eyes and looked upon this earth,
arrayed in blue cloth spangled with golden rays,
and saw this world's ways, studded with pleasures and pains,
in an instant did this unknown, unbounded
mystery seem as entirely familiar
as my mother's breast, very much mine.

Unmanifest, beyond cognition, this awesome power
has, to my eyes, assumed the shape of a mother.

No. 90

Nor do I know death. Today at times
I'm shivering with fear of it. When I think
I have to bid adieu to this world, my eyes moisten
and with both arms I try to hang on to life,
calling it mine.

            Fool, who had made this life, this
world, unawares to yourself, so much your own,
from the moment of your birth, even before
your own volition? Thus at death's dawn
you'll see once more the face of that unknown
and instantly recognise it. I have loved
my life so dearly that I am convinced
when I meet death, I shall love it just as much.

Removed from one breast, a child cries in alarm,
but given the other breast, is immediately calmed.

FROM *Smaran* (1903)

No. 5

No, no, she's no longer in my house!
I've looked in every corner. Nowhere to be found!
In my house, Lord, there's such precious little space –
what goes away from it cannot be retraced.
But your house is infinite, all-pervasive,
and it's there, Lord, I've come to look for her.
Here I stand, beneath this evening sky,
and look at you, tears streaming from my eyes.
There's a place from where no face, no bliss,
no hope, no thirst can ever be snatched from us.
It's there I've brought my devastated heart,
so you can drown, drown, drown it in that source.
Elixir of deathlessness no longer in my house –
may I recover its touch in the universe!

No. 14

A few old letters I found –
a handful of tokens
belonging to love-drugged life,
memory's toys, which with such particular care
and secrecy you had hoarded in your room.
From mighty time's destructive deluge
which sweeps away so many suns and moons
you had in dread stolen these few trifles
and hidden them, saying to yourself,
'No one else has a right to these riches of mine.'
And who is going to look after them today?
They belong to nobody, yet they exist.
As your affection had guarded them once,
isn't anyone guarding you likewise today?

[Bolpur, 17 December 1902]

❦

Empathy

If I wasn't your little boy,
but just a puppy-dog,
would you tell me off,
lest I tried to taste
rice from your dinner-plate?
Tell me truly,
don't trick me, Mum!
Would you say, 'Off, off, off!
Whence has it come, this dog?'
Then go, Mum, go.
Let me get off your lap.
I won't eat from your hand,
I won't eat from your plate.

If I wasn't your little boy,
but just a parrot, your pet,
would you chain me, Mum,
lest I should fly away?
Tell me truly,
don't trick me, Mum!
Would you say, 'Wretched bird!
He wants to escape, does he?'
Then let me get off, Mum.
You don't have to love me any more.
I don't want to stay on your lap,
I'd rather go off to the forest.

[Rainy season 1903?]

An Offer of Help

Mum, why do you look so upset?
Don't you want to take your boy on your lap?
Feet stretched out in a corner of the room,

just sitting, so lost in your thoughts, –
    you haven't even plaited your hair yet.
Why open the window? What d'you want to see?
It's raining. You're getting your head wet.
    Your clothes will be splashed with mud.
D'you hear that? It's four o' clock!
End of school. My brother'll be back.
    You don't seem to remember that!
It's getting late.
What's the matter today?
    Haven't you had a letter from Dad?
From his bag the postman
left a letter for everyone,
    why not one from Dad every day?
He keeps 'em in his bag
to read 'em himself.
    The postman's very smart, a crafty beggar!

    Listen, Mum, you just take my advice.
    Don't you worry about that any more.
Tomorrow's market day.
Just ask the maid
    to get some paper and a pen.
You'll see, I'll make no mistakes;
from *ka* and *kha* to cerebral *na*
    I'll write Dad's letter for him, I promise!
Come on, Mum, what's the meaning of that smile?
You think, don't you, I can never write
    as good a hand as Dad can?
I'll draw the lines first,
then the rest big and neat.
    When you see it, you won't believe it!
When the letter's written,
d'you think I'd be silly
    like Dad and put it in the bag?
Never! Myself
I'll read it out to you,
    for they don't deliver good letters.

[Rainy season 1903?]

146

Hide-and-Seek

If I played a naughty trick on you, Mum,
 and flowered as a champa on a champa tree,
and at sunrise, upon a branch,
 had a good play among the young leaves,
then you'd lose, and I'd be the winner,
for you wouldn't recognise me.
 You'd call, 'Khoka, where are you?'
 I'd just smile quietly.

All jobs you do in the morning
 I'd watch with my eyes wide open.
After your bath, damp hair loose on your back,
 you'd walk this way, under the champa tree.
From here you'd go to the chapel
and smell flowers from afar –
 you wouldn't know that it was
 the smell of your Khoka's body in the air.

At noontime, when everyone's had their lunch,
 you'd sit down, the *Mahabharat* in your hands.
Through the window the tree's shade
 would fall on your back, on your lap.
I'd bring my little shadow close to you
and sway it softly on your book –
 you wouldn't know that it was
 your Khoka's shadow moving before your eyes.

In the evening you'd light a lamp
 and go to the cow-shed, Mum.
Then would I, my flower-play done,
 fall down plonk on the ground.
Once again I'd become your little boy,
go up to you and say, 'Tell me a story.'
 You'd say, 'Naughty! Where have you been all day?'
 I'd say, 'I'm not telling you that!'

[Rainy season 1903?]

☙

No. 7

Like a musk-deer
maddened by my own scent,
a maniac, I roam
from forest to forest.
The south wind blows
upon a night of Phalgun.
I quite lose
my power of orientation.
What I want
I want by mistake.
What I get
I do not want at all.

My desire – it flies out
from my breast.
Like a mirage
it shifts from place to place.
I want to hug
and press it against my chest,
but never again
does it return to my breast.
What I want
I want by mistake.
What I get
I do not want at all.

My flute – it wants
to hang on to its own song,
like one deranged, gone
totally off the rails.
But what is caught
and bound so fast, so fast –
from it, alas,
all melody evaporates.
What I want
I want by mistake.
What I get
I do not want at all.

The Auspicious Moment

O Mother, listen: the king's darling son
    will ride past my room this very day!
How can I cope with housework
    this morning?
Tell me, please, how I should dress myself,
in which style my hair should be braided,
how my body should be draped
    and in which tint.

Ah, Mother, why do you look at me like that
    with such surprise?
I know too well he'll never cast a glance
at the spot by my window where I'll stand and bide.
It will all be over in the twinkling of an eye
    and to a distant city away he'll ride.
Only from some field a minstrel–flute
    may play a wistful melody for a while.

Yet, knowing that the king's darling son
    will ride past my room this very day,
what can I do but get myself dressed up
    just for that moment?

[Bolpur, 29 July 1905]

The Renunciation

O Mother, listen: the king's darling son
    just rode past my room!
How the golden crest of his chariot gleamed
    in the morning sun!
At my window I removed my veil
and just for a moment stole a glance at him.

I tore my chain of jewels, flung it on the dust
    right before his path.

Ah, Mother, why do you look at me like that
    with such surprise?
Of course, he didn't pick up the chain-torn jewels:
his wheels ground them to dust.
His wheel-track is all you can see now
    before our house.
No one knows what I gave to whom:
    it's covered by dust.

Yet, seeing that the king's darling son
    was riding past my room,
what could I do but fling the jewels of my breast
    before his path?

[Bolpur, 29 July 1905]

᳀

FROM *Gitanjali* (1910)

No. 106

Gently in this hallowed place
        wake up, o my mind –
on this seashore of India's grand
        concourse of humankind.
                        Here I stand and stretch my arms,
                                saluting God-in-Man;
                        in grand rhythm, with great delight
                                I praise Him as best I can.
        This mountain-range so steeped in meditation,
        these plains clutching their rosaries of rivers:
        here for ever the sacred Earth
                we may find,
        on this seashore of India's grand
                concourse of humankind.

No one knows who called them to this place –
        such streams of humanity!
Whence did they issue, in impetuous cascades,
        to lose themselves in the sea?
                    Here Aryans and non-Aryans,
                            Chinese and Dravidians,
                    Scythians, Huns, Pathans, Mughals
                            dissolved in one body.
        Now that the West has opened its door
        we're bringing ourselves gifts from that store.
        We shall give and receive, mingle and harmonise:
                there's no turning back
        on this seashore of India's grand
                concourse of humankind.

Those warrior-hordes who sang of conquest
        with a demented din,
through desert trails and mountain passes
        all those who poured in:
                    they are all within me still,
                            none are far from me!
                    In my blood their music hums
                            in all its diversity.
        Resound, resound, awesome vina,
        so those who still despise and shun us
        may burst the barriers and gather around us.
                Yes, they'll congregate
        on this seashore of India's grand
                concourse of humankind.

Here once without cease
        the great sound of *Om*
had vibrated in heart-strings
        asking us to be one.
                    With ascesis it strove to cast
                            the Many in the fire of the One,
                    to forget divisions and set in motion
                            one gigantic heart.
        The entrance to that sacred space
        where such a sacrament took place
        is now open, so with good grace
                we must humbly congregate:
    on this seashore of India's grand
                concourse of humankind.

151

Look! That sacrificial fire
      is streaked today with suffering's red glare.
Within our spirits this burning we must bear –
      it is written in our fate.
                  My mind, be strong to endure this affliction
                        and listen to unity's call.
                  Your sense of fear, embarrassment, humiliation –
                        banish them, conquer them all.
      The intolerable pain will come to an end.
      Behold what a huge new life is about to be born!
      The night glides to daybreak, the mother-bird wakes
            in her colossal nest –
      on this seashore of India's grand
            concourse of humankind.

Come, Aryans, non-Aryans,
      Hindus and Muslims alike.
Come you too – you, English people.
      Come, come, Christians!
                  Come, Brahmins, with chastened minds,
                        and hold everyone's hands.
                  Come, outcastes, bidding goodbye
                        to your burden of affronts.
      Make haste to Mother's consecration,
      where the ritual jars are waiting to be filled
      with water blessed by the touch
            of all and sundry's hands –
      today on this seashore of India's grand
            concourse of humankind.

[Bolpur-Santiniketan, 2 July 1910]

No. 107

Where the lowliest live, the poorer than poor,
      it's there that your footsteps ring:
            behind all, below all,
                  amongst those who've lost everything.
      When I make an obeisance to you,
      somewhere my gesture comes to an abrupt end.

To those lowest depths of hurt and insult, where your feet descend,
    my gesture of homage, alas, cannot bend:
        behind all, below all,
            amongst those who've lost everything.

Pride can never reach you where you wander
    in humble clothes, bereft of adornments:
        behind all, below all,
            amongst those who've lost everything.
    Where wealth is heaped, where honour is piled up,
        it's there that I expect your company,
but where you dwell as a friend of friendless men,
    to that low abode my heart, alas, cannot bend:
        behind all, below all,
            amongst those who've lost everything.

[Bolpur-Santiniketan, 3 July 1910]

No. 108

My ill-fated country, those you have affronted –
with them you must be equalised by sharing the same affront.
    Those you have denied
    human rights,
allowed to stand before you but never invited in –
with all of them you must be equalised by sharing the same affront.

Day after day you have avoided the human touch,
showing your contempt for the deity that dwells in man.
    One day the Creator's ruthless fury
    will make you sit by famine's doorway
and share with others what there is to eat and drink.
With all of them you'll have to be equalised by sharing the same affront.

There, where you have pushed them away from sharing your seat,
even there you have banished your own powers, carelessly.
    Crushed by feet,
    those powers now crumble to dust.
You must come down to that level, or else you can't be redeemed.
Today you have to be equalised with others by sharing the same affront.

153

Whoever you fling to a lower level will bind you to that level.
Whoever you keep behind your back is only dragging you backwards.
　　Whoever you keep occluded,
hidden in ignorance-darkness,
is shaping a chasm between you and your own welfare.
You must be equalised with all of them by sharing the same affront.

A hundred centuries have rained indignities on your head,
yet you still refuse to acknowledge the innate divinity of man.
　　But can you not see
　　when you lower your eyes
that the God of the downtrodden, the outcaste, is there in the dust with
　　　　　　　　　　　　　　　　　　　　　　　　　　them?
You must be equalised there with all the others by sharing the same affront.

You cannot see Death's messenger at your door:
he has already inscribed a curse on your caste-pride.
　　If you don't send out a call to all
　　and still insist on staying apart,
wrapping yourself on all sides with your conceit,
then surely in death, in the pyre's ashes, you will be equalised with all.

[Bolpur-Santiniketan, 4 July 1910]

❦

FROM *Balaka* (1916)

No. 6

Are you just a picture upon a piece of paper?
　　Those distant nebulae
　　who jostle in the sky's nest,
　　　　those who, day and night,
　　light in hand, are in transit through the dark,
　　　　planets and stars –
　　are you not as real as they are?
　　　　Alas, picture, are you just a picture?

154

In the midst of the ever-restless why are you calm?
  O you without a path,
    find a travelling companion!
  Must you, night and day,
be amongst all and still be so far away,
    for ever fastened to fixity's inner niche?
      Why, this dust that lifts
the grey end of its cloth
    and wind-blown, runs amuck,
in Baishakh strips the widowed earth of jewels,
    decks the anchoress in saffron attire,
        in spring's coupling-dawns
            covers her limbs with the tracery of patterns:
        even this dust is real, alas,
                like this grass,
            almost hidden under the feet of the universe.
Because they are mutable, they are real.
      You are immutable, you are a picture.
      You are just a picture.

One day you walked this road by our side.
  Your breast stirred with your breathing.
    In your limbs
        your life created its very own rhythms
            in songs and dances
            keeping time with the cosmos.
    Ah, that was so long ago, that was!
        In my life
      and my world
          how real you were once!
      In every direction,
        wherever my eyes glanced,
it was you who inscribed
    the graphics of art's delight with beauty's brush.
In that morning it was you who was
    the word of the cosmos made flesh.

As we travelled together,
    behind the screen of one night
        you came to a stop.
    I've kept going
        with so much pleasure and pain
      for days and nights.

Flood-tide and ebb-tide
in light and dark, sea and sky;
on either side of the road the flowers march past,
quietly, with all their dyes.
Life's wild river rushes in a thousand streams,
ringing death's bells.
The unknown calls me;
I walk further, further,
drugged by my passion for the road.
But where you stood
when you got off the road –
there you are stuck.
This grass, this dust, those stars, that sun, that moon –
screened by them all,
you are a picture, you are just a picture.

What a poetic delirium this is!
You – a picture?
No, no, you are not just a picture.
Who says you are bound by still lines
and mute cries?
Nonsense! That joy could have ceased only if
this river had lost its flow
or this cloud
had wiped this golden writing off itself.
If the shadow
of your fine hair had vanished for ever,
then one day
the murmuring shade
of wind-blown madhabis too
would have been a dream.
Had I forgotten you?
It is because
you lodge in my life's roots
that the error arises.
With absent minds we walk,
forgetting the flowers.
Don't we forget the stars?
And yet
they sweeten the air we breathe,
fill with tunes
the emptiness that dwells within our errors.

Being unmindful – I don't call it oblivion:
you've swayed my blood from your seat in my amnesia's core.
    Before my eyes you are not;
        right within my eyes are you installed.
        That is why
you are the green of my greens, the blue of my blues.
        My whole world
    has found its inner harmony in you.
        No one knows, not even I,
           that your melodies reverberate in my songs.
You are the poet within the poet's heart.
You are not a picture. No, not just a picture.
    Early one morning I found you,
        then lost you at night.
And in the darkness you return, unawares to me.
You are not a picture. No, you are not a picture.

[Allahabad, 20 October 1914]

No. 36

Glimmering in evening's colours, Jhelum's curved stream
    faded in the dark, like a sheathed
        curved sword.
The day ebbed. Night, in full flood,
rushed in, star-flowers afloat in its black waters.
    In the darkened valley
        deodars stood in rows.
Creation, it seemed, had something to say in its sleep,
    but couldn't speak clearly:
clumps of inarticulate sound moaned in the dark.

    Suddenly that instant I heard
        a sound's lightning-flash in the evening sky:
    it darted across that tract of empty space,
then receded – further, further – till it died.
    Wild birds,
        how your wings drunk on the wine
           of violent gales raised billows of surprise
and merriment's loud laughter in the sky!

That sumptuous whoosh – it was
a sonorous nymph of the heavens swishing across,
disturbing stillness seated in meditation.
They quivered with excitement –
the mountains sunk in darkness,
the deodar-glen.

What those wings had to say
seemed to conduct
just for an instant
velocity's passion
into the very heart of thrilled stillness.
The mountain wished to be Baishakh's vagrant cloud.
The trees – they wanted to untie themselves from the earth,
to spread wings
and follow the line of that sound,
to lose themselves in the quest for the sky's limit.
The dream of that evening burst and ripples rose,
waves of yearning for what was far, far away.
Vagabond wings!
How the universe cried with longing –
'Not here, no, not here, somewhere else!'

Wild birds,
you've lifted the lid of stillness for me tonight.
Under the dome of silence
in land, water, air
I can hear the noise of wings – mad, unquiet.
The grass
beat their wings on their own sky – the earth.
Millions of seed-birds
spread their sprouting wings
from unknown depths of subterranean darkness.
Yes, I can see
these mountains, these forests
travelling with outspread pinions
from island to island, from one unknown to another.
Darkness is troubled by light's anguished cries
as the wings of the very stars vibrate.

Many are the human speeches I've heard migrating
in flocks, flying on invisible tracks

from obscure pasts to distant inchoate futures.
     And within myself I've heard
               day and night
          in the company of countless birds
a homeless bird speeding through light and dark
     from one unknown shore to yet another.
On cosmic wings a refrain echoes through space:
'Not here, no, but somewhere, somewhere else!'

[Srinagar, between 27 and 31 October 1915, at night]

No. 39

The day you rose, world poet, above a far shore,
England's horizon found you close to her breast
and reckoned you were her treasure, hers alone.
She kissed your radiant forehead and for a while
held you tight in the clasp of her sylvan boughs,
hid you for a while behind her stole of mists
on a playground of fairies, dewy, dense with grass,
where wild flowers blow. As yet the island's groves
hadn't woken up to hymn the poet-sun.
Thereafter, slowly, to the infinite's silent signals
you left the horizon's lap, and hour by hour
climbed, through the centuries, brilliant, to the zenith,
taking your place in the centre of all directions,
lighting all minds. Hear how, in another age,
on the shore of the Indian Ocean the quivering fronds
of massed coconut-groves ring with your triumph.

[Shilaidaha, 29 November 1915]

Getting Lost

My little girl,
having heard the call of her mates,
stopping and starting nervously in the dark,
was making her way down the stairs.
She had a lamp in her hand,
which she carefully guarded with her sari's end.

I was on the roof-terrace
on that night of Chaitra, full of stars.
Suddenly hearing my daughter's cry, I rushed
to see what the matter was.
It seemed that as she'd been going down the stairs,
the wind had blown out her lamp.
'What's up, Bami?' – I asked.
She cried from below, 'I'm lost!'

On that night of Chaitra, full of stars,
back on the roof-terrace, looking up at the sky,
a girl just like my Bami I thought I saw –
slowly, without companions, walking by,
lamp-flame shielded by dark-blue sari's end.
Should her light have gone out, making her suddenly stop,
she would have filled the sky with her cry – 'I am lost!'

The Last Establishment

They always say: 'Has gone', 'Has gone away'.
Yet let me add this:
don't say he or she is not.
That's a lie.
Therefore I cannot endure it.
It hurts my soul.

160

Coming and going
to men are so clearly partitioned
that their language
bears but half a hope.
But I would unite myself to that ocean
where *is* and *is-not*, in their fullness, are equipoised.

ॐ

FROM *Lipika* (1922)

The Old House

1

A family rich for generations has become poor;   it's to them that
the house over there belongs.

Each day the bad times dent it a bit more.

Walls crumble into sand;   sparrows dig into broken floors
with their claws, flapping their wings in the dust;   in Chandi's
chapel pigeons congregate like flocks of torn rain-clouds.

No one has bothered to find out when a door-leaf on the north
side broke off.   The other leaf – left on its own like a grieving
widow – bangs again and again in the wind; nobody looks at it.

A house in three parts.   Only five rooms are inhabited, the
rest being locked up.   Like an old man of eighty-five, most of
whose life is occupied by memories in ancient padlocks, –   with
only one area available for the movement of modern times.

Dribbling sand and baring its bricks, the house stands on the
edge of the street like an apathetic tramp dressed in a patched
kantha,   as unmindful of himself as of others.

2

In the early hours of one morning a wailing of women rose from
the direction of the house.   The last son of the family, who used
to scrape a living by playing Radhika in amateur open-air theatricals,
had just died at the age of eighteen.

The women wailed for a few days,   then one heard no more
about them.

After that *all* the doors in the house were padlocked.

Only that *one* widowed door on the north side, which neither broke off nor could stay shut,   kept slamming in the wind crash crash like the beating of an agonised heart.

3

One afternoon one heard the noise of children in that house.

A red-bordered sari was hanging from the balcony.

After so many days a portion of the house has been let.
The tenant has modest wages and numerous children.   The exhausted mother gets fed up and spanks them,   and they roll on the floor and howl.

A middle-aged maid toils all day and has rows with the mistress;   she says 'I'm leaving!' but never does.

4

This part of the house is seeing a little bit of maintenance every day.

Cracked panes have been papered over;   gaps in the balcony railing have had bamboo slats over them;   a broken bedroom window is propped up by a brick;   the walls have had a coat of whitewash, though the black patches haven't altogether disappeared.

On the cornice of the roof-top terrace the sudden apparition of an impoverished pot-plant of variegated leaves feels ashamed of itself before the sky.   Right next to it the foundation-cracking peepul tree stands erect,   its leaves appearing to laugh cheekily at the other leaves.

A great decline of a great prosperity.   Trying to conceal it with the little tricks of little hands has only laid it bare.

No one, though, has ever bothered to look at the empty room on the north side.   Its mateless door still keeps thrashing in the wind –   like a wretch beating his breast.

[1919?]

One Day

I remember that afternoon.   From time to time the rain would slacken, then a gust of wind would madden it again.

It was dark inside the room, and I couldn't concentrate on

work.   I took my instrument in my hand and began a monsoon song in the mode of Mallar.

She came out of the next room and came just up to the door. Then she went back.   Once more she came and stood outside the door.   After that she slowly came in and sat down.   She had some sewing in her hand;   with her head lowered, she kept working at it.   Later she stopped sewing and sat looking at the blurred trees outside the window.

The rain slowed, my song came to an end.   She got up and went to braid her hair.

Nothing but this.   Just that one afternoon twined with rain and song and idling and darkness.

Stories of kings and wars are cheaply scattered in history.   But a tiny fragment of an afternoon story stays hidden in time's box like a rare jewel.   Only two people know of it.

[1919?]

Grief's Ingratitude

It was at daybreak that she took her leave.

'Everything's unreal,' said my mind, attempting an explanation.

'Why?' – I asked in a cross mood –   'Aren't these all real – the sewing-box on the table,   the flower-pot on the roof-terrace, the name-inscribed hand-fan on the bed?'

My mind replied, 'But still you have to consider that –'

'Stop it,' I interrupted.   'Look at that book of stories with a hair-pin stuck half-way through the pages.   Clearly, she hadn't finished reading it.   Is that unreal as well?   If so, why should she be even more unreal than that?'

My mind fell silent.   A friend came and said, 'What's good is real and never perishes.   The whole world cherishes it, keeping it on its breast like a jewel in a chain.'

'How do you know?' – I asked angrily –   'Isn't the body good?   Where's that body gone?'

As a little boy in an angry mood vents his violence on his mother, I began to lash out against whatever was my refuge in this universe.   'This world's a traitor,' I said.

Suddenly something startled me.   It seemed to me that some-one whispered, 'Ungrateful!'

Looking out of the window, I saw the moon, the third of the waning phase, rising behind a casuarina tree.   It was like the hide-and-seek of the laughter of her who had gone.   A rebuke came to me from the star-sprinkled darkness, 'That I had let myself be caught – was *that* illusory?   And why this fanatical faith in the screen that's come between us?'

[1919?]

The Question

1

The father returned from the crematory.

The boy of seven – his body bare, a gold amulet round his neck – was alone by the window above the lane.

He was unaware of his own thoughts.

The morning sun had just touched the tip of the neem tree in front of the house opposite.   A man selling green mangoes came to the lane, called several times, then went away.

The father came and took his little boy in his arms.   The little boy asked: 'Where's Mummy?'

The father lifted his head upwards and said: 'In heaven.'

2

That night the father, weary with grief,   sobbed intermittently in his sleep.

A lantern glimmered by the door.   A pair of lizards kept watch on the wall.

The room faced an open terrace.   At some point the little boy went outside and stood there.

All around him the houses with their extinguished lights looked like guards at a giant's palace,   sleeping in a standing position.

The naked child stood staring at the sky.

His bewildered mind was asking a question of someone: 'Where's the road to heaven?'

The sky didn't answer;   only the stars trembled with the dumb darkness's tears.

[1919?]

Sunday

Monday, Tuesday, Wednesday, and others –
    they come so fast, so fast.
I suppose their fathers must be owners
    of vast motor cars.
But Sunday, but Sunday –
    why does she delay?
Slowly, slowly she walks
    after all the other days.
Her home beyond the skies –
    is it further than the homes of the others?
  Like you, Mum, she must be
  the daughter of a poor family.

Monday, Tuesday, Wednesday, and others –
    all hell-bent to stay.
They won't go home. Amazing
    how they simply won't go away!
But Sunday, but Sunday –
    someone treads on her heels.
Every half-hour they ring the hour!
    What a flurry! She keels!
In her home beyond the skies
    has she more chores than the others?
  Like you, Mum, she must be
  the daughter of a poor family.

Monday, Tuesday, Wednesday, and others –
    grim-faced old stewpots!
They don't like little boys. With us
    they are always cross!
But as I get up in the morning
    at the end of Saturday night,
who should I spy but Sunday,
    her face lit up by a smile!
How she cries when she says goodbye
    and gazes with yearning at us!
  Like you, Mum, she must be
  the daughter of a poor family.

[21 September 1921]

Remembering

I don't remember my mother.
   Only this: sometimes when I'm at play,
      suddenly, for no reason at all,
a tune begins to buzz
      and ring in my ears,
and my mother comes
      and merges with my play.
Maybe she used to sing,
      rocking me.
She has gone
      and left her song behind.

I don't remember my mother.
   Only this: when in Ashwin
      at dawn among shiuli trees
the scent of their flowers
      is borne by the dewy breeze,
somehow then she comes back to my mind –
      my mother.
Long ago perhaps she gathered shiulis,
      filling her basket.
So the scent of Puja
      returns as her scent.

I don't remember my mother.
   Only this: when I sit by the window
of my bedroom
      and look at the far blue sky,
it seems to me my mother's looking at me
      with steady eyes.
Long ago she used to hold me on her lap
      and look at my face.
That's the look she has left
      in all the sky.

[25 September 1921]

❦

166

Gratitude

'I won't forget,' I had said, when your moist eyes
had silently gazed at my face. Forgive me if I did forget.
Ah, that was such a long time ago! On that day's kiss
so many madhabi petals of early spring
fell in layers and withered, so many times
noon's dove-cooings pressed weary sleep,
going and returning. Your black eyes' gaze
had written on my spirit that letter of first love,
so shy, so nervous! On that autograph of your heart
restless lights and shadows have through the hours
waved their brush-strokes, so many evenings have splashed
golden oblivion, so many nights have left
their own dream-writings in crisscrosses of faint lines,
covering it quite. Each minute, second going by
leaves its souvenir-script upon the mind,
like the deformed doodlings of a heedless boy,
each obscuring the other, weaving amnesia's net.
If this Phalgun I have perchance forgotten
the message of that earlier Phalgun, if the flame
has silently died on grief's lamp, forgive me then.
Yet I know, because you had once appeared,
harvests of song had ripened in my life,
which continue; once the light of your eyes
had played its vina, wringing the innermost notes
from sunlight itself. Gone is your touch,
but what a touchstone you have left within my heart,
which shows me still, at times, the undying
panorama of this universe, makes me drink
causeless joy's full cup. Forgive my oblivion.
I know you had once called me into your heart,
which is why I myself forgive my own fate,
forgetting all those miseries, those griefs
which it has heaped on my days: how it has snatched
thirst's water-cup from my lips, conned me with smiles,
betrayed my confidence, suddenly upset
my laden ship within sight of shore: all I forgive.

You are no more. You have hopelessly receded.
Evenings are mournful, charged with your smothered vermilion.
My mateless life in an empty house has no grace.
All this I accept, and above all, that you were here once.

[On board the *Andes*, 2 November 1924]

The Apprehension

The more you heap my hands
    with the coins of love,
won't it expose the more the deceit's depth
    that's within me?
Better for me to pay my piling debts
    and sail away in an empty boat.
Better that I should starve and you withdraw
    your heart filled with nectar
        and go away.

To dull my pain
    I might wake it in you;
to lighten my load
    I might press it on you;
my anguished cry of loneliness well might
    keep you awake at night –
such are my fears, why I don't speak freely.
    If you can forget,
        please do.

On a lonesome trail I was, when you came along,
    your eyes set on my face.
I thought I'd say, 'Why not come with me?
    Say something to me, please!'
But all of a sudden, as I gazed at your face,
    I felt afraid.
I saw a dormant fire's secret smoulder
    in the obscure depths
        of your heart's darkest night.

Anchoress, should I suddenly fan
    the flames of your penance into a blazing fire,
wouldn't that stark light slash all veils asunder
    and lay my poverty bare?
What have I got to offer as sacred fuel
    to your passion's sacrificial fire?
Therefore I say to you with humility:
    With the memory of our meeting
        let me return alone.

[Miralrío, San Isidro, near Buenos Aires, 17 November 1924]

The Skeleton

There on the plain, on the way-side, an animal's skeleton
        is lying on the grass,
the same grass that had once given it strength
        and gentle rest.

They lie, bleached bones in a heap,
        time's loud dry laughter,
like death pointing its finger, insinuating:
        Where the beast ends
    there you end as well; there's no distinction;
        in your case too, when life's wine's been drained,
the broken cup will be left like that in the dust.

I said: Death, I don't believe what you say
        mockingly of emptiness.
My life's not the sort that becomes a total pauper
        at its journey's end,
        that at the end of the day
pays with hollow bones its last bill of board and bed.
All that I've thought and known, spoken, heard with my ears,
    all that has burst from me in sudden songs
        were not contained in a life hemmed by death.
        What I've received and what I've given back –
            on this earth of mortals where can that be measured?

Many a time has my mind's dance transcended
life and death, and gone where beauty lives
    eternally. Can it then stop for ever
        at the boundary of bones?
    My true identity
    cannot be measured by flesh.
The hours and minutes don't wear it out by their kicks,
    nor does the wayside dust pauperise it.

For in the lotus of manifest form I've drunk the honey of the
                                formless,
in the bosom of suffering found the dwelling of joy,
    heard within me the voice of eternal silence,
seen the way of stars through the dark empty spaces.
        No, I'm not a big joke of the Creator,
not a grand holocaust built with infinite riches.

[Chapadmalal, near Mar del Plata, Argentina, 17 December 1924]

The Exchange

Flowers of laughter she brought, and I
    the fruits of suffering's monsoon piled in a basket.
And I said to her, 'If we do an exchange,
    tell me who'll be the loser!'
The beauty laughed, mightily amused,
    and said, 'Come, let's do it!
Have my flower-chain. Let me take your fruits
    filled with the juice of tears.'
I looked at her face, and right enough
    a belle dame sans merci she was.

She picked up my basket of fruits, laughed and clapped,
    mightily amused.
I took her garland of flowers,
    pressed it to my breast.
'Mine's the victory!' she cried, and never stopped laughing
    as she scampered off.
The sun, he meanwhile clambered to the zenith

170

to burn the earth.
The hot day ended. In the evening I discovered
    that all my flowers had perished.

[On board the *Giulio Cesare*, going away from Argentina, 17 January 1925]

❦

FROM *Mahua* (1929)

The Identity

In rain-stopped afternoon clouds
        fear still lurked,
    as the wind blustered at times,
            mouthing sharp rebukes.
Above, in the sun's red, cloud-torn, Durvasa's wrath
    flared in oblique glares of bloodshot eyes
            and dun matted locks.

In that dismal weather I brought you an afternoon gift,
        kadambas in a basket.
    In the rain's sombre shadow
            in a songless dawn
those despair-dispelling flowers in a lampblack-hour
had stocked, in their ecstatic pollen, visions of the sun.

When sluggish clouds, hard pressed by easterly clouds,
        had rushed to the sky's rim,
    and on a Srabon night
            the woods, hit by a cataclysm, had wept,
even then the bold kadamba had shed its scent
to birds' nests, stalks unwearied, not yet felled.
        With such a flower, symbol of my confidence,
            I made you a present.

In the dripping evening, friend, you brought me
     a single ketaki.
        I was by myself,
          my lamp unlit.
In the tossed dense green of a row of areca-palms
fireflies flitted, unflagging in their quest.

You stood outside my door,
     secretly smiled.
   'What have you brought?'
     I asked, curious.
Raindrops fell pitter-patter on the leaves;
I stretched my hand in the fragrance-laden dark.

Abruptly did my limb reverberate
     to a staccato of thorns.
   How that barbed touch caught me unawares
     like a pleasure's sharp twang!
It wasn't an offer of surrender, easily gained,
but splendour within, sheathed in spiky pain.
     A homage hedged in by don'ts
       was what you gave me.

[Calcutta, 20 August 1928]

Disappearance

On the canvas of disappearance I see your eternal form.
You've finally arrived in my invisible inner domain.
    The jewel of everlasting touch have I obtained.
You've yourself filled the gap made by your absence.

When life darkened, I found
you'd left within me evening's chapel-lamp.
    Through separation's sacrificial fire
passion becomes worship, lit by suffering's light.

[Santiniketan, July 1928 (26 Ashadh 1335)]

❦

172

Kopai

Padma meanders away under far skies:
    I see her in my mind.
On one side sandbanks,
    fearless, for they're destitute, without attachments;
on the other side bamboo and mango groves,
    old banyans, derelict cottages,
   jack-trees of many years' standing, with fat trunks,
    a field of mustard by a pond,
    wayside jungles of rattan,
an indigo factory's ruined foundations, a hundred and fifty years old,
   tall casuarinas murmuring in its garden night and day.
There's the neighbourhood of the Rajbangshis,
   where their goats graze on cracked fields,
    and a granary with a tin roof stands by the market-place.
    The whole village trembles with fear of the cruel river.

    Hallowed in legends is that river's name.
    Mandakini flows in her pulse.
She is free. She passes by human dwellings,
    endures them, but doesn't acknowledge them.
    Her uncorrupted high-born metre holds
the memory of desolate mountains and the call of lonely seas.

On her sandbank-moorings it was once my lot to dwell,
   in solitude, far from crowds.
    Seeing the morning star, I would rise at dawn,
   and at night sleep on boat-deck
    under the Great Bear's eyes.
   Her indifferent streams would flow
    past the margins of the multitudinous thoughts
    of my lonely days and nights,
    even as a traveller skirts
    a householder's joys and sorrows, near yet far.

   Then at the end of my days of youth I came
    to this savannah's edge

where shaded Santhal villages make a fringe of massed green.
River Kopai is my neighbour here.
Not hers the glamour of an ancient line.
Her name's non-Aryan,
linked to the laughter-rich
sweet speech of generations of Santhal women.
With the village she's on intimate terms:
between land and water there's no conflict here
and dialogue's easy between her two banks.
Fields of san-hemp are in flower, brushing right against her body;
green rice seedlings have risen.
Where the footpath stops, meeting her bank,
she gives way to the farer,
letting him walk across
her murmuring crystal current.
Not far, the fan-palm rises from the plain;
mangoes, jaams, amlokis jostle on the banks.

She speaks the tongue of common men;
nobody would call it literary.
Her rhythm binds land and water together;
there's no rivalry between the liquid and the green.
Her slim body twists and turns
through light and shade,
dancing in simple steps to hand-clappings.
In the rains her limbs are touched with ecstasy
like a village girl drunk on mahua wine:
she doesn't break or cause to drown,
just twirls and twirls the eddies of her skirts,
gives little pushes to both her banks,
and laughing loudly, races along.
At the end of the post-rains her waters become limpid,
her flow becomes thinner,
showing the sand below,
yet the pallor of that shrunken celebration
cannot shame her,
for her affluence isn't arrogant, nor is her poverty a disgrace:
she is lovely in both –
like a dancer who dances, jingling her jewels,
and sits quietly, tired,
laziness in her eyes
and the hint of a smile in the corner of her mouth.

174

Kopai has made a poet's rhythm her own companion today,
a rhythm that reconciles an idiom's land and water,
what in speech is song and what is homely.
Walking to that flawed measure, a Santhal boy will trip across,
bow in hand;
a bullock-cart will cross over
with stacks of straw;
the potter will trot to market,
his pots slung from a pole,
followed by the village dog
and the three-rupees-a-month schoolmaster,
a torn umbrella over his head.

[August 1932 (1 Bhadra 1339)]

By the Pond

From the first-floor window eyes can see
a corner of the pond
brimful in the month of Bhadra.
Trees, deeply reflected, tremble in the waters
with the sheen of green silk.
Clumps of kolmi and heloncho grow on the borders.
On the sloping bank arecas face each other.
On this side are oleanders, white rongons, one shiuli,
two neglected tuberoses showing impoverished buds.
A henna hedge with bamboo reinforcements;
beyond it, orchards of banana, guava, coconut.
Further off, among trees, a house's roof-terrace
with a sari hanging from it.
A fat bare-chested man, a wet cloth round his head,
sits on the ghat's paved steps, his fishing-line cast.
Hour after hour passes.

The day wanes.
Rain-rinsed sky.
Abnegation's pallor in the ageing light.
A slow breeze stirs,
rippling the waters of the pond;
shaddock leaves quiver and glint.

175

I look, and it seems to me
 that this is the pale reflection of another day,
  bringing me, through the gaps in the fence of modernity,
   the image of someone from a far-off age.
Her touch is tender, her voice gentle,
 her black eyes are enchanted and naïve.
The wide red border of her white sari
  falls circling her feet.
She spreads a mat for her guest to sit on the yard;
  she wipes the dust off with her sari's end;
  she fetches water in the shades of mangoes and jacks;
then the magpie robin calls from the shajina branch
 and the black drongo swings its tail among date trees.
  When I say goodbye to her and come away,
   she can hardly say anything, –
just leaves the door ajar
   and stands there, looking at the road,
    and her eyes dim.

[August 1932 (25 Srabon 1339)]

Dwelling

By the River Mayurakshi.
 As my pet deer and calf are on friendly terms,
  so are the sal and mahua trees.
 They shed their leaves
  and these are blown to my window.
 In the east the fan-palm stands erect:
   morning's oblique light
casts its stolen shadow on my wall.
 A footpath skirts the river
   over red soil,
 its dust strewn with the kurchi's fallen flowers.
  The aroma of shaddock blossoms
    hugs the wind;
 there's rivalry between jarul and polash and madar;
  the shajina's floral tassels swing in the air
 and the chameli winds all along the fence
   by the River Mayurakshi.

Paved with red stones,
       the steps of a modest ghat descend to the river.
    By the ghat stands a champak of many years
         with a fat trunk.
Over the river I've built a bamboo bridge
    and placed on either side in urns of glass
       jasmines, bels, tuberoses, white oleanders.
       The waters are deep in places,
    with pebbles below,
  where swans come floating,
while on the sloping bank
graze my russet milch-cow
and brinded calf
    by the River Mayurakshi.

A pale blue rug on the floor
  is embroidered with dark brown flowers.
    The walls are saffron
      with borders of black lines.
A little veranda looks towards the east;
  there I sit even before the sun rises.
And I've found a person
from whose throat the notes splash
  like light from a dancer's bracelets.
    She lives in the cottage next door,
a passiflora trailing over her roof.
  It's when she sings to herself
    that I hear her at all,
      for I never ask her to sing.
Her husband's a good chap:
  he likes my writings,
  has a sense of humour, knows where to laugh,
can converse with ease on most humdrum topics,
  but can also suddenly hold forth
in what people patronisingly call a poetic style
    at eleven p.m. in the sal forest
      by the River Mayurakshi.

    Behind their cottage
      they have a kitchen garden
and about two bighas of land where they grow rice,
    plus orchards of mango and jack

hedged in by ash-sheoras.
In the morning my neighbour croons
  as she churns yoghourt to make butter,
while her husband rides off to supervise the farm
      on a red pony.
  On the river's other side stretches a road
    and beyond the road a dense forest;
  from there comes the sound of Santhal flutes
    and gypsies come there for their wintering
      by the River Mayurakshi.

That's all. This dwelling of mine
I've never built, nor ever will.
  Never have I even seen the Mayurakshi.
    Her name I don't hear with my ears:
      upon my eyes I see it.
  It rubs the unguent of dark blue magic
    on my eye-lids.
And I despair
  of my mind ever settling elsewhere.
    Taking leave of everything, indifferent to all else,
      my soul yearns to rush off
        by the River Mayurakshi.

[August 1932 (3 Bhadra 1339)]

Memory

A town in the west country.
  On its secluded edge
a neglected house beats the day's heat
    with a thatch that dips low on all four sides.
Eternal shadows lie prostrate in the rooms
  and a musty smell lives as a permanent prisoner.
      A yellow rug on the floor
is printed with images of gunmen hunting tigers.
    Under a shishu tree a road of white soil heads north:
      there the wind blows
        like a fine-spun wrap on the fierce sunlight's limbs.

178

On the sandbank in front are fields of wheat, cajan, melons,
              water–melons.
        Ganga glitters in the distance.
          Boats being towed
            look like ink sketches.
On the veranda, Bhajiya, silver bangles on her wrist,
        grinds wheat between stones
         and sings in a monotonous drone.
Girdhari the doorman has been sitting next to her
     for a long time, under who-knows-what pretext.
          Beneath the old neem tree the gardener draws
           water from a well with a bullock's help.
          The midday's wistful with its creaks
          and the field of sweetcorn shimmers in water-streams.
The warm wind wafts the faint scent of mango buds
and tells us that bees have gathered on the mahaneem's flowers.

    Later in the afternoon a young woman comes from the town.
       She is foreign to these parts and her sad face
         is drawn and pale from the heat.
         In a low voice she teaches the poetry of a foreign poet.
In a room where a tattered blue screen obscures the light
        and the damp odour of vetiver fills the air,
    enters the pain of a human heart from beyond the seas.
My early youth goes seeking its own expression
     in a foreign tongue,
         even as a butterfly flits
           among beds of cultivated seasonal European flowers,
         in their crowds of colours.

[August 1932 (7 Bhadra 1339)]

The Boy

He was about ten years old,
     an orphan raised in a home that wasn't his own,
   like a weed that springs up by a broken fence,
      not tended by a gardener,
     receiving sunlight, gusts of wind, rain,

insects, dust and grit;
which sometimes a goat crops off
or a cow tramples down,
which yet doesn't die, gets tougher,
with a fatter stem
and shiny green leaves.

From the jujube tree he'd fall, trying to pluck its drupes,
and break his bones,
faint after eating poisonous berries,
get lost on his way to the Chariot Festival;
but nothing could destroy him:
half dead, he'd revive,
lost, he'd return,
caked with mud, his clothes ripped;
would be spanked hard
and yelled at in torrents,
and when freed, he'd run off again.

Weeds had choked a dried river's curve;
herons stood on its edges;
a jungle crow rested on a boinchi branch;
high above flew a white-breasted kite;
a fisherman had fixed long bamboo poles for his net;
a kingfisher perched on a pole;
ducks dipped their heads and picked water-snails.
It was the middle of the day.
The shimmering waters were alluring;
the water-weeds swayed with their leaves outspread;
fishes darted about.
Further down, weren't there serpent-maidens
who combed their long tresses with gold combs,
casting those moving shadows on the ripples?

The boy fancied a dip precisely there,
in those green transparent waters
as smooth as a snake's body.
'Let's see what there is' was his greedy approach to everything.
So he plunged, got caught in the weeds, –
screamed, gulped water, and went down down down.
When a herdsman grazing his cows on the near-by bank
pulled him up with the help of a fishing-boat,
he was unconscious.

For days thereafter he remembered that feeling
    of losing his grip on things:
        how the world went dark
    and the image of his long-lost mother
        returned only to yield
            to the black-out.
        It was quite exciting, really, –
    like death, that big experience.
'Go on,' he urged a playmate to dare the same,
    'Just try to drown once, with a rope tied round your waist.
        I'll pull you up again.'
    But the playmate wouldn't agree to do it.
    'Coward!' he fumed, 'Coward! What a coward!'

Like an animal he'd slink to the Buxy family's orchard,
    getting plenty of blows, but eating many more jaams.
        'Monkey!' they'd say at home, 'Aren't you ashamed?'
        Why should he be ashamed?
    The lame Buxy boy limped as he gathered fruits,
        heaping them in baskets.
            Branches got broken;
                fruit got trampled.
            Was *he* ashamed of it?

One day the second Pakrashi boy showed him a tube
    with glass at its end and said, 'Just peep inside!'
        A pattern of colours he saw,
            which shifted with each shake.
        He begged, 'Give it me, please.
            You can have my polished shell
                for peeling green mangoes
            and my flute made from green mango kernel.'

It wasn't given to him.
    So he had to nick it.
        He wasn't acquisitive,
    didn't wish to hoard anything, just wanted to see
        what was inside.
    Cousin Khodon twisted his ear and said,
        'Why did you nick it?'
            The scamp replied,
                'Why didn't he give it me?'
        As if the real blame lay with the Pakrashi boy.

Neither fear nor loathing did his body know.
　　He would pick up a fat frog just like that
　　　　and in a hole in the garden meant to take a pole
　　　　　keep it as a pet,
　　　　　　　nourish it with insects.
He'd stow beetles in a cardboard box,
　　　　feed them on dung-balls,
　　　raise hell if anyone tried to chuck them.
He'd go to school with a squirrel in his pocket.
One day he put a harmless snake inside the teacher's desk,
　　thinking, 'Let's just see what Sir does!'
The gentleman opened his desk, leaped, and ran –
　　his flight was quite a thing to see.

　　　A pet dog he had,
　　　　not pedigreed by any means,
　　　　　　very much a native of the soil.
　　He looked quite like his owner,
　　　　behaved like him too;
　　　couldn't always find food,
　　　　so had to steal it;
had to pay for his crime by having his leg number four lamed.
　And the chastisers, by some causal connection,
　　had the fence of their cucumber field broken.
　Save in his master's bed the dog couldn't sleep
　　at night, nor his master without him.

　　　One day the dog met his end,
having stuck his muzzle into a neighbour's just-served dinner.
　　The worst torment hadn't drawn a tear from the boy,
but now he spent two days hiding from others and crying.
　　　He wouldn't eat or drink.
　　　Koromchas had ripened in the Buxy orchard;
　　　　he wasn't interested in pinching any.
　Those neighbours had a nephew, seven years old,
　　on whose head he dumped a broken pot.
　From under the pot came a whining, like from an oil mill.

Decent people wouldn't have him in their homes.
　　Only Sidhu the milkwoman brought him in
　　　　and gave him milk to drink.
Seven years ago she had lost her son.

The two boys' birthdays had been three days apart
   and they'd had the same looks:
      dark skin, flat nose.
On this milkwoman auntie of his the boy played his latest tricks,
   cutting off the string which tethered her cow,
      hiding her pails,
      staining her clothes with catechu.
To the tune of 'Let's see what happens' went his experiments,
   which would only cause the milkwoman's love to flow
      even more, and if any told him off,
she would simply side with her favourite, and that would be it.

Ambika the schoolmaster regretted to me,
   'Even your poems written for children don't appeal to him.
      That's how thick he is.
      Mischievously cuts the pages
         and says the mice did it,
            the monkey that he is.'
I said, 'The fault is mine.
   If there was a poet truly of his own world,
the beetles would come out so vivid in his verse
   the boy wouldn't be able to leave it.
Have I ever managed to write with authenticity
   about frogs, or that bald dog's tragedy?'

[August 1932 (28 Srabon 1339)]

The Last Letter

The empty house seems displeased with me.
   I've done something wrong
      and it's keeping its face averted.
   I wander from room to room,
      feeling unwanted,
         come out panting with exhaustion.
I'm going to let this house and go off to Dehra Dun.
   For such a long time I couldn't go into Amli's room:
      it would twist my heart.
Now that the tenant will come, the room must be cleared,

183

so I undo the padlock and go in.
A pair of Agra shoes, a comb,
  hair oil, a bottle of perfume.
On a shelf her school-books.
  A small harmonium.
  A scrap-book
covered with cut-and-pasted pictures.
  On a clothes-rack towels, dresses, saris of homespun cotton.
In a small glass cabinet a variety of dolls,
    bottles, empty powder tins.

I sit silent on the seat
        in front of the table.
There's the red leather case
    she used to take to school.
From it I pick up an exercise-book,
    a maths one, as it happens.
      Out slips an envelope, unopened,
        with my own address
        in Amli's childish hand.

    They say when a man drowns,
      pictures from the past
        in one moment press before his eyes.
    So does that letter in my hand
  in an instant bring back so many things to my mind.

Amala was seven
  when her mother died.
    The fear that she wouldn't live long
      began to haunt me.
    For there was something sad about her face,
      as if the shadow of an untimely parting
    had tumbled backwards from a future time
      to fall on her big black eyes.
  I was so afraid to leave her alone.
      Working at my office,
        I would suddenly wonder
  if something awful had happened at home.

  From Bankipore came her mother's sister on holiday.
    She said, 'The girl's education's in a mess.

Who's going to bear the burden of an ignorant girl
in this day and age?'
Ashamed to hear her words, I blurted out,
'I'll get her admitted to Bethune School tomorrow.'

Admitted she was, but her holidays seemed to grow
more in number than days of academic work.
There were days when the school bus came and went without her.
Her father was involved in those plots.

The following year her aunt came on holiday again.
'This just won't do,' she said,
'I'll take her with me and put her in a boarding-school
in Benares, for she must be saved
from her father's loving excess.'
So she went away with her aunt,
dry-eyed, but deeply hurt
because I let her go like that.

I set out on a pilgrimage to Badrinath
in a sudden desire to run away from myself.
For four months there were no communications.
Thanks to my guru, I reckoned,
the knot that tied me had slackened.
In my mind I placed my daughter in God's hands
and my chest felt lightened.

After four months I came home.
I was running to Benares to see Amli,
but on my way got a letter.
What's there to say? –
It was God who had taken her.

But I don't want to talk about those things.
Sitting in Amala's room, I open the unopened letter
and read:
'I want to see you so much.'
There's nothing else on the paper.

[August 1932 (31 Srabon 1339)]

185

Camellia

Her name's Kamala:
I've seen it written on her file.
She was on the tram-car, with her brother, on her way to college.
I was on the seat behind.
The clear outline of a side of her face I could see,
and the soft hair-wisps on her nape, under the hair-coil.
On her lap were books and files.
I couldn't get off where I should have done.
From then on the time I left home was adjusted
not so much to fit my own needs at work
as to match with the time when these two left home.
And often we met.
I thought, unconnected as we were,
at least she and I were travellers together.
Her mind's clarity
shone in her countenance.
The hairs were combed away from the delicate forehead;
the bright eyes were without a hint of embarrassment.
I wished a crisis would occur,
so that I could help her and glorify myself:
some sudden disturbance
or a ruffian's insolence,
not infrequent these days.
But my fate resembled a puddle of turbid waters
which wouldn't hold historical episodes,
where the tame days croaked like monotonous frogs
and neither sharks nor crocodiles, nor swans came for a swim.

One day the car was packed with jostling crowds.
A Eurasian was sitting next to Kamala.
I wished I could just knock the hat off his head,
grab him by the neck and shove him into the street.
My hand itched to do it, but could find no excuse.
Then he got out a fat cheroot
and began to smoke.
I came close to him and said, 'Chuck that cheroot.'
He pretended he hadn't heard
and puffed out even bigger whorls of smoke.
I pulled the cheroot off his mouth

and flung it to the street.
He clenched his fist and glared at me for an instant,
but said nothing, just got off the car in a leap.
He might have recognised me,
for in football I happen to be a name, –
quite a big name, in fact.
The girl's face reddened.
She opened a book, lowered her head,
and pretended to read.
Her hands shook, but she didn't spare
one sidelong glance at her heroic champion.
'You did the right thing,' said the office workers in the car.
The girl soon got off, not at her usual stop,
and hailed a taxi and went away in it.

The next day I didn't see her,
nor the next.
On the third day I spied her
going to college in a rickshaw.
I knew then how stupid I'd been.
She was a girl who could look after herself.
She didn't need me.
Once again I muttered to myself
how my fate was just a puddle of muddy waters
where the memory of a heroic act kept croaking
like a frog's sick joke.
I resolved to make amends.

I found out that in summer they went to Darjeeling.
I too felt keenly the need for a change of air.
Their villa was small. They called it Motiya.
It was in a nook, a bit below the road,
sheltered by trees
and facing snowy peaks.
When I got there, I heard they weren't coming that year.
I was thinking of coming back, when I ran into a fan of mine, –
Mohanlal,
tall, thin, and in specs, –
whose weak digestion revived in Darjeeling.
He said, 'My sister Tonuka
won't be happy until she's introduced to you.'
She was a shadow of a girl

with a minimal body,
more interested in books than in food.
Hence her strange admiration of the football star.
My coming for a chat was taken as a rare kindness.
What an irony of fate!

Two days before my scheduled descent from the hills
Tonuka said, 'I would like to give you something
by which you'll remember us. A flowering shrub.'
This was a nuisance. I kept quiet.
Tonuka said, 'It's a rare, precious plant.
Survives in this country only with masses of care.'
I asked her, 'What's it called?'
She replied, 'Camellia.'
A shock pulsed in me, –
another name rippled through my mind's darkness.
I smiled and said, 'Camellia?
Is her heart not easy to win?'
I don't know what Tonuka thought. She blushed,
seemed pleased as well.
I started my journey with the potted shrub
and found her, my fellow-traveller, not an easy neighbour.
In a two-room carriage
I hid the pot in the bathroom.
But never mind that travel-story.
Let's skip, too, the next few months' triviality.

In the Puja holidays the curtain rose on the farce
in the Santhal Parganas.
It's a small place. I don't wish to mention its name.
Change-of-air fanatics haven't heard of it yet.
Kamala's mother's brother, a railway engineer,
had built a house there
in the shade of sal forests, the squirrels his neighbours.
There one could see the blue hills in the distance;
nearer, a stream of water ran through sand.
Silkworms had woven their cocoons in the polash woods;
a buffalo was grazing under a myrobalan,
a naked Santhal boy astride its back.
A guesthouse was nowhere to be seen,
so I camped right by the river.
Nor had I a companion
save the potted camellia.

Kamala was visiting with her mother.
      In the dewy breeze
    before the sun was fierce
she went for walks in the sal woods, a parasol in her hand.
    The meadow-flowers beat their heads against her feet,
        but do you suppose she looked at them at all?
          She crossed the shallow stream
            to the other side
        and sat and read a book under a shishu tree.
    And the way she steadily ignored me made it plain
        that she'd recognised me.

One day they were picnicking on the sands by the river.
I wished I could go and ask, 'Couldn't I be useful in some way?'
      I could fetch water from the river,
    hew logs from the woods.
        Besides, wouldn't the near-by jungles harbour
          at least a respectable bear?

Among the group I noticed a young man, –
      in shorts, and a silk shirt of foreign make, –
        sitting next to Kamala, his legs stretched out,
          a Havana cigar in his mouth.
Kamala was absent-mindedly tearing to pieces
    the petals of a white hibiscus flower.
      Beside her lay
        a foreign magazine.

Instantly I knew that in that private spot
    of Santhal Parganas I was strictly superfluous:
        there was no room for me.
I would have left at once, but had one last thing to do.
      In a few days the camellia would flower.
      I'd send it to her. Then I'd be free to go.
Gun on shoulder, I spent the days hunting in the woods,
      returned before dark to water my shrub in its pot
        and see how far its bud had developed.

  The day arrived.
      I called the Santhal girl
        who fetched wood for my stove.
        I would send it in her hand
          on a platter made from sal leaves.

I was sitting inside my tent reading a detective story.
A sweet voice spoke outside, 'Sir, why did you call me?'
I came out and saw the camellia
    on the Santhal girl's ear,
        lighting up her dark cheek.
She asked me again, 'Why did you call me?'
I said, 'Precisely for this.'
    After that I came back to Calcutta.

[August 1932 (27 Srabon 1339)]

A Person

An oldish man from India's north,
    skinny and tall.
White moustache, shaved chin,
        face like a shrivelled fruit.
Chintz shirt. Dhoti in wrestler-style.
    Umbrella on left shoulder. Short stick in right hand.
Shoes with turned up toes. He's walking to town.
    Bhadra morning.
    Sun muted by thin clouds.
After a muffled, stifling night
    a fog-damp breeze
vacillates through young amloki twigs.

    The wayfarer appeared
on the outermost line of my universe,
where insubstantial shadow-pictures move.
    I just knew him to be a person.
He had no name, no identity, no pain,
    no need whatsoever of anything.
        On the road to market
    on a Bhadra morning
        he was just a person.

    He saw me too
on the last limits of his world's waste land,
    where, within a blue fog,

connections between men there were none,
　　　　　where I was – just a person.

At home he has a calf,
　　　a myna in a cage,
a wife, who grinds wheat between stones,
　　　fat brass bangles on her wrists.
He has his neighbours, – a washerman,
　　　a grocer with his shop.
He has his debts, – to merchants from Kabul.
　　　　　But nowhere in that world of his
　　　　　is there me – a person.

[Post-rains, 1932 (17 Bhadra 1339)]

Writing a Letter

You gave me a gold-capped fountain-pen
　　and so many accessories to writing.
　　　　The little desk
　　　　　　made of walnut-wood.
　　Notepaper with printed heads
　　　　in different sizes.
A paper-cutter of enamelled silver.
　　Scissors, pen-knife, sealing-wax, reel of red tape.
　　　　Paper-weights of glass.
　　Pencils – red, blue, and green.
You said I must write you a letter
　　　　every other day.

Here I am, sitting down, ready to write you a letter.
　　I've had my bath already, – earlier in the morning.

I can't think of a subject to write about.
　　There's only one piece of news:
　　　　　　you've gone away.
　　That's an item of news known to you too.
　　　　Yet it seems
　　you may not know it that well.

191

Well then, what about letting you know
　　　　that you've gone away.
　　But each time I begin to write
I find that piece of news by no means easy to report.
　　　I am no poet:
I cannot give language a voice
　　　　or put into it the way eyes look.
　　　　　The more I write, the more I tear up.

Past ten o'clock.
　　Time for your nephew Boku to go to school.
　　　Let me go and give him his meal.
　　　　Before I go, let me write this for the last time:
　　　　　　you've gone away.
　　　The rest are scribbles
　　and doodles on the blotting-paper.

[Rainy season 1932 (14 Ashadh 1339)]

❦

FROM *Shesh Saptak* (1935)

No. 1

So sure was I that you were mine
　　　　that it never even came to my mind
　　　to check the real value of your gifts.
Nor did you claim a price.
　　　　Day went after day, night after night.
　　　　You gave, emptying your baskets.
　　　　　　Glancing sideways, with an absent mind
　　　　　　I would put them away in my store
　　　　　　　and not remember them the next day.
　　　　　The new spring's madhabi
　　　　　　added its presence to your gifts;
　　　　　the post-rains full moon
　　　　　　　lent them its special touch.

Covering my feet
   with your black hair's flood, you said,
     'What I give you is much less
        than the revenue due to your realm;
           more I cannot give
             for I have no more.'
As you spoke, your eyes filled with tears.

      Now you are gone.
    Day comes after day, night after night,
      but you don't come.
After all these days I've opened my treasure-chest.
    I'm looking at the jewelled necklaces you gave me,
      pressing them to my breast.
My pride that partook of indifference
  is bent to the ground –
     there, where your two feet have left their imprints.

    In pain I pay you now the price of your love,
    and thus, having lost you, I have you fully at last.

[Santiniketan, mid-November 1932 (1 Agrahayan 1339)]

No. 2

Through the interstices of a casual conversation
  in an unforeseeable smile
    one day you set rocking
      my youth drunk on itself.
A filament of deathlessness
    sparked then suddenly across your face,
      never to be seen again.
The play of waves at flood-tide cast from the deep
    a gem-fragment of the ever-rare
    on the sea-beach of a million incidents.

    Thus does an unfamiliar moment's abrupt pain
      knock us on the breast in a trice,
        through our half-open inner window borne

in a farer's song
        from a far forest's edge.
So does the never-been-before with its unseen fingers
        set our heart-strings in separation's ache,
moving through microtones in slides from note to note,
        in our rain-resonant lonely hours abroad,
    in the evening jasmine's sad and gentle scent,
        leaving us the unexpected, invisible
            caress of its slipped cape.

Then one day
    for no reason at all, at an odd time
    that instant, surprise-unquiet, returns to our minds, –
        say, in a winter midday,
        when we're passing the time, staring
    at a field shorn of crops, where cattle are grazing,
        or in the darkness of a lone twilight, when
            from sunset's other shore the pain
                of a soundless vina begins to vibrate.

No. 3

Days of Poush are coming to an end.
    Inquisitive dawnlight
        pushes fog's wrap aside.
Suddenly I see
    on the dew-moist shaddock tree
        budding new leaves.
The tree looks astonished at itself.
As once Valmiki, on Tamasa's edge,
        was himself amazed
        at his own breathed out metre,
            so looks this tree to me.

From a long silent neglect into the crimson light
    these few leaves have
        brought their unabashed speech,
like those few words which you alone could have said
    but left unsaid when you left.

Then was spring near
   and between you and me
      hung the curtain of unfamiliarity.
Sometimes it fluttered;
   sometimes a corner went flying;
but the south wind, though it grew bold,
   never blew it off entirely.
      Unshackled interval didn't come to pass.
      The bell tolled
   and at the day's end
      you went away
         into the unspoken's darkness.

No. 9

Fallen in love, the mind said,
   'All my kingdom I give unto you.'
      The childish wish exaggerated, of course,
         for how could such a thing be given?
All of it: how could I get hold of that?
      A continent
         broken up by seven seas,
   it lives alone with its distances,
      speechless, not to be traversed.
Its head rises in cloud-capped mountain peaks,
      feet descend into cavernous darkness.

Like an inaccessible planet is this my being,
in a vaporous mantle, where there are occasional gaps,
   and these alone are what the telescope prods.
What I can call my wholeness
      hasn't been named.
      When will its ongoing design be completed?
And who is it that'll have direct commerce with it?
   The identity the name so far conveys
         is a patchwork of pieces gathered from the edge
            of the undiscovered.

The sky is scattered with the flickering shadows and lights
        of desires, vain and filled.
From there fall tinted shadows of so many aches
        on awareness's earth;
    the winds are touched by winter or by spring;
and who has clearly seen
            that restless play of the unseen?
Who can hold it
        in language's cupped hands?
A margin of life's territory is firm
        with the ruggedness of work's diversity;
on another futile labours vaporise,
        turning into clouds, ascending into space, –
        mirages busy at their sketches.

This world of the individual shows itself amongst men
    in the narrow corridor connecting birth and death.
In its obscure provinces
    massed in vast unknownness
            are powers oblivious of themselves,
        greatnesses that haven't received their dues,
    seeds of success, unsprouted, ensconced in the soil.
There crowd the shy one's timidity,
    concealed self-abasements,
    histories not bruited about,
            the many accessories
    to conceit and disguise.
There much hidden thick muck
    waits to be mopped up by death's working hands.

This undeveloped, unmanifest myself:
    for whom is it, and for what?
So many beginnings it brought, so many expressions;
    with so much toil was its language-building fraught,
        so much not reaching the felicity of speech, –
to perish abruptly in no-meaning's abysmal pit!
    Such childishness of creation: how can it be borne?

The maestro works with his study's curtain half drawn;
        the blossom stays veiled in the bud.
The artist's unfinished picture's not for the public:
        a few hints may be had,
but full viewing's forbidden.

In me his vision's not completed yet,
    which is why so much dense silence surrounds me,
    why I'm unfamiliar, unattainable.
Circled by an impenetrable guard,
    in his hands is this creation still;
        the time's not ripe to hold it to any eyes.
            All are far from me, –
and those who said 'I know', knew not.

[Santiniketan, 27 March 1935]

No. 11

In the dawn half-light
    the koel's intermittent calls
        are like fireworks of sound.
    Torn clouds disperse,
        on each a fragment of a golden script.

Market day.
    Bullock carts trundle
        on the track that crosses the field.
    Sacks of rice, fresh cane molasses in pitchers,
        and carried on the hip-baskets of village girls,
            kochu greens, green mangoes, shajina sticks.

Six a.m. in the school clock.
    The bell's ding-dong and the tint of the young sunshine
        merge with my mind.
    By the wall of my little garden
        I sit on a chair
            under an oleander.
    From the east the sun's strength casts
        an oblique shadow on the grass.
    Two coconut trees standing side by side
        toss their branches unquietly in the breeze
        like twin children making an enormous fuss.
    Sheltered by shiny green,
        young fruit peep from the pomegranate tree.

197

The month of Chaitra's moored to its last week.
  The sail slackens
      in the sky-floating raft of spring.
        The grass is starved and thin;
  by the gravel path
      the European seasonal flowers
          have lost their bloom and are withered.
A west wind blows,
      a foreigner in Chaitra's yard.
      Reluctantly I wrap myself.
The water shivers in the pond with the paved surround;
      the leaves of the water-lilies tremble;
          the few red fish grow restless.

  The lemon-grass is rampant
      in the rockery.
From the leafage peeps a figure,
      four-faced, in ochre stone.
On the far margin of flowing time it lives,
      indifferent, untouched by seasons.
Art's language it speaks,
      which has no likeness to what the trees have to say.
The care that seeps from earth's inner rooms
      day and night to all branches and leaves –
          that statue there stands outside the limits
              of that vast kinship.
A long time ago man immured in it
      his own secret speech
  like a spirit-guarded hoard of buried treasure:
      with nature it cannot communicate.

The clock strikes seven.
      The scattered clouds have gone.
The sun climbs above the wall:
      tree-shadows shorten.
          Through the back gate
              a girl enters the garden.
Tasselled plaits swing on her back;
      in her hand is a slender bamboo stick.
She's brought a pair of swans
      and their young ones to feed.
The swans look grave,

aware of their responsibilities as a pair.
　　　Even greater is the responsibility of the girl,
in whose young mother-mind love's liquid throbs
　　　to the demands of living creatures.

　　　I've wished to preserve
　　　　　this fragment of a morning.
　　　So easily it came
　　　　　and will so easily leave.
　　He who sent it
has paid for it already
　　from his own treasury of joy.

No. 13

A Baul busker walking along the street
　　came and stopped by your front door.
He sang, 'Behold! The unfamiliar bird
　　comes flying into the cage!'
　　Yes, and seeing it, the silly mind thinks –
　　Aha! I've caught the uncatchable!

You were standing at the window
　　after your bath,
　　　your damp hair cascading on your back.
The uncatchable was on the lids
　　of your far-away eyes,
in the loveliness of your rounded
　　　bangled wrists.
You sent him alms.
　　　He went away.
You didn't know
　　it was you the song spoke about.

Like a melody you come and go
　　on the ektara's string.
　　　That instrument is your manifest form's cage
　　　swaying in the breeze of spring.
　　I roam, hugging it to my breast;

199

I colour it, pattern flowers on it,
    just as I please.
When it sounds, then I forget its form:
    its string vibrates into invisibility.
Then does the unfamiliar come out to play in the universe,
    rippling right across the forest's green,
        merging with the dolonchampa's fragrance.

You are the unfamiliar bird
    dwelling in the cage of mating,
        that cage with many embellishments,
where separation's ache is eternal in bird-wings,
    in flight's postponement.
            Bird without address,
flying love-wards to the horizon's rim
            where all visibles vanish.

No. 22

Right from the beginning he's been hanging on to me,
    that old chap, that antique of a bloke,
    camouflaging himself by blending with me,
But today I'm letting him know
    that we're going to part, we are.

Along the bloodstreams of millions of forefathers
    he has come, bearing the hunger
of so many ages, and so much thirst;
all those pains had churned many days and nights
    in a long, continuous past;
        with all that baggage he decided to colonise
    this vessel of new-born life –
        that ancient, that crafty beggar.

Ethereal messages come from upper worlds:
    he fouls them up by the din he makes.
I arrange offerings on a ceremonial platter:
    he reaches out his hand and grabs them himself.

Desires burn him,
   wither him, day in, day out.
He smothers me with his decrepitude –
   me, who am ageless.
Minute by minute he has squeezed pity out of me,
   so that when death-throes grip him,
     I'm really frightened, I am –
      I, who am deathless.

So I've decided to part from him today.
   Let him stay outside the door –
     that old, starving wretch.
Let him beg and enjoy what scraps he gets.
Let him sit and patch his tattered wrap.
Let him live precariously on gleanings
   in that little field, earth-ridge-bound,
     between birth and death.

   I shall sit at my window and watch him,
     that long-distance traveller
     who's been travelling for so long
      along the road-curves of many bodies and minds,
       across the ferries of such various deaths.
I shall sit upstairs
   and watch his different crazes,
the see-saws of his hopes and despairs,
   the chiaroscuro of his mirths and sorrows.
I shall watch, as people watch a puppet-show;
     I shall laugh to myself.

   I'm free, I'm translucent, I'm independent;
     I'm eternity's light;
     I'm the flowing joy of creation's source;
      a total pauper am I;
     I own absolutely nothing that is walled in
      by ego's pride.

No. 27

Under the cascading stream
             I place my little pitcher
and sit
   all morning,
      sari-end tucked into waist,
      dangling my legs
            on a mossy slippery stone.

In an instant the pitcher fills
   and after that it just overflows.
      Curling with foam, the water falls, –
   nothing to do, no hurry at all, –
   the flowing water has its holiday play
         in the light of the sun
   and my own play leaps with it
         from my brimming mind.
The green-forest-enamelled valley's
                  cup of blue sky.
Bubbling over its mountain-bordered rim,
         falls the murmuring sound.
            In their dawn sleep
               the village girls hear its call.
   The water's sound
         crosses the violet-tinted forest's bounds
         and descends to where the tribal people come
               for their market day,
            leaving the tracks of the Terai villages,
climbing the curves of the winding uphill path,
         with the ting-a-ling-a-ling
            of the bells of their bullocks
      carrying packs of dry twigs on their backs.

   Thus I while away
the day's first part.
   Red's the colour
      of the morning's young sunshine;
         then it grows white.
      Herons fly over the mountains
            towards the marshes.

A white kite flies alone
within the deep blue,
   like a silent meditative verse
      in the far-away mind
of the peak with its face upturned.

Around noon
   they send me word from home.
      They are cross with me and say,
         'Why are you late?'
      I say nothing in reply.
Everyone knows
   that to fill a pitcher it doesn't take long.
      Wasting time which overflows with no work –
      who can explain to them the strange passion for that?

No. 29

Just one day among many days
   had somehow got caught
      in a picture, metre,
         or song.
   Time's envoy had managed to keep it stranded
      outside the path of traffic's constant current.
In the image-immersion rituals of the epoch
   many were the things that sped beyond the ghats.
      No one knew when that one day got stuck
         in a dry bend of the river.

In the Magh forests
   so many mango blossoms budded,
      so many fell down.
In Phalgun flowered the polash
   and carpeted the ground.
Between the Chaitra sun and the full-blown mustard-field
   in sky and earth
      it was a contest between bards.
But no brush of any season
   left its mark
      on that day of mine that got stuck.

I was once right in the middle of that day.
   The day was recumbent
      amongst so many things,
  all of which crowded round me, before me.
    I saw them all
       without taking it all in.
    I loved,
       but didn't really know
          how much.
       So much was wasted,
      absent-mindedly left
        undrunk in the juice-cup.

That day, as I knew it then,
    has changed its looks.
So much is dishevelled, so much is topsy-turvy;
    details have vanished.
She who emerges from it all –
    I see her today against the background of distance:
a new bride of those days.
      Her body was slim
       and her sari-end, peacock-neck-coloured,
    reached her head just above the hair-coil.
I couldn't make time
    to tell her everything.
Much was said at random now and then,
    but they were trivial things.
      And soon the time was up.

Today her figure has re-appeared,
     quietly stood
    at the fence between shadow and light.
She seems to want to say something
     and can't.
How I long to go back to her side,
     but there's no way to return.

No. 31

I'm letting the neighbourhood club
have use of my ground-floor room.
    For that, they've praised me in the local paper,
    called a meeting, put a garland round my neck.

For eight years now
   my home's stood empty.
      Now when I come back from work, I find
      in a portion of that room
someone reading a newspaper,
   his legs thrust on a table,
      others playing cards,
others locked in some furious argument.
    The enclosed air
        gets stuffy with tobacco smoke;
          ashtrays pile
        with ash, matchsticks,
            burnt-out cigarette ends.

With such turbid conversation's din
      day after day
  in huge quantities
    I fill the emptiness of my evenings.
Then after ten p.m. a stretch of time
like a meal's left-overs piled on dirty plates
   is vacated for me once more.
The noise of passing tram-cars invades the room
    and at such times I sometimes listen to songs
          on the gramophone –
the few records I have, the same
        over and over again.

Today none of them are here.
   They've all gone off to Howrah Station
      to give an ovation
  to someone who's just brought
    hand-clappings from across the seas
      clipped to his own name.

I've turned off the lights.
What's called 'current times' –
after many days
    that current time, that herald of everyday
        isn't in my room this evening.
Rather, I sense a lingering pain
clinging to everything
    from a touch that was air-dispersed,
a faint scent of hair
    that was here eight years ago.
My ears are alert,
    as if to receive a message.
        The old empty seat
            with its floral cover
                seems to have someone's news.

        An old muchukunda tree
            from my grandfather's days
                stands in front of the window
                    in the black night's darkness.
                In the scanty sky that there is
                    between this tree
                    and the house on the road's other side
                        a star shines brilliantly.
I stand staring at it
    and it begins to ache inside my chest.
        How many evenings had seen that star reflected
            in the flood-tide waters of our life together!

        Amongst so many things
            one tiny incident makes a special come-back.

That day I'd been too busy
    to read the paper in the morning.
    In the evening I'd at last sat down with it
        in this very room,
            by this window
                and on this armchair.
    She came ever so quietly behind me
        and quickly snatched the paper from my hands.
We tried to grab it from each other
    with bursts of loud laughter.

I recovered my plundered property,
     cheekily once more sat down to read it.
  Suddenly she turned off the light.
That defeat-acknowledging
   darkness of mine that evening
envelops me totally today
     even as her victorious arms,
      loaded with silent, teasing, mischievous laughter,
had encircled me
    in that light-turned-off seclusion.

  Suddenly a wind
     rustles the tree's branches.
  The window creaks.
The doorway curtain
    flaps restlessly.
'Love,' I blurt out,
'From death's kingdom have you
  come back to your very own home today
    with your brown sari on?'
A breath brushes my body;
   a strange voice speaks,
'To whom can I return?'
  I ask,
    'Can you not see me?'

  I hear,
    'He whom I knew
      most intimately on this earth,
that ever-youthful lover of mine
    I no longer find
     in this room.'
I ask, 'Is he nowhere?'
   Quietly she says,
     'He is precisely where
      I am and nowhere else.'

An excited hubbub reaches me from the door.
  They've come back
    from Howrah Station.

No. 46

I was then seven years of age.
   Through the dawn window I would spy
      the upper lid of darkness lifting,
         a soft light streaming out
            like a newly opened kantalichampa flower.

Leaving my bed, I would rush into the garden
      before the crow's first cry,
         lest I deprived myself
   of the rising sun's preliminary rites
      among the trembling coconut branches.

Each day then was independent, was new.
      The morning that came from the east's golden ghat,
         bathed in light,
         a dot of red sandal on its forehead,
   came to my life as a new guest,
         smiled to me.
Not a trace of yesterday would there be on its body's wrap.

   Then I grew older
      and work weighed me down.
   The days jostled against one another,
      losing the dignity that was unique to each.
   One day's thinking stretched itself to the next day.
   One day's job spread its mat on the next day to sit down.
   Time, thus compacted, only expands,
      never renews itself.
   Age just increases without pause,
      doesn't return
   from time to time to its eternal refrain,
      thus to re-discover itself.

Today it's time for me to make the old new.
      I've sent for the medicine-man: he'll rid me of the ghost.
         For the wizard's letter
            every day I shall sit in this garden.
             A new letter each day
            at my window when I awake.

Morning will arrive
　　to get introduced to me;
will open its eyes, unblinking, in the sky
　　and ask me,
　　　　'Who are you?'
What's my name today
　　　　won't be valid tomorrow.

The commander sees his army,
　　not the soldier;
sees his own needs,
　　not the truth;
doesn't see each person's
　　unique, creator-shaped form.
Thus have I seen the creation so far –
　　like an army of prisoners
bound in one chain of need.
And in that same chain
　　I have also bound myself.

　　Today I shall free myself.
Beyond the sea
　　I can see the new shore before me.
I won't tangle it with
　　　　baggage brought from this shore.
On this boat I'll take no luggage at all.
　　　　Alone I'll go,
made new again, to the new.

❦

The Indifferent One

When I called you to the arbour,
fragrance still lingered in the mango grove.
Don't know why your thoughts were elsewhere,
why your door was closed.
One day fruit-clusters filled the branches;
you ignored my full cupped hands.
Your eyes were blind to fulfilment.

In Baishakh, in harsh pitiless storms
gold-hued fruit fall tumbling down.
'My gifts,' I said, 'which lie in the dust, –
may they find their heaven in your hands!'
Your mind, alas, was still unresolved!

Unlit was your evening
and by your dark door I played my lute.
My mind, in unison with star-light,
on the resonating strings danced.
Not a flutter in your heart!

A yearning bird in a sleepless nest
sent vain calls to some lost mate.
The hour passed, the moment slipped.
You kept to your room, in indifference dipped,
though the moon was still in the sky.

Who can thought-read? My silly heart
had wanted to pour itself in words.
I had reckoned on some surplus remaining, –
a memory lingering, drenched in tears.
Perhaps there was a beat in the anklets.

At dawn's feet the pallid moon
slipped down from night's necklace.
Was the lute's lament some company for you?
Did it raise waves below sleep's brink?
Was there some pleasure, even if in dreaming?

[Santiniketan, July 1934 (9 Srabon 1341)]

ꠇ

No. 5

Evening arrived, her hair let down,
    having just had her bath in the sunset-ocean.
Dreams' incense seemed to be rising
        towards the stars.
In that quiet moment, – compact, magic-wrapped, –
    she, – I won't mention her name, –
her hair just plaited, a sky-blue sari on,
        was singing on the open roof-terrace, all alone.
    I was standing behind her:
    she mightn't have known that, or she might have.

To the tune of Sindhu Kafi went her song, and said –
    If this is what's in your mind, that you'll go away –
    then I won't call you back, no, I won't.
    I don't – do I? – ask the morning star to stay. –

As I listened, the world's utility-sheath
    slipped, and as though from its bud, –
revelation not vouchsafed before –
the unknowable opened, fully blown,
    scattering its light aroma in the sky.
        It was the unattainable's protracted sigh,
    the unuttered language of difficult hope against hope.

Vedic words, dispellers of death-grief,
    had once averred, unveiling the universe,
        that honeyed is this earth's dust.
In the same tune my mind said –
    'This earth's dust is musical, it is.'
'Death, honeyed death,'
    cried my mind, –
'On the wings of song
    you carry me to another world.'

I saw her.   She was like a nymph
    sitting at a ghat the colour of touchstone, dipping

her red-dyed feet in evening's black waters.
Soft ripples of tunes ruffled the shoreless lake,
    and charged with my own heart's trembling, the wind
    circled and touched her.

I saw her.   She was like a bride
    in nuptial chamber waiting, lights turned off,
        all the veins in her limbs in one pulsation
            in the imminent's ecstatic expectation.
The Pole Star's unflickering eye looked on from the sky
    and the Shahana Ragini's tenderness hung in the air.

I saw her.   She seemed to have returned
    to a fore-existence, to that obscure haze
        where the familiar jostles with the unfamiliar.
    Bent on recovering that epoch's escaped phrases,
        she was turning and casting her song's net,
        seeking, seeking, with the caresses of her notes,
            an identity that was lost.

Before us, a nut tree's head rose higher than the roof.
    Above it slipped the moon, the fourth of the waning phase.
        I called her by her name.
Sharply she stood up, turned to me, frowned,
                and said –
        'How unfair! Why did you steal up like a thief?'
        I didn't reply,
    didn't say, 'There was no need
for this trite play-acting. Today you could have happily said, –
    "Come, I'm glad to see you."   A pall of dust
        fell and settled on the honeyed.

The next day was a market day.
    I sat at the window, staring, next to me
        that open roof-terrace, where now the sun burned,
    wiping off, with its clear light,
            last night's spring-excess.
Without making distinctions the light fell –
    on field and road, the merchant's tin roof,
        trays and baskets of greens,
            stacks of straw,
        piles of clay pots,

                pitchers of fresh molasses,
        touching with its golden stick
            blossoms emerging on the mahaneem tree.

By the roadside rose a peepul, twined round a palmyra trunk.
        In its shade sang a blind mendicant, drumming a pot –
            – *Went away, saying 'I'll come tomorrow'.*
            I'm gazing at that morrow, I am. –

    The hubbub of buying and selling was like a fabric
        on which the notes embroidered with their art
    a motif of the entire universe's tense disquiet –
                'I'm gazing, I am.'

A pair of buffaloes with longing eyes wide open
            went along the road, dragging a laden cart.
        Bells jingled at their necks;
        the wheels groaned at each turn.
A field-flute's tunes
        seemed to be hung out in the firmament's light.
        Embracing all, the mind was entranced.

    To the beat of the Vedic verse my mind repeated –
            'Honeyed is this earth's dust.'

Before the kerosene shop
        my eyes spied a latter-day Baul.
    Tied to the waist of his patched mantle
                was a drum.
    A crowd had gathered round him.
I laughed, seeing the absurd too was harmonious here:
        this man too had come to fill the market's canvas.
        I called him to my window
                and he began to sing –
        To market I came, in search of the uncatchable.
        Everyone pulls me about, saying 'Hither! Come hither!'

[Santiniketan, 25 October 1935]

213

No. 7

Eyes fill with sleep
    and from time to time I wake up.
As the water of a new monsoon's first shower
    seeps through the ground to tree-roots,
so has the light of the young autumn trickled
    through my sleep to my unconscious mind's roots.
The day draws towards mid-afternoon.
Thin white wisps of clouds
    are afloat but still in the Kartik sunshine –
        paper boats made by the children of the gods.

    From the west a fast wind begins to blow,
    shaking the branches of the tamarind.
    A road goes north to the neighbourhood of dairymen:
from there bullock-carts spread saffron dust
                on the pale-blue sky.

  In the quiet hours of this afternoon
        my mind drifts in the currents of non-work
            on the raft of a day without cares.
    This day has torn its mooring from the world's ghat:
        to no need is it tied.
    Crossing the river of colours, in the evening it will vanish
        into the black ocean of unruffled sleep.

In pale ink is this day's mark left on time's page
        and will soon fade.
    In man's fate-writings it is the luck of some days
          to be inscribed in the thickest alphabet:
        between such scripts this is an empty space.
    A tree's withered leaves fall on the ground:
        the tree too tries to pay its debt to the earth.
    The fallen leaves of these lazy days of mine
        have given nothing back to humanity's forest.

    Yet my mind says:
        to accept is also a way of giving back.
      I have accepted in my body and mind
      the juice of creation's fountain dripping from skies.

That coloured stream has given its tint to my life,
    as it has to rice-fields,
      to forest leaves, and to the wrap
    of the migrant cloud of the post-rains.
All of them together have filled today's world-picture.
That a burst of light has flashed through my mind,
    that autumn's warm breath has ruffled the waters where sleep
    and waking mingle, like Ganga and Jamuna –
aren't these too to be found in the cosmic picture?
    My gladness without reason that gleams
      with the peepul's restless leaves in the juice-hall
    of water, land, and sky may not leave its mark
upon the history of this universe,
yet its art is among the universe's expressions.
    These moments, drowned in creativity's juice,
      are the seeds of my heart's red lotus being threaded
    into a chain in the seasons' royal court –
    a garland made of the gladness of all my life.
Nor has this not-famous day of an idle chap
    left a gap in that chain:
this day too has witnessed the threading of a seed.

By this window I spent last night alone.
Stuck to the forest's forehead was the moon's curve –
    the fifth of the waxing phase.
    The same universe was that,
save that the maestro had changed its melody
    with the ascents and descents of hazy light.
    The earth, that busy wayfarer,
    was then motionless, sari-end spread on the yard,
no longer heeding the household by her side,
listening to the legends murmured by starlight.

    Childhood memories came back – from a far-off vaporous age.
      The trees were still,
    the massed embodiment of the night's quiet,
their shadows cast in a row on the obscure green of the grass.
In the daytime, by the road of daily living
    those shadows had been nurses, companions
giving refuge to herdsmen,
    peace from noon's fire.
Now in the moonlit night, with no more duties to discharge,

they sat, silhouetted in the night's light:
brothers and sisters had together made with brushes
compositions as their whims had dictated.
My diurnal mind
had changed its sitar's pitch.
I was like one transported to a neighbouring planet,
watching through a telescope.
The deep feeling that gathered mass in my mind
throughout creation I have dispersed.
That moon, those stars, those trees – clusters of darkness –
became one, became vast, became complete
in my consciousness.
That the cosmos has found me
and in me has found itself
is surely a triumph for an idle poet.

[Santiniketan, autumn 1935 (Kartik 1342)]

No. 8

They brought me this wild plant, its leaves
a yellowish green, its flowers
like crafted cups of a violet hue
for drinking the light.
I ask, 'What's it called?'
No one knows.
It belongs to the universe's infinite unfamiliar wing,
where the sky's nameless stars also belong.
So I've made it captive in a pet-name
to get to know it by myself in private.
I call it 'Peyali', Miss Cup.
Invited by the garden, they've all come –
dahlia, fuchsia, marigold.
But this one enjoys the unspotted freedom that comes
from not being cared for, not being bound by caste.
It's a Baul, living on society's edge.

In no time at all its flowers have fallen off.
The sound that the falls made
couldn't be caught by ears.

The conjunction of moments that make up this plant's horoscope
    is infinitesimal.
The honey stored in its bosom
    is a minute drop.
Its journey's complete in a tiny spot of time,
    even as the fire-petalled sun completes its flowering
        in an eon's span.
This plant's little history's written by the cosmic scribe
    with a very small pen in the corner of a very small page.

Yet at the same time is that vast history unfolded,
    where sight cannot climb from one page to the next.
    The currents of centuries that flow without intermission
        like slow-motion waves, carrying in their course
            the rises and falls of so many mountain-chains,
        in seas and deserts so many costume-changes –
the same endless time's long flow has advanced
        through creation's conflicts
            this floweret's primeval purpose.

For millions of years in the path of its flowering and falling
    that ancient purpose has stayed new, alive, mobile.
        Its finished, finalised picture's not appeared yet.
This purpose without body, that picture without lines –
    in which invisible's vision do they live without end?
In the infinite imagination of the same invisible
    which holds me and the history of all men
        of the past and of the future.

[Santiniketan, 5 November 1935]

No. 11

As day by day the woodlands slowly cause
                Phalgun's colourful mood to fade away
                    into dry Baishakh's bareness, so have you,
enchantress, in wanton neglect,
                withdrawn your witching arts.

Once with your own hands you had spread magic on my eyes,
        set my blood swinging, filled me with drunkenness –
                my cup-bearer!
Now you've emptied the cup,
    dashing the magical juices against the dust.
        You've ignored my compliments,
            neglected to summon the surprise of my eyes.
                There's no accent now in the way you dress yourself,
                    nor, in my name, any of that hushed vibration
                        which had once made it musical.

They say that once winds whirled
                round the moon's body.
    Then had it the craft of colours,
        the witchery of music.
            Then was it ever-new.
    Indifferent to all that, why did it, over the days,
            block the flow of its own play?
Why did it grow weary of its own sweetness?
    Today all it has
        is the unfriendly duality of light and shade:
            flowers don't bloom there,
                nor do murmuring streams glide.

That silent moon you are to me today.
    And this is my sadness – that you are not sad about it.
Once, sorceress, you were wont to renew yourself
    with my own delight's dyes.
Today you've drawn over that scene
    the black curtain of an epoch's end,
        colourless, tongue-tied.
You've forgotten that the more you gave yourself,
    the more you found yourself in diverse ways.
    Today, by depriving me,
        of your own triumph you've deprived yourself.
    The ruins of the era of your sweetness remain
        in the strata of my mind:
    the crumbled gates of those days,
        foundations of palaces,
    garden paths choked with weeds.

Among the scattered fragments
    of your fallen grandeur I live,
        groping for the darkness that lies beneath the ground,
           picking up and saving what my fingers knock against.
And you dwell
    in the wan desert of your own miserliness,
which has no water to slake thirst,
    nor even the means
        to con thirst by mirages.

[Santiniketan, 16 February 1936]

❣

FROM *Shyamali* (1936)

Dream

In the deep dark night
    the rainy wind
        lashes indiscriminately around.
           Clouds rumble,
             rattling windows,
           causing doors to vibrate.
             I look outside:
        rows of areca and coconut palms
           are restlessly tossing their heads.
        Lumps of darkness
           heave in the jack's thick branches
             like ghosts conspiring together.
        A ray of light from the street
           touching a corner of the pond
        is as sinuous as a snake.

And I remember the old lines –
    'Deep the night of Shaon, deep the thunder's moan...
    at such a time I dreamt...'

219

Behind the picture of the Radhika of those days
near the poet's eyes
there was a girl,
a bud of love just sprouting in her mind.
Shy she was,
her eyes shaded with lamp-black,
and 'wringing, wringing' her blue sari, she went
home from the ghat.

This stormy night
I want to bring her to my mind –
as she was in her mornings, evenings,
manner of speech, way of thinking,
the glance of her eyes –
that daughter of Bengalis the poet knew
three hundred years ago.
I don't see her clearly.
She's in the shadow of others, and these –
the way they fix their sari-ends on their shoulders,
the way they curve their hair into knots
sloping slightly on their necks,
or the way they look you straight in the face, –
well, such a picture
wasn't in front of the poet three hundred years ago.

Yet – 'Deep the night of Shaon...
at such a time I dreamt...'
That Srabon night the rainy wind did blow
as it does tonight,
and there are likenesses
between the dreams of yore and the dreams of nowadays.

[Santiniketan, 30 May 1936]

220

The Lost Mind

You are standing outside the doorway, screened by the curtain,
   wondering whether to come into my room.
     Just once I heard the faint tinkle of your bangles.
I can see a bit of your sari-end, pale brick-red,
     stirring in the wind
        without the door.
     I can't see you,
        but I can see that the western sun
     has stolen your shadow
and cast it on the floor of my room.

Below your sari's black border I see
   your creamy golden feet hesitating
     on the threshold.
               But I won't call you today.
Today my light-weight awareness has scattered itself
     like stars in the deep sky of the moon's waning phase,
        like white clouds surrendering themselves
           to the blue of the post-rains.
My love
   is like a field long abandoned by the farmer,
     its boundary-ridges in ruins,
        on which absent-minded primal nature
     has re-asserted her rights
        without giving it so much as a thought.
Grass has grown over it,
     weeds without names have sprung.
It has merged with the wilderness around it,
     as at the end of night the morning star
        lets its own light's pitcher sink
           into the light of the morning.

Today my mind's not hemmed in by boundaries,
   so you might misunderstand me.
All the old signs are wiped out.
You won't be able to hold me together anywhere
     tight in any trussing.

[Santiniketan, 1 June 1936]

221

Tamarind Flower

Many were the riches I didn't gain in my life,
    for they were beyond my reach,
but much more I lost because
    I didn't open my palms.
    In that familiar world
      like an unsophisticated village belle
        lived this flower, its face covered,
ignoring my neglect without a grudge –
      this tamarind flower.

A squat tree by the wall,
  stunted by the niggardly soil,
    its bushy branches growing so close to the ground
      that I hadn't realised its age.

Over there lime flowers have opened,
  trees have filled with frangipani blossoms,
    kanchons have budded in the corner tree,
      and in its prayerful striving for flowers
        the kurchi branch has become a Mahashweta.
        Their language is clear:
they have greeted me and introduced themselves to me.

Suddenly today some whispering from beneath a veil
  seemed to reach my ears.
      I spied a shy bud in a spot of the tamarind branch
      on the wayside,
        its colour a pale yellow,
          its scent delicate,
        a very fine writing on its petals.

In our town house there is
    an aged tamarind tree I've known since childhood,
      standing in the north-west corner
        like a guardian-god
    or an old family servant
      as ancient as Great-grandfather.
    Through the many chapters of our family's births and deaths
      quietly it has stood

like a courtier of dumb history.
The names of so many of those
     whose rights to that tree through the ages were undisputed
are today even more fallen than its fallen leaves.
     The memories of so many of them
          are more shadowy than that tree's shadow.

Once upon a time there used to be a stable below it,
          in a tiled shed
     restless with hooves.
The shouts of excited grooms have long departed.
     On the other bank of history is that age
          of horse-drawn carriages.
The neighing's silent
     and the canvas has changed its tints.
The head coachman's well-trimmed beard,
     his proud disdainful steps, whip in hand,
have, with the rest of that glittering paraphernalia,
     gone to the great greenroom for costume-changes.

In the morning sunshine of ten o'clock
     day after day from under that tamarind tree
          came a carriage without fail to take me to school,
     dragging a young lad's load of helpless reluctance
          through the crowded streets.

No, you won't recognise that boy today –
neither in his body, nor in his mind, nor in his situation.
But poised and serene, the tamarind tree still stands,
          indifferent to the rises and falls
               of human fortunes.

I remember one day in particular.
     From the night on the rain had poured in torrents
          till by daybreak the sky was the colour
               of a madman's eyeballs.
     Directionless, the storm blew everywhere
          like a huge bird beating its wings
               in an invisible cosmic cage.
               The street was water-logged,
          the yard flooded.
     Standing on the veranda I watched

how that tree lifted its head to the sky, like an angry sage,
    reprimands in all its branches.
On each side of the lane the houses looked like nitwits:
    they had no language with which they could complain
    against the sky's torment.
Only that tree in the tumult of its leaves
    could voice rebellion
    and hurl arrogant curses.
Ringed by the mute insensibility of brick-and-wood,
    it alone was the forest's delegate,
and on the rain-pale horizon I saw its commoved greatness.

But when, spring after spring,
    others got their honours, like ashok and bokul,
I knew the tamarind as a stern and stoical porter
    at the outer gate of the monarch of all seasons.
Who knew then how beauty's softness lurked
    in that harsh giant's bosom, or how high it ranked
    in spring's royal court?

In its floral identity I see that tree today:
like the Gandharva Chitrarath,
    vanquisher of Arjun, champion charioteer,
practising singing, lost in his art, alone,
    humming to himself in the shades of Nandan-garden.
If then, at an appropriate moment, the eyes
    of the adolescent poet of those days had spied
    the furtive youth-drunkenness of the middle-aged tree,
    perhaps in the early hours of some special day,
made restless by the buzzing wings of bees,
    I might have stolen just one bunch of those flowers
and placed it, with trembling fingers, above
    someone's joy-reddened earlobes.
And if then she'd asked me, 'What's its name?'
    I might have said –
    'If you can think of a name
for that sliver of sunshine that has fallen across your chin,
    I shall give this flower the same name.'

[Santiniketan, 7 June 1936]

The Nap

Unsummoned, I came,
　　planning to play a trick,
　　　meaning to take by surprise
the busy housewife with her sari-end tucked into her waist.
　　No sooner had I stepped on the threshold than I saw
　　　her form stretched out on the floor
　　　　and the beauty of her nap.

In a far neighbourhood in a house of wedding a shanai
　　played to the tune of Sarang. The day's first part
had gone in that morning drooping in Jyaishtha's heat.
　　Her two hands in layers under a cheek,
　　　she slept, her body relaxed,
　　　　fatigued by a festive night,
　　beside her unfinished housework.
The current of work was waveless in her limbs,
　　like River Ajay's last waters, exhausted,
lying in the margins in a season of no-rain.
In her slightly open lips hovered
　　the sweet unconcern of a closing flower.
The dark lashes of the sleeping eyes had cast
　　shadows on the pale cheeks.

In front of her window the weary world
　　trod softly, going about its business
　　　to the rhythm of her tranquil breathing.
　　　　The clock's hints
　　　ticked on a corner table in the deaf room.
A calendar swung in the wind against the wall.
The mobile instants, stalled in her resting awareness,
　　had converged into one steadfast moment,
　　　opening its bodiless wings
　　　　over her deep sleep.
Her weary body's sad sweetness was spread on the ground
　　like a lazy full moon that hadn't slept all night
　　　and now in the morning was at an empty field's last limits.

Her pet cat miaowed by her ear,
　　reminding her of its need for milk.

Startled, she woke up, saw me, quickly pulled
her sari over her breast and said with pique,
'Shame! Why didn't you wake me before?'
Why? I couldn't give an adequate answer to that.

Even someone we know very well we don't know entirely –
this is something that is suddenly revealed to us.
When laughter and conversation have come to a halt,
when the vital wind is stilled within our minds,
what is it then that appears
in the depths of that unexpressed?
Is it that sadness of existence
that can't be fathomed,
or that mute's question to which the answer plays
hide-and-seek in the bloodstream?
Is it that ache
of separation which has no history? Is it a dream-walk
along an unknown path to the call of an unfamiliar flute?
Before which silent mystery did I pose
that unspoken question, 'Who are you? In which world
will your final identity unfold itself?'

That morning, across the lane in a primary school
children were shouting their tables in a chorus;
a jute-laden buffalo cart was wringing the wind
with its wheels' groans; somewhere near by
builders were banging into place a new house-roof;
below the window in the garden
under a chalta tree
a crow was dragging and pecking
at a discarded mango stone.

Over all that scene time's distance has now cast
its rays of enchantment.
In the indolent sunshine of a perfectly commonplace
midday lost in history those details
ring the picture of a nap, giving it a halo
of beauty never seen before.

[Santiniketan, 10 June 1936]

The Uncoupling

You came with the soft beauty
     of the green years,
  brought me my heart's first amazement,
     the first spring-tide to my blood.
  The sweetness of that love, born of half-knowing,
     was like the first fine golden needlework
  on dawn's black veil, the sheath
     of furtive unions of gazes.
          As yet birdsong was
     inchoate within the mind; the forest's murmur
          would swell and then fade away.

In a family of many members
  in secrecy we began to build
     a private world for the two of us. As birds
  gather straws and twigs, a few every day, to build,
     so the things we gathered for that world of ours were
          simple, collections of bits
               fallen or blown from moments that passed by.
          The value of that world lay
     not in its material, but in the way
          we created it.

Then one day from that dual management of the boat
          you went ashore at some point, by yourself;
     I kept drifting in the current, while you sat
  on the further bank. In work or play
          our hands never joined again. The twosome split,
     the structure of our life together was cracked.
  As a green islet, newly painted upon
     the canvas of the sea's dalliance-restless waves,
          can be wiped off by one tumultuous flooding,
  so did it vanish – our young world
          with its green beauty of new sprouts
               of joys and sorrows.

Since then many days have passed.
  When, of an Ashadh evening pregnant with rain,
     I look at you in my mind, I see you still

227

ringed by the magic of that emerging youth.
    Your age has not advanced.
In the mango buds of your springtime the aromas
    still assert themselves; your middays live,
        just as separation-pained, even today,
    with the call of doves, as before.
        To me your memory's remained
    amongst all these ageless identities of nature.
        Lovely you are in immutable lines,
        fixed on a steadfast foundation.

My life's flow never stopped
    at any one spot.
        Through depths, difficulties,
          conflicts of good and bad,
            thoughts, labours, aspirations,
sometimes through errors, sometimes through successes,
    I've come far beyond
        the bounds that were known to you.
    There I'd now be a foreigner to you.
If you could today, this thunder-echoing evening,
    come and sit before me, you would see
        in my eyes the look of a man who's lost
        his sense of direction
        on the beach of an unknown sky,
            in his track through a blue forest.

Would you then, sitting by my side,
    speak in my ears the remnants of bygone whispers?
        But look, listen: how the waves are roaring,
        how the vultures are screaming,
          how the thunders are rumbling in the sky,
        how the dense sal forests are tossing their heads!
    Your speech would be a surfing raft of sport
        in a vortex of mad waters.

In the old days my whole mind
    joined with your whole mind in unison.
That's why new songs surged
    in the joy of first creation
        and it seemed
that the yearnings of epochs had fulfilled themselves

in you and me.
Then did each day bring word
of the arrival of a new light,
like stars opening their eyes in primeval times.

Hundreds of strings have
mounted my instrument these days.
None of them are known to you.
The tunes you practised in those days
may be shamed on these strings.
What was then the natural writing of felt emotions
would now be copying, tracing a model hand.

Yet the tears spring to my eyes.
On this sitar had once descended the grace
of your fingers' first tenderness.
That magic is still within it.
It was you who gave this boat the very first push
from the green banks of adolescence: it still has
the momentum from that.
So when in midstream today I sing my sailing songs,
your name may get caught
in some sudden melodic expansion.

[Santiniketan, 20 June 1936]

A Sudden Encounter

A sudden encounter in a train compartment,
just what I thought could never happen.

Before, I used to see her most frequently in red,
the red of pomegranate blossoms.
Now she was in black silk,
the end lifted to her head
and circling her face as fair and comely as the dolonchampa.
She seemed to have gathered, through that blackness,
a deep distance round herself,
the distance that is in a mustard-field's far edge

229

or in a sal forest's dark kohl.
My mind paused, seeing someone I knew
touched with the solemnity of the unknown.

Suddenly she put her newspaper down
        and greeted me.
The path for socialising was opened
        and I started a conversation –
'How are you? How's the family?' and so forth.
She kept looking out through the window in a gaze
that seemed to be beyond the contamination of near-by days,
    gave one or two extremely brief replies,
        left some questions unanswered,
    let me understand through her hand's impatient gestures
        that it was pointless to raise such matters,
            better to keep quiet.

        I was on another seat
            with her companions.
She beckoned me with her fingers to come and sit next to her.
    I thought it was bold of her to do so
            and did as asked.
Softly she spoke,
        her voice shielded by the train's rumble,
            'Please don't mind.
    We've no time to waste time.
    I've got to get off at the next station
        and you'll go further.
        Never again shall we meet.
    I want to hear from your mouth
the answer to the question that's been postponed so long.
        Will you speak the truth?'

'I shall,' said I. And she,
    still looking out – at the sky – put this question,
        'Those days of ours that are gone –
            have they gone entirely?
            Is nothing left?'

For a minute I held my tongue,
    then replied,
        'The stars of night are all within the deep
            of the light of day.'

I was bothered with my answer. Had I made it up?
    She said, 'Never mind. Now go back to your seat.'
      They all got off at the next station;
          I continued alone.

[Santiniketan, 24 June 1936]

❧

FROM *Prantik* (1938)

No. 5

Dogged follower at my heels, my unfulfilled past,
shadows of unslaked thirst risen from a ghost-land,
determined to keep me company, zealous in back-beckoning,
soft-playing on a sitar a tune that drugs, obsesses,
like a bee, hive-dislodged, humming in a hushed
deflowered garden: from the back onto the path before me
you cast the sunset-peak's long shadow, fabricate
a tedious farewell twilight, ashen and pale.
Companion at my back, tear the bindings of dreams;
and those treasures of suffering, tinted futilities of desires,
which you have snatched and guarded from death's grasp –
give them back to death. Today I've heard
in the cloudless post-monsoon's far-gazing sky
a packless vagabond's flute, and I'll follow it.

[Santiniketan, 4 October 1937]

No. 14

Time for the bird to go. Soon its nest,
stripped, dislodged, song-silenced, will slip to the dust
in the forest's tumult. With dry leaves and withered flowers

at dawn I'll fly to the trackless emptiness
beyond the sunset-sea. For long has this earth
been host to me. Heady with mango blossoms,
greetings have come to me, sweet with Phalgun's gifts;
ashok-buds have sign-solicited my tunes
and I've given them, love-juice-filled; while at times
Baishakh's storms have gagged me with hot dust,
maimed my wings. Yet with all that I'm blest
with the honour of being alive. And when this shore's
tiring journey ends, back-glancing for a moment,
I'll honour, before I go, in humble salutation
the divinity that inhabited this incarnation.

[Santiniketan, summer 1934 (15 Baishakh 1341)]

No. 18

She-serpents hiss everywhere, exhaling poison-breaths.
Soft words of peace will sound like hollow jests.
    Before I take my leave
    let me invoke
  those who, in human homes, are preparing themselves
    to wage war against the monsters.

[Santiniketan, Christmas Day 1937]

❦

FROM *Akashpradip* (1939)

The Dark Girl

  Her colour a luminous dark, a coral necklace round her neck.
    In amazement I had gaped.
  She'd been staring too, without a trace of embarrassment,

her big eyes lampblack-stained, –
    a girl approaching adolescence,
        close to my age.
Clearly I recall the scene. The room's south door
    open to the morning sun. The nut tree's crown
with its fine thick foliage against the sky's pale blue.
    Her young tender body draped in white,
the black border encircling her limbs,
        then falling at her feet.
    Two gold bangles ringed her shapely wrists.
    Such was the reflection that fell on the stories I read
in vacation noontides. At times she beckoned me to lands
    where the creator's whims in many guises weave
unattainable mirages skirting a boy's dreams.
    A bodied enchantment
    cast its invisible shade
on my body and mind, subtle yet tactile.
    I dared not speak to her. My heart ached
        with the softest tune that hummed –
        'She's far, far away,
    as far as the shirish tree's furthest branches from where
        slowly the faint scent drips to our inner depths.'

        One day she left me a card inviting me
            to her dolls' wedding.
    Boisterously merry were her guests, whilst I, a shy lad,
        dreadfully embarrassed, kept to a corner. The evening passed
            in vain, and I can't even recall
what I had to eat at the party, but I observed
    how her nimble feet went busily back and forth
        with the black border dancing round their movements.
    From the corner of my eyes I noticed how her bangles
        seemed to have tied the solid sun to her hands.
        Her gentle, coaxing voice I also heard,
    which, when I came home, echoed in my head
            for half the night.

        Then one day
    I got to know her without impediments. One day
I called her by her pet name. My awe went
        and even banter was exchanged.
Sometimes we made up charges against each other

and made angry scenes – all in pretence.
Sometimes cruel jokes in cutting words
    hurled real hurt.
  Sometimes she gave me a bad name,
    calling me careless.
Sometimes I saw her in casual disarray,
    busy with cooking, quite unembarrassed.
How many of my male follies she would deride
    with her sharp, female pride!

    One day she said, 'I know how to read palms.'
My hand in hers, her head lowered, she read the lines,
    then said, 'Your temperament
shows a poverty in love.' I gave no rejoinder at all.
False calumny it was, but the sting was anaesthetised
    by her touch, my true prize.

      Yet the pain
    of incomplete knowing still remained.
    Beauty's distance never seems to wane –
so near, and yet so far, without end.

On the western horizon the days fade,
    mixed with gladness and with sadness's shade.
The essence of blue was distilled by Chaitra skies,
    and now this Ashwin light
  plays its holiday shanai in the gold rice-fields.
Slowly drifts the boat, to no port, weighed with dreams.

[Santiniketan, 31 October 1938]

Green Mangoes

Three green mangoes were lying under the tree
    in the mild sunshine of the Chaitra morning.
  When I saw them, my hands didn't itch to get them
    with a restless impatience.
  Then I knew, sipping my tea,
    how the wind had changed on my sails,

how the ferry-ghat in the east had dimmed.
Once upon a time, the chance getting of a green mango or two
    was my golden key, unlocking the secret cell
        of a whole day's gladness. Now
    there's no such padlock, nor is a key required.

    Let me begin at the beginning.
For the first time in my life a bride was coming
    from another family to ours.
My mind, which was then like a boat at anchor,
      was suddenly tossed by a flood-tide.
    Overflowing the bounds of what I'd been allotted
      came fate's bounty to me,
  shaking off all those old, torn, mundane days
    and nights from the whole house.
The marvellous opened
    Three times a day for some days
    the wedding music played, changing the daily language
around us, and in all the rooms
    the lights made a fuss in lanterns and chandeliers.
The marvellous opened
    in the midst of the too familiar.
Decked in colours, feet dyed in lac,
    someone came, hinting she wasn't a person
of limited value, belonging to this world,
    but was unique, past compare.
For the first time to the boy's eyes was revealed
something that could be seen, but couldn't be known.
    The flutes stopped playing,
      but not what they implied:
        our bride remained,
      girded by marvel's invisible rays.

Her treaties, quarrels, sports were all with her groom's sister.
    Conquering shyness, I would try to get a little close,
    my mind in a whirl because of her sari's stripes,
  but her frowns would soon let me know I was just a kid,
    nor was I female, but of a different tribe.
She was just a month or two older
    or perhaps younger than I was.
    Yet I had to concede
      we were made with different ingredients.
How I yearned to build a bridge towards her

with something, no matter what!
One day this unfortunate fellow acquired from somewhere
    some gaudy handwritten books.
    He thought they would stun her,
        but she laughed, and said,
            'What shall I do with these?'
Such tragedies, ignored by history, cannot draw
    sympathy from any source.
This one crushed the boy, heaping on him humiliation
    for whole days and nights.
Who was the judge who could assess and declare
        the value of those handwritten books?

Despite all that, I found that the lady of rank
    was quite interested in claiming petty dues:
there her wooden seat was at floor-level.
    She loved to eat green mangoes
    mixed with shulpo greens and chillies.
There was a tiny door through which such treats could be shared
    even by a boy and a mere kid like me.

Climbing trees was strictly forbidden.
    Whenever the wind blew, I would rush into the garden
and if, by a stroke of luck, found even one fruit
        snatched from its minor rarity, I would see
how green, how shapely, how beautiful,
    what a wonderful gift of nature it was.
The glutton who splits and eats it hasn't seen
    its incomparable beauty.

One day I gathered mangoes in the middle of a hailstorm.
    She said, 'And who asked you to fetch these?'
    I said, 'Nobody,'
left the whole basket on the floor and went off.
    Another time I got stung by bees.
She said, 'There's no need to take so much trouble to get fruit.'
    I kept quiet.

    I grew in years.
Once I got a gold ring from her;
    there was something memorable inscribed on it too.
I lost it, bathing in the Ganges,

couldn't recover it.
Even now the green mangoes fall
   under the trees, year after year.
      There's no way I can find her again.

[Santiniketan, 8 April 1939]

🌿

FROM *Nabajatak* (1940)

Birthday

No, I don't know
         the figure you folks have fashioned
with so many decorations,
      nor does He who dwells within me know
that effigy of my name inscribed with your signatures.
The bounds of His creation
      are beyond the range of your vision.

On time's ocean's shore
   the Maker of forms
shapes that image, by Himself, in secrecy
   behind a screen of varied mysteries.
         From the outside
   through mingled dark and light
some see it in one way, some in another.
   Fragments of forms and shadows,
      tricks of the imagination,
gaps in between: even so is an identity fashioned
               against the backdrop of the unknown.
   In His temporal playroom
   the Sculptor shaped me as a toy,
worked with clay and light,
            black and white.
Who doesn't know its brittleness,
how time's wheel will crush it to smithereens?

The gift it bears
professes, for a brief while, to be deathless,
    then in a trice eludes us,
        leaving behind a few handfuls of dust
and that death-night that washes all traces away.
    Sportive crowds,
        do you suppose the puppet you have made
will escape the grasp of great and greedy dust
        and abide for ever in light?
I wonder today
        if my own secret Maker
    smiles in a corner of His eye
when you imagine
        such an event.

[Written at Puri on his birthday in 1939 (25 Baishakh 1346)]

Romantic

Yes, they call me a romantic.
    And I accept it:
        I am a traveller to delight's sacred springs.
    Love, I have indeed
dyed the shawl that wraps me.
    When I come to your door,
        I sing dawn's Bhairab, invoke its furor.
I pluck the scent of spring
            in tuberoses
        and invade your lonely room's gentle breezes.
    Softly I read you poems
        which are rhythmic.
            The rhythms are interspersed
with structured statements artfully prepared.
            When you hear such things,
                the smile on your lips acquires a drunken tinge.
            When I play Multan
                on my flute,
    my inner mystery finds its melodic route.
        I place you at the centre of a sphere of fantasies,

238

carefully peeling off its dusty sheath:
    myself I make that world.
      I trick the Creator,
picking colours and flavours from His workshop,
      nicking a touch of His magic.
    Much of that is fantasy, I know;
      much, indeed, is a shadow.
When you ask me – 'Can this be realistic?' –
    I say, 'Never, for I am a romantic!'
    There it is – the realistic world;
  I know too well how to get there
    and get back.
      I pay back what I owe it –
    that's not done in words, and I do know it –
    I fully accept my liabilities.
There's poverty there, and disease, and ugliness;
    women there are placed under duress.
  There I discard my shawl and don my armour,
    for jobs must be done that know no mercy whatsoever.
Let drums give us courage where we must renounce and suffer:
  never let me be an amateur realist out there.
    There let beauty walk hand in hand
      with the terrifying.

[1939? First published in the magazine *Kavita*,
Poush 1346 (December–January 1939–40)]

ꘖ

FROM *Sanai* (1940)

Coming and Going

Love came
    with such quiet steps
I thought her a dream.
    I didn't ask her to sit down.
When she took her leave, no sooner had she opened the door
    than I heard the sound.

I rushed out to call her back.
By then she was a bodiless dream
        fading into the night's dark,
  in the far path her lamp-flame
            a reddish mirage.

[Santiniketan, 28 March 1940]

Impossible

When separation, I reckoned, was total,
I was walking all alone, without an aim,
Srabon clouds dark-leaning on the wood's head,
keenest lightning cleaving apart night's breast;
River Baruni's liquid purr from afar. –
My mind kept saying: Impossible, it's impossible!

On many such nights, her head against my arm,
she'd heard a poet's own humming of kajari chants.
Trees thrilled by densest downpour's drumming,
in flesh and spirit at one with one's leman:
came such a night, with the same Srabon abundance. –
My mind kept saying: Impossible, it's impossible!

On I drifted in the darkest deep of night,
the rain playing sky's music on my veins.
A honey-whiff from a jasmine grove, wind-borne,
the tidings I used to get from chains on her braids:
it rose again, the fragrance of those flowers. –
My mind kept saying: Impossible, it's impossible!

In a reverie, I wandered by thought's error
to the window which had so often beckoned me.
I heard a sitar playing a musical air,
a song of mine, twined with a hint of tears.
You left the poet, but kept the poet's honour. –
My mind kept saying: Impossible, it's impossible!

[Santiniketan, 16 July 1940]

No. 22

In the noontide between sleep and wake
perhaps in a dream I saw
the sheath of my being slip
and fall in the stream
of an unknown river,
carrying with it my name, my reputation,
all of a miser's heap,
shameful memories signed by
delicious moments.
Glories and infamies
floated away on the waves,
couldn't be brought back.
Then did I, ego-less, argue within myself:
of all my losses
which one hurt me the most?
It wasn't my past, with which in joys and sorrows
my days and nights had passed.
It was my future,
which I'd never had,
in which my desires,
like seeds within the earth's womb,
had, with their sprouting hopes,
dreamt through the long night
of the light that hadn't arrived.

[Santiniketan, 24 November 1940]

No. 38

When the god of death gave the command for annihilation,
men took on themselves the task of self-destruction.
Depressed, I've thought: why doesn't a sudden disaster
hit this errant planet which has veered from its course,
so we all die together, in one big blazing pyre?

But then I reflect: if through suffering on suffering
sin hasn't rotted, its seed will surely sleep
in the ashes of the holocaust, and on the breast
of a new creation
once more raise its thorns.

[Santiniketan, 5 December 1940]

ॐ

FROM *Arogya* (1941)

No. 7

Silently comes the fierce night, batters down
the sapped body's enfeebled door-bolt,
enters within, commences to ravish
life's glorious loveliness, till the mind,
under darkness's attack, acknowledges it's beaten.
When the shame of that defeat, that infirmity's ignominy
have done their worst, suddenly upon the horizon
appears the day's banner, drawn in golden rays,
and as if from some far centre of the firmament
arises a clamour – 'Lies! All lies!'
In the morning's serene light I see myself
as one who has conquered suffering, on the tower
of the exhausted body's fortress.

[Santiniketan, 27 January 1941]

No. 9

In creation's vast field
the play of fireworks in the skies
with suns and stars
is on a cosmic scale.
I too came from the invisible without beginning
with a minute fire-particle to a tiny spot

of space and time.
Now as I enter the last act, the lamp's flame
flickers, the shadows reveal
the illusory nature of this play.
Joys and sorrows, dramatic disguises,
slowly become slack.
Hundreds of actors and actresses through the ages
have left their many-coloured costumes outside the door
of the theatre. I look and see
in the greenroom of hundreds of extinguished stars
the king of the theatre standing still, alone.

[Santiniketan, 3 February 1941]

💥

FROM *Janmadine* (1941)

No. 28

This life of mine's been nurtured by a river.
In its arteries flow
the gifts of mountain-peaks.
Its fields have been shaped by many alluvial layers.
Mysterious vital juices from diverse sources
have spread themselves in harvests upon harvests.
From the east and the west networks of song-streams
lull its sleep and wake.
Ambassadress of the cosmos, that river,
she who brings the far near, bids us greet
the unknown at our doorsteps, – it was she
who wove the day of my birth. And for ever
on her streams, untied, my mobile home
drifts from bank to bank.
I am an outcast. I am a vagabond.
Boundless bounty piles my birthday plate
again and again with food, making no bones about it.

[Santiniketan, 23 February 1941]

💥

No. 5

One more time, if I may,
I would like to find that seat
on the lap of which is spread
a caress from a foreign land.

Runaway dreams from the past
may flock there yet again
and with their inchoate hummings
build a nest for me once more.

Resurrecting the happy hours,
it may make my waking sweet
and to the flute that has fallen silent
restore the melodious airs.

At the window, arms outstretched,
it may waylay the scents of spring
as the great silence's pacing
is heard in the midnight universe.

It will lock for ever in my ears
the whispers of that beloved woman
who has spread this seat for me
with her love from a foreign land.

It will keep for ever unsleeping
that message, so sad, so tender,
of that woman whose language I did not know
but whose eyes were eloquent.

[Santiniketan, 6 April 1941]

No. 11

On Rupnarayan's bank
I awoke
and knew the world
was no dream.
In blood's alphabet
I saw my countenance.
I knew myself
in blow on blow received,
in pain on pain.
Truth is hard,
and I loved the hard:
it never deceives.
This life's a penance of suffering unto death,
to gain truth's terrible price,
to clear all debts in death.

[Santiniketan, 13 May 1941]

No. 13

When existence first manifested itself,
the first day's sun asked:
'Who are you?'
There was no answer.
Years passed.
The day's last sun
put its last question
on the shore of the western ocean
in a hushed evening –
'Who are you?' –
but got no answer.

[Calcutta, 27 July 1941]

No. 14

Time and again the obscure night of suffering
has knocked at my door.
Its only arms, as far as I've been able to make out,
are the tortuous poses of pain, grotesque gestures of terror –
in brief, its role as a conjuror in the darkness.
Each time I've believed those horrid masks to be true,
disastrously I've lost.
This game of winning and losing, life's false jugglery,
nightmare that clings to our steps from childhood on,
replete with torment's jests.
Fear's variety show on film –
death's smart artistry projected onto the dark.

[Calcutta, 29 July 1941]

No. 15

Your creation's path you've spread with a magical net
of tricks, enchantress,
laying with expert hands the snares
of false beliefs
for life's innocents.
With this trickery you've stamped human greatness:
for such a one you haven't left veiled nights.
The path that your stars
show him
is his inner way,
ever transparent,
ever illuminated
by his simple faith.
However crooked outside, it's straight within:
that's his pride.
Others say he's been deceived,
but he receives
truth within, bathed in his inner light.

Nothing can cheat him:
he carries his last reward
to his own storehouse.
He who easily endures your tricks receives
from your hands
a lasting claim to peace.

[Calcutta, 30 July 1941]

Songs

All the songs can be found in *Gitabitan*, the standard collection of Tagore's songs, which is available separately or as part of his collected works. Any other work where a particular song occurs is mentioned along with the place and date of composition. If there is an uncertainty about the date of composition, any information available on its first publication is given. Several new songs have been added in the present edition. All the songs are arranged in a chronological sequence as far as possible, except that the bunch of songs from *Gitanjali* have been kept together for convenience and presented in the order intended by the poet, as indicated by their serial numbers.

1.

O beggar, you've made me a beggar,
    what more do you need?
My mendicant, what's this beseeching song
    you sing as you walk by?
  Every morning with riches new
  to please you was my heart's desire,
    my mendicant!
Alas, in a flash I placed all at your feet;
    nothing's now left.
O beggar, you've made me a beggar,
    what more do you need?
With my own breast's cloth-end
  I've clothed your nakedness.
For your pleasure I've
    emptied my universe.
  My heart, my mind, my life's springtime
  already lie in your cupped palms,
    my mendicant!
Should you want more, give me something first;
    then can I hand it back.

[Potisar, 27 September 1897. In *Kalpana* (1900).]

2.

I live with so little
that what I lose, I lose.

248

A particle goes
and 'Woe is me!' cries my soul.
Like a river-bank, in vain
I try to grasp the passing flow.
One by one they knock against my breast
and then they move away – the waves.

Whatever passes and what remains:
if I could surrender all to you,
then would nothing perish
but everything awake
in your resplendent greatness.
In you are so many suns and moons:
not a molecule, not an atom's lost.
Will not my crumbs of lost jewels be at your feet?

[1900/1901? In *Naibedya* (1901).]

3.

I want, I want, I want with all my strength,
and you save me – by denying me what I crave.
My life's a garner of your mercy's duress.
　　　All that you've given me without my asking for them –
　　　this sky, its light, this body, this mind, life's pulse –
　　　daily you see to it that I deserve such precious gifts,
　　　　　delivering me
　　　　　from the crisis
　　　　　of too much desire.

I am sometimes forgetful, and sometimes I walk
on the track that leads in your direction.
And you are cruel: you move away from my sight.
　　　That this is your kindness – I know, I know, alas!
　　　You send me away because you wish to receive me.
　　　You are filling my life so it deserves union with you,
　　　　　delivering me
　　　　　from the crisis
　　　　　of flagging desire.

[Calcutta, 27 June, 1907. No. 2 of *Gitanjali* (1910).]

4.

So many unknowns you made me know,
        in so many homes allotted me some space!
What was far you made near, friend!
        and gave the stranger a brother's face.
                When I leave a familiar dwelling-place,
                I panic, wondering 'whatever's coming next?'
                That you abide in all that's new to me
                        is at that moment from my mind effaced.
                What was far you made near, friend!
                        and gave the stranger a brother's face.

In life and death in this wide universe
        wherever your fancy takes me,
surely you, whom I've known all my life,
        will yourself introduce me to each face!
                Once you are known, there are no strangers,
                no interdictions, no scary dangers.
                Uniting all, you remain watchful:
                        may you always be in my gaze!
                What was far you made near, friend!
                        and gave the stranger a brother's face.

[1906-7 (1313)? First published in the rainy season of 1908 (Srabon 1315).
No. 3 of *Gitanjali* (1910).]

5.

'Save me in danger!' is never my prayer to you:
        I would rather be unafraid of danger.
If you can't comfort me in sorrow, never mind:
        it's sorrow itself I would like to conquer.
                If there's none to support me,
                let my own strength wake,
                and if in this world I face loss
                        or heaps of deceit,
                may my own mind never concede defeat!

'Redeem me, please!' is never my prayer to you:
    I would rather have the strength to cross over on my own.
If you can't lighten my load, never mind:
    may I have the strength to carry it myself!
        In happy days with deep humility
        I'll get to know your face,
        so that in nights of sorrow
            when the whole world seems to cheat,
    I don't doubt your grace!

[Calcutta, 26 June 1907. No. 4 of *Gitanjali* (1910).]

6.

Sunshine and shadows play hide-and-seek today
    in the paddy-fields!
These white cloud-rafts soft-floating in the sky's blue –
    who has set them adrift?
        Today the bees forget to gather nectar:
        they just fly about, they're blind drunk on light!
        And why are pairs of chakravaka birds
            milling on the river's sands?

Listen, mates, we ain't going home today –
    no! not indoors!
We'll smash the sky and plunder
    what's outdoors!
        Like crests of foam on tidal waters
        laughter scuds along the wind today.
        We're gonna skip work
            and play the flute all day!

[Bolpur-Santiniketan, Bhadra 1315 (post-rains 1908)? No. 8 of *Gitanjali* (1910), and also in the play *Sharadotsab* (September 1908).]

7.

A soft wind stirs the white sail without a spot.
Never, never have I seen such navigation.
From which shore does it bring its alien riches?
My mind wants to glide with it,
leaving on this edge all wanting and all getting.

Water drips behind. Low thunder calls.
Clouds give way. On a face the red rays fall.
Who are you, pilot? Whose beloved are you?
I wonder, but have no answer.
In which mode will you tune your instrument?
What are the magic words you'll intone?

[Bolpur-Santiniketan, 19 August 1908 (3 Bhadra 1315).
No. 12 of *Gitanjali* (1910) and also in the play *Sharadotsab* (1908).]

8.

Clouds have gathered on clouds,
          darkness descends.
Why do you keep me sitting alone
          by the door?
                    In working days, busy with different chores,
                    I keep the company of diverse men,
                    but today I'm waiting to have a rendez-vous
                              with you, only with you!
                    Why do you keep me sitting alone
                              by the door?

If you slight me,
          if you don't show yourself,
how will I pass such a
          day of the monsoon blues?
                    My eyes wide open,
                    I can only stare at the distance,
                    while my soul weeps and wanders
                              with the storm-wind's roar.
                    Why do you keep me sitting alone
                              by the door?

[Bolpur-Santiniketan, rainy season, 1909 (Ashadh, 1316).
No. 16 of *Gitanjali* (1910).]

9.

Where's the light? Where, where is the light?
Kindle it in separation's blaze!
    A lamp exists, but has no flame –
    was this written in my fate?
Death, surely, would be better than this state!
Light the lamp in separation's blaze!

Pain, she-messenger, croons:
'Listen, soul, for your sake God wakes,
    in deepest darkness
    calls you to keep love's tryst,
tests you with affliction to uphold your nobleness.
For your sake God wakes!'

The dome of the heavens has filled with heaps of clouds,
the rain continues to fall, does not abate.
    In such a night for what
    does my soul awake with a start
feeling tender yearning's sudden onslaught?
The rain continues to fall, does not abate.

The lightning's gleam just casts a moment's brightness,
only to plunge the eyes in denser darkness.
    Far away – don't know exactly where –
    a melody in bass notes commences,
tugging all my soul towards the road's distance,
plunging the eyes in even denser darkness.

Where's the light? Where, where is the light?
Kindle it in separation's blaze!
    The thunder calls. Loudly the tempest bawls.
    If the hour is missed, the tryst will not be kept.
Well-advanced and touchstone-black is the night.
Light love's lamp with your soul, let it blaze!

[Bolpur-Santiniketan? Rainy season, 1909 (Ashadh 1316).
No. 17 of *Gitanjali* (1910).]

10.

It is a stormy night
and you are coming to meet me,
o my friend, my soul-mate!

The sky weeps like
someone in despair,
my eyes know no sleep.
Beloved, I throw open my door
and look out again and again.
O my friend, my soul-mate!

Outside I can see
nothing at all, nothing!
I wonder what kind of
track you might be treading.

Along the bank of
what distant river,
skirting the edge of
what dense-knit forest,

in what depth of darkness
are you coming across,
o my friend, my soul-mate!

[Houseboat on the Padma, July-August 1909 (Srabon 1316).
No. 20 of *Gitanjali* (1910).]

11.

O master singer, how marvellously you sing!
All I can do is listen to you, entranced.
Melody's light overspreads the earth's expanse,
gales of melody scale the sky's ramparts;
bursting rocks, melody's Ganga flows
torrential in its speed.

In my heart of hearts I wish to sing like you,
but such rich notes elude my vocal cords.
I want to say something, but falter in my speech.
I am trumped! My inmost being weeps.
What a trap this is, where I find myself ensnared,
with your web of melodies woven all around me!

[Bolpur-Santiniketan, night of 26 August 1909.
No. 22 of *Gitanjali* (1910).]

12.

No! It won't do to evade me like this!
Steal secretly into my heart's seat:
nobody will know it, or talk about it!

No matter where I roam, abroad or at home,
your game of hide-and-seek is patent to me.
     Say now
you won't trick me,
will let yourself be caught
in an obscure corner of my mind's retreat!
It won't do to evade me like this!

Yes, yes, my heart is hard, I know,
not soft enough for your feet!
Yet should your breeze blow upon it, friend,
wouldn't it thaw a bit?

I may lack self-discipline's grit,
but should your tender mercy's droplets fall,
wouldn't blossoms unfold in an instant,
fruits ripen, too, in a sudden burst of heat?
It won't do to evade me like this!

[Bolpur-Santiniketan, night of 27 August 1909.
No. 23 of *Gitanjali* (1910).]

13.

If I don't see you, Lord, in this life,
let me remember that fact –
that I never had the chance to meet and get to know you.
Let me not forget it. Let it hurt my sleep and dreams.

I may spend days in this world's market-place,
my two hands may get piled with stupendous riches.
Yet let me remember that I haven't gained anything at all.
Let me not forget it. Let it hurt my sleep and dreams.

If I sit down idly on the road,
carefully spread my bed-roll in the dust,
let me remember all my paths are still untrod.
Let me not forget it. Let it hurt my sleep and dreams.

No matter how loudly peals of laughter ring
or how long the flute plays in my house,
no matter how lavishly I decorate all the rooms,
let me remember that I haven't had you as my guest.
Let me not forget it. Let it hurt my sleep and dreams.

[Bolpur-Santiniketan, 28 August 1909.
No. 24 of *Gitanjali* (1910).]

14.

My eyes keep vigil for you, Lord,
      but I don't see you.
         I scan the road:
    and I like that too!

        Sitting in the dust by the gate,
        my beggar's heart
            solicits your mercy, alas!
                Your pity I don't get,
                    I just ask for it:
             and I like that too!

Today in this world
so many, so busy, so happy,
        have rushed past me and sped ahead of me.
            I can't find a companion,
                it's *you* I want:
            and I like that too!

            Around me the green
            yearning honeyed earth
                draws from me such tears of tenderness!
                No sign of you, none!
                    O yes, it hurts:
                but I like that too!

[Bolpur-Santiniketan, night of 30 August 1909. No. 28 of *Gitanjali* (1910).]

15.

My heart's ravisher,
        this is your love indeed:
this light's golden dance
        upon the leaves!
            These clouds, sweetly sluggish,
            drifting in the heavens,
            this breeze dripping manna
                on my skin:
            my heart's ravisher,
                these are your love indeed!

Streams of morning light
        have flooded my eyes.
Your words of love
        have entered my inmost being.
            I've seen your face bend down
            and fix its gaze on my face.
            Today my heart has touched
                your very feet.

[Bolpur-Santiniketan, 1 September 1909. No. 30 of *Gitanjali* (1910).]

16.

For how many aeons
        have you been coming towards me –
        to be united with me!
Where possibly could your suns and moons
        keep you hidden!
                In the mornings and evenings
                of how many ages
        have your footsteps reverberated!
And a secret messenger
                has etched your call on my breast!

O wayfarer,
        today in all my being
I think I sense
        joy's fitful shivers.
        It is as if the hour had finally come,
                and all I had to do was at last done.
                O great king, how the wind does blow
                with your perfume on itself!

[Bolpur-Santiniketan, 1 September 1909. No. 34 of *Gitanjali* (1910).]

17.

The song I came to sing here stays unsung.
It's still the scales, just the wish carrying me along.

I haven't yet hit the notes. I haven't yet fixed the words.
Within me there's just a song's disquiet.
The bud's still closed. Just a breath of air has stirred.

I haven't yet seen his face. I haven't yet heard his speech.
From time to time I just hear his pacing feet.
He comes and goes just without my door.

The whole day's gone in just preparing a seat.
My room's unlit. How can I ask him in?
I hope to have him, for I haven't had him yet.

[Calcutta, 12 September 1909. No. 39 of *Gitanjali* (1910).]

18.

That is why
you take such pleasure in me,
why you have come down!
Lord of the three worlds,
were it not for me,
your love would have been naught!

Here with me
you have framed a fairground's play;
inside my heart the emotions are swaying;
within my life in diverse manifestations
your will is in wave motion.

That is why,
though you are a king of kings,
you still seek my heart
and wander in such captivating costumes,
always alert.

That is why
it is your love that pours
in the love of one who adores:
it is where two are united
that your likeness
is fully manifest.

[Janipur, River Gorai, 12 July 1910. No. 121 of *Gitanjali* (1910).]

19.

All life's acts of worship
        not completed –
even those, I know,
        aren't utterly lost, forfeited.
The flower that fell to earth
before opening its eye,
the river that lost its way
        in desert sands –

even those, I know,
        aren't utterly lost, forfeited.

Jobs undone that
        trail behind me still –
I don't believe
        they'll only add up to nil.
I hear them ring
on your own lute-strings,
which I haven't reached
        or plucked with my fingers yet.
I just don't believe
they're totally trashed, defeated.

[Bolpur-Santiniketan, 8 August 1910. No. 147 of *Gitanjali* (1910).]

20.

She won't take no for an answer.
I look away. She says, 'No, no, no!'
I tell her, 'It's day. The lamp is pale.'
Her eyes on my face, she says, 'No, no, no!'
Wild and flustered in the blustering wind,
Phalgun yawls in the flower-garden.
I tell her, 'Well then, time for me to go.'
She stands at the door, says, 'No, no, no!'

[Spring 1909? In the play *Prayashchitta* (1909).]

21.

The dawn in which you called me
                is known to none.
That my mind weeps to itself
                is allowed by none.
Restless, I stalk
and stare at others' faces.

Traction such as yours
　　　　　is matched by none.
The fifth note quakes,
the shuttered room vibrates.
But, without, my door
　　　　　is knocked by none.
Whose unquiet in the sky
and news in the wind that flies?
Along this path that secret
　　　　　is borne by none.

[Shilaidaha? Rainy season 1911? In the play *Achalayatan*, which
was first published in the magazine *Prabasi* in September–October 1911
(Ashwin 1318), then in book form in 1912.]

22.

When my pain escorts me to your door,
come, open the door yourself and call her in.
Starved of your arms, all else has she forsworn
and runs to meet you along a path of thorns.

When pain plucks my strings, my notes vibrate.
That song pulls you so, you gravitate.
It flounders down like a bird in a night of storm.
Come you then. Come out into the darkness.

[Calcutta, 28 February 1914. In *Gitimalya* (1914).]

23.

That fire of music you ignited in me –
how its flames have reached out everywhere!
All around me on branches of dead trees
tarum tarum it dances in rhythmic beats
and stretches its hands skyward to someone above.
The stars are stunned. They look on in the darkness.
And from somewhere a mad wind charges at us.

261

See: in the midnight's bosom this immaculate
lotus unfolding its petals – so aureate –
this fire –
who knows its power?

[Santiniketan, 7 April 1914. In *Gitimalya* (1914).]

24.

Not just your words,
o my friend, my beloved,
please give my spirit
your touch as well at times!
My long day's thirst,
long journey's weariness
I can't figure out
how to slake or alleviate:
assure me, please, that this darkness
is filled with you!

My heart doesn't just want to take,
it also longs to give!
It toils and trudges,
carrying all it's hoarded.
Extend your hand
and place it, please, in mine –
let me hold it, let me fill it,
let me keep it with me
to charge my lonely wayfaring
with beauty!

[Santiniketan, 4 September 1914. In *Gitali* (1914).]

25.

There's no end to it,
so who's to say the last word?
What came as a blow

will later glow as a fire.
When clouds have had their show,
rain will pour.
When snow has piled,
it'll melt into a river.

What comes to an end
ends only to the eyes,
walks through the door of darkness
into light.
Bursting the heart of the old,
the new will of itself unfold.
When life's flowering's over,
death's fruits will appear.

[Surul, 14 September 1914. In *Gitali* (1914).]

26.

I shall not beguile you with my beauty,
I shall beguile you with my love.
I shall not open the door with my hand,
but with my song I shall make it come open.

I shall not load you with the weight of jewels,
nor cover you with chains of flowers.
My tenderness will be the garland
which I shall swing from your throat.

No one will know what typhoon it is
that makes waves heave within you.
Like a moon by invisible pull
I shall raise the tide.

[Date of composition unknown. Though it is stated in some sources that this song was first published as part of the play *Raja*, it is in fact not in the first edition of the play (1911). It was first added to *Raja* in a special edition of various works of Tagore published from Allahabad, *Kavyagrantha*, vol. 9, 1916, and was thereafter included in the play *Arupratan* (1920) and the second official edition of *Raja* (1921) which became the standard text of the play.]

27.

I couldn't keep them in the golden cage –
my days, my many-coloured days.
They couldn't take it – the bondage of laughter and tears –
my days, my many-coloured days.

The language of my heart's very own songs
they might pick up: even such was my hope.
But they flew away before learning all the words –
my days, my many-coloured days.

Now I dream that expecting someone there,
they hop around that broken cage of mine –
my days, my many-coloured days.

So much feeling – could it have been in vain?
Were they all made of shadows – those birds?
Did they take nothing at all with them to the skies –
my days, my many-coloured days?

[Santiniketan, 1918/1919? First published with notation
in *Gitibithika* in April–May 1919 (Baishakh 1326).]

28.

A fire of flowers has hit the blue horizon.
A flame of fragrance in springtime has risen.
The sky is cozened,
thinks the sun's there imprisoned.
Perhaps in the earth it seeks its consummation
and so as flowers in a mustard-field has risen.

It is my ache that's hit the blue horizon.
What I've wished to say for years has risen.
From some lost Phagun of mine a gusty wind
has returned with its unreason.
This Phagun, maybe, it seeks its consummation
and so as waves in a mustard-field has risen.

[1922? First published in *Nabagitika*, vol. 1, in 1922.]

29.

Tonight the fire-flames burn in a million stars
   beneath a sky without sleep.
That grand marquee of heaven, drunk on light –
   there was I once a guest, in another age.
But my mind –
my mind wouldn't settle there.
So I sailed away across the ocean of time
   beneath a sky without sleep.

Such dulcet whispers between land and water
   in this green earth of ours.
   Floral pigments dappling the grass,
   light and darkness in their sylvan clasp.
I liked it here –
yes, I liked it so much here
that I thought I'd stay
and spend my days in play
   in this green earth of ours.

[1922? Notation published in *Nabagitika*, vol. 2 (December 1922).
In *Prabahini* (1925).]

30.

Lest he goes without telling me,
my eyes can't go to sleep.
I stay near him as best I may,
yet an ache won't leave.
The farer who by his faring's error
has hit upon my heart's border
may have his error's spell broken
and go off upstream.
When he came, he
came by snapping my bolts.
He may run off
through the same open door.
The maniac that may rise in him,
stirred by a capricious wind,

may well not, so late in the day,
be barred by appeals.

[Santiniketan, summer (May–June) 1925? First published in the post-rains
of that year (Bhadra 1332). In the play *Chirakumar-sabha* (1926).]

31.

Come to the kadamba grove, under the shady trees,
come bathe in the showers of the new monsoon!
Let your dark black tresses hang down;
drape your body in a cloud-blue dress.
Kohl in your eyes, a jasmine-chain round your neck,
come to the kadamba grove, under the shady trees!

Friend, let a smile flash from time to time
in your lips and eyes!
Let your honeyed voice sing a song in raga Mallar,
giving shape to the forest's murmur.
In the dense downpour, in the gurgling of water,
come to the kadamba grove, under the shady trees!

[Santiniketan? Rainy season 1925? First published in the pamphlet
of songs which accompanied the first performance of the musical play
Shesh Barshan on 11 September 1925 (26 Bhadra 1332).]

32.

Lost to myself,
I'm feeling so high,
waiting for you to come.
Cup-bearer, won't you
keep filling my cup?
This stream of juice,
nectar-filtered,
with a hint of musk,
sends its bouquet
along the wind and

maddens me from a distance.
Look at me, love,
with your own hands' favour
just for a night
make me immortal.
Many are the flowers
that blow in Nandan.
Rare, rare is
such enchantment.
Where else could one
discover such fragrance?

[Agartala, February–March 1926 (Phalgun 1332).]

33.

So many times I've been along this trail
and never once lost my way.
Are its traces lost today?
Has the wild grass covered it all?

Still, in my mind I know there's nothing to fear,
for a wind in my favour suddenly begins to blow.
I shall surely know you   the time will come –
for you know me.

Lamp in hand, I used to go alone.
Its flame's gone out.
Yet in my mind I know the address is written
in the language of the stars.

The wayside flowers,
I know, will check my errors
and guide me gently
by their scents' secret codes.

[Santiniketan, 8 April 1926.]

34.

Shiuli flower! Shiuli flower!
What an error! Such an error!
By what sleight
did the breeze of night
bring you here
to the forest shade?
No sooner it's dawn
than you want to return.
Every day's the same.
Why such longing?
There's dew in your eyes.
What's the idiom
of your goodbyes?
And your scent –
what does it portend?
Ah, away they go –
minute by minute
heaps and heaps
of bokuls also.

[Spring 1927. In the musical play *Nataraj-riturangashala* (1927).]

35.

The two of us had swung in the forest that day,
    swing-ropes twined with chains of flowers.
Recall it, please, from time to time!
    Never forget it, never!

That day the wind was laced, you know,
    with my mind's delirious chatter,
and in the heavens, scattered in plenty,
    were similes of your laughter.

As we walked along the path that evening,
    the full moon rose in all its lustre.
Ah, what a splendid hour it was
    when you and I met together!

Now I have no time of my own.
   I'm far from you and must bear it alone.
But the friendship's thread I tied to your heart –
   never untie it, never!

[Written on a train from Bangkok to Penang, 17 October 1927.
Included in the musical play *Shapmochan* (edition of 1933).]

36.

The moon's laughter's dam has burst:
light spills out.
Tuberose, pour your odour.

The crazy wind – he can't make out
who calls him and whence;
whomever he visits in the flower-garden
he fancies straight away, he does.

Sandal smothers the blue sky's forehead
and Saraswati's swans have escaped.

Moon, what d'you think you're doing,
strewing the earth with all this parijat pollen?
Which of you women in Indra's heaven
have lit yourself this nuptial lamp?

[1929? In the play *Paritran* (1929, revised version of *Prayashchitta*).
The publication date of the play is May-June 1929 (Jyaishtha 1336).
But there is a possibility that the play was first published in the Puja
issue of a magazine two years earlier in 1927 (post-rains 1334). If the song
was there then, its date of composition would have to be pushed back.]

37.

House-bound men, open your doors.
It's swinging time.
In land and water and sylvan spots

it's swinging time.
Open your doors.

Red is the laughter piled in polash, ashok.
A red drunkenness marks the morning clouds.
The new-born leaves are tinged with ripples of red.

The south wind makes the bamboos murmur.
Butterflies dangle from tall grass-stalks.

The bee is after the flowers' bounty,
playing on its wings its busker's vina.

In the madhabi arbour the wind is fragrance-drugged.

[Spring 1931? In the musical play *Nabin* (published
in Phalgun 1337, i.e., February–March 1931).]

38.

Where does the road end? What's at the end of the road?
Desires, our labours' prayers: where do they go?
Up and down
roll the waves of weeping.
Ahead us
the deepest darkness falls.
In which country is the shore?

In this trail of a mirage –
it seems to me –
thirst may not end,
and that's the fear that clings.
Pain, helmless,
its sails ripped to shreds,
drifts nowhere.

[1933? In the play *Chandalika* (1933).]

39.

In the dead of night you brought me devastation.
What your feet broke was also blessed by them.
I'll thread the pieces in a chain of blood-red stones.
On my breast they'll hang and heave with hidden sadness.

You took a sitar on your lap and slid between notes,
pulled the strings sideways so cruelly that they broke.
You left it behind on the ground.
Its silenced song, I know, is your gift to me,
riding the Phalgun winds in phantom ascents and descents.

[This song has a slightly different poem-version, written in
Sriniketan on 12 July 1939 and included in *Sanai* (1940).]

40.

You gave me the monsoon's first kadamba flower.
I've brought you a present, my Srabon song.
I've kept it wrapped in the dark shadows of clouds,
this sheaf from my music's field, its first gold corn.

You bring me a gift today;
you mightn't tomorrow.
Your branches of flowers
may be bare by then, – who knows?

But this my song
will ride your amnesia's tide,
return each Srabon,
boat bearing you ovation.

[30 July 1939. A slightly different poem-version, written
on 10 January 1940, is included in *Sanai* (1940).]

41.

Take the last song's diminuendo with you.
Speak the last word as you go.

Darkness falls,
there's little time.
In the dim twilight
the farer loses his way.

The sun's last rays now fade from the western sky.
From the tamal grove comes the last peacock-cry.

Who is she who searches the unknown
and for the last time opens my garden-gate?

[1939? Possibly published in Bhadra 1346 (August–September 1939).]

NOTES & GLOSSARY

Notes

(In these notes the word *stanza* refers to any kind of verse-paragraph, whether in metrical structure or in free verse.)

For convenience of reference certain works are referred to in the notes in abbreviated form, and their details are as follows:

Ketaki Kushari Dyson, *In Your Blossoming Flower-Garden: Rabindranath Tagore and Victoria Ocampo* (Sahitya Akademi, New Delhi, 1988).

Krishna Kripalani, *Rabindranath Tagore: A Biography*, 2nd edition (Visvabharati, Calcutta, 1980).

Prasantakumar Pal, *Rabijibani*, nine volumes; the first two volumes were initially published by Bhurjapatra of Calcutta in 1982 and 1984, but are no longer available in that edition; all nine volumes are currently available from Ananda of Calcutta.

Rabindranath Tagore, *Rabindra-rachanabali* (Collected Works), the older Visvabharati edition in 30 volumes.

Rabindranath Tagore, *Chhinnapatrabali* (Visvabharati, 1963 reprint).

Rathindranath Tagore, *On the Edges of Time* (Visvabharati, 2nd edition, 1981).

Heinrich Zimmer, *Myths and Symbols in Indian Art and Civilization* (paperback edition, Harper and Brothers, New York, 1962).

Other references are given in full where they occur.

80-81. The Suicide of a Star (*Sandhyasangit*, Evening Music): When translating this poem, I had to decide whether the star should be a *he* or a *she*. The star is clearly anthropomorphised, but as I have explained in the Introduction, Bengali does not distinguish between *he* and *she*, so a decision had to be reached. In the first edition of this book, I had rendered the star as a *he*. It was a nerve-racking decision, as my gut instinct told me that this star should be seen as a female figure.

According to Prabhatkumar Mukhopadhyay, the author of the first major biography of Tagore in Bengali, this poem refers to a first suicide attempt Kadambari Devi is supposed to have made in 1880. He reckons that the poem must have been written in Calcutta shortly after the incident, perhaps in September of that year. Prasantakumar Pal rejected this suggestion, maintaining that the poem reflected no more than a generalised mood of youthful romantic agony. According to him, whether Kadambari had made an early suicide attempt or not cannot be definitively established, and even if she had, Tagore would not have referred to it in this way. Not only was the poem openly published in the Tagore family magazine *Bharati* in the summer of 1881, but it also uses the words *jyoti* (light, radiance) and *jyotirmay* (luminous, radiant). Pal argued that if the poem had any conscious reference to Kadambari's presumed first suicide attempt, then those words would amount to deliberate and crude punning on Jyotirindranath's name, something one does not expect from his sensitive younger brother. (See Pal, vol. 2, 2nd edition, p. 109, where Prabhatkumar Mukhopadhyay's different view on this matter is also quoted.)

Translating the poem for the first edition, I accepted Pal's argument and ruled out any conscious reference to Kadambari, but went on agonising over a possible unconscious connection. Suicides often do make one or two initial unsuccessful attempts at self-destruction, succeeding better in their final attempt, and there can be no doubt that any such failed attempt on Kadambari's part would have been effectively hushed up by the family. A romantic toying with the ideas of unbearable anguish and frustration, and of escape through death, could have been part of the ambience of both the young people, Rabindranath and Kadambari. As a person who dipped a great deal in European romantic literature, Rabindranath could have even introduced some of these ideas to his sister-in-law.

In this connection we need to remember Tagore's collection *Bhanusimha Thakurer Padabali* (The Songs of Bhanusimha Thakur), published by him in 1884 after Kadambari's death and dedicated to her. The poems had actually been written much earlier and had been accumulating when she was still alive. Tagore says in the dedication that she had often urged him to publish these verses, but while she was alive, he did not do so. The poems and songs in this volume were deliberately written in a mock-medieval style, mimicking the old Baishnab poets. In one of these poems, Radha in a fit of love-pique, addresses Death as her Lover. She says she would prefer Death to Krishna and go to meet him, because Death would never abandon or hurt her, Death would never let her down. The poet, under the pseudonym of Bhanusimha Thakur, tries in an arch manner to dissuade Radha from this project. When in 1931, at the age of 70, Tagore published his Selected Poems under the title of *Sanchayita*, he chose this poem to begin the collection, thereby giving it a symbolic aura. It was as if he was saying to the dead woman, 'I advised you not to, but you still went ahead and did it. Look – I am not guilty of your death in any way.'

Translating 'The Suicide of a Star' for the first edition, I reluctantly decided that any direct identification of the star with Kadambari had to be avoided, so translating the third person pronoun with a *she* was out. I persuaded myself that in view of the strong bond of sympathy between the young poet and the suicidal but brilliant star, *he* was a logical enough choice. But deep down I was unhappy about this decision, because the original poem with its unisex third person pronoun kept twinkling brightly and ambiguously at me in the manner of a star-maiden. I felt that the poem was laughing at the translator's predicament like a mischievous, cross-dressed Shakespearean heroine.

When I first undertook this translation project, I knew that I had to start my selection with one or two poems from *Sandhyasangit*, the first volume of his poetry that according to the poet himself was stamped with his real poetical personality. At that time I did not pay much attention to Tagore's works from the very early years. Barring *Bhanusimha Thakurer Padabali*, which he admitted to the hall of his Collected Works, the rest of the early works had been banished to two volumes of juvenilia, dubbed *Achalita Sangraha* or 'volumes no longer in circulation', which effectively functioned as appendices to his oeuvre. These books had been out of print for a long time, and Tagore had been quite reluctant to re-issue them. They were really re-published for historical and archival reasons, and under pressure from his entourage. In the 1990s, in course of a completely different project in which I was involved – on how Tagore's slightly problematic colour vision had affected his writings and

276

visual art – I decided to survey all the volumes of the *Rabindra-rachanabali* in the older Visvabharati edition, including the two volumes of the *Achalita Sangraha*. It was then that I read the early poetic texts with proper attention. These certainly contain plenty of romantic anguish, but they also contain some more startling elements: violent imagery, the near-operatic explosion of jealousies, death-wishes, and wallowings in the idea of self-harm. Today we might be inclined to identify such material with the release of pent-up youthful sexual frustration. Here was the dark underbelly, as it were, of the God-fearing, Brahmo-Victorian nurturing the junior members of the Tagore family were receiving: the underground rebellion of one hyper-sensitive soul against a repressive regimen. Rabindranath did indeed survive the passage through such gruelling contradictions, and his subsequent personal bereavements to boot, by turning his entire life into one furious frenzy of creativity at multiple levels. But Jyotirindranath's young wife, perhaps depressive by nature, more easily hurt, and trapped in a childless marriage with a talented and somewhat eccentric man ten years her senior, within a patriarchal setting where there were far fewer opportunities for females to express and fulfil themselves in non-domestic contexts, succumbed. Most critics agree that Kadambari's suicide delivered a profound shock to Rabindranath's psychology, maturing him. Looking at the early texts, one senses that the event caused him to pull himself together and move away from the edge of an abyss. One understands why Tagore was reluctant to re-issue the early texts.

In *Kabi-kahini* (The Tale of a Poet, 1878), Tagore's first work published in book-form, a very romantic, nature-loving poet leaves his beloved Nalini, who is almost Nature herself personified as a young girl, to travel abroad; when he returns, he finds her dead. The grieving poet is, however, allowed to reach a ripe old age and become a mellowed philosopher, compassionate to all creation. The plot of *Bana-phul* (Forest-flower, 1880) is more disturbing. Although published as a book after *Kabi-kahini*, *Bana-phul* was written earlier, begun when he was only fourteen and published serially in a magazine in 1876, when he was fifteen. It is Tagore's first completed poetic opus and described in the title-page as a verse-novel. In it Kamala, a Miranda-like figure, is given shelter by Bijoy after she is left an orphan at the death of her father. Kamala, however, falls in love with Bijoy's friend Nirad who has shoulder-length hair, while a maiden named Niraja seems enamoured of Kamala's Bijoy. It could have been a prankish story like *A Midsummer Night's Dream*, but it changes course and moves towards *Romeo and Juliet*. Nirad says he has been told by Bijoy to leave, and he is on his way, but he suddenly falls to the ground, injured, with a knife stuck on his back, while Bijoy is seen slinking off with bloody hands. There is a terrific scene in which Nirad is consumed in a funeral pyre, and at one point we wonder if Kamala is going to throw herself on the flames too, but she doesn't. She chooses to hurl herself from a snowy mountain peak, falling into a foaming stream which carries her off.

So the young Tagore was quite capable of imagining hopeless love-tangles, conflicts between love and friendship and between old loyalties and new attractions, sexual jealousy and murderous impulses, suicides driven by hurt feelings or love's despair. In *Bana-phul* we see him indulging in an extremely risqué tragicomic pun involving his own name (Rabi) and that of his elder brother (Jyoti). Kamala's suicidal fall from the top of a mountain is described as 'the fall of a bright star from the sky'. This clinched it for me: I decided that

277

should there be a new edition of my translations, I would change the gender of the star in 'The Suicide of a Star' to a *she*.

In the book in which my research colleagues and myself gave the results of our investigations into the effects of Tagore's protanopic vision on his literature and art, I indicated *en passant* that I was moving away from the position that the poem 'The Suicide of a Star' had nothing to do with Jyotirindranath and Kadambari (Dyson, Adhikary et al., *Ronger Rabindranath*, Ananda, Calcutta, 1997, p. 15).

What is intriguing is the freedom with which the young Tagore could openly publish his angst-ridden, erotically charged adolescent texts. The value of the freedom of expression was indeed very much in the air, and perhaps his guardians thought that it was better that he should get his obsessive preoccupations out of his system. Attention could be deflected from risky details by delaying publication, re-arranging the sequence in which a series of poems had been written, and by editing. 'The Suicide of a Star' was first published in *Bharati* in the summer of 1881. That is to say, if Kadambari had really tried to kill herself the previous year, a decent length of time had elapsed and the matter had been hushed up. The poem could now be understood symbolically. And the following year the poet could happily include it in *Sandhyasangit*, acknowledged as his first adult collection. But some anxiety did keep him editing the text of the poem between different editions of this collection, perhaps in an effort to erase the traces of any reference to a real incident and to emphasise the poem's symbolical nature. Dr Sumana Das of the Bengali Department of Rabindrabharati University, Calcutta, has drawn my attention to an edition of *Sandhyasangit* which collates the variant readings of the poems in the collection (Visvabharati, revised reprinting of 1993). Looking at the variant readings of 'The Suicide of a Star' here, one realises that Tagore was indeed trying to cover some traces, de-emphasise some aspects of the poem and re-emphasise others. In an article recently published in the departmental journal of her university, Dr Sumana Das has written how surprised she had been to find that in my translation I had rendered the star as a *he*, for she had always imagined this star as a *she* (' "Tomar srishtir path..." ' Rabindranather kabitar anubad ebong prasangik kichhu bhabona', *Rabindrabharati Visvavidyalay: Bangla Bibhagiya Patrika*, vol. 25, June 2008).

81-83. **Invocation to Sorrow** (*Sandhyasangit*): This poem may have been written in Kartik 1287 (mid-October to mid-November of 1880 A.D.) when Jyotirindranath and Kadambari were away in western India on a long holiday and Rabindranath was living in their rooms adjoining the second floor terrace of the Jorasanko house, devoting himself to writing poetry (Pal, vol. 2, 2nd edition, p. 89). One suspects this long holiday was meant to be therapeutic, for curing Kadambari's depression. Whether or not she had tried to kill herself, she might have had a bout of depression, and in those days 'a change of air' would be the enlightened remedy for such a condition, as indeed for many other maladies. Prabhatkumar Mukhopadhyay seems to have supported such a hypothesis. Pal does not commit himself on the health issue, but thinks that Jyotirindranath and Kadambari were away in the hilly regions of western India (Pal, vol. 2, 2nd edition, pp. 69-70, where there is also a relevant quotation from Mukhopadhyay). I am inclined to think that both 'The Suicide of a Star' and 'Invocation to Sorrow' spring from the same emotional turmoil in roughly the same period. If the first one was directly triggered by a suicide attempt on the part of Kadambari (or her depression), in the second one the agitation is increased by the departure of Jyotirindranath and Kadambari to western India for a long period. The variant readings for the second poem, collated in the edition of *Sandhyasangit* referred to before (Visvabharati, 1993), show the same anxiety to edit material. Some 52 lines which existed in the poem once were cut out and never restored. Four such discarded lines can be translated thus: 'Having fun has fatigued me exceedingly,/ I can no longer smile a skeleton's smile,/ fleshless, just teeth and bones!/ Just laughter, just laughter, nothing else!' Readers can see for themselves the strong echo of 'The Suicide of a Star'.

83-84. **Endless Death** (*Prabhatsangit*, Morning Music): This is an interesting example of the young poet trying to understand the meaning of life and death in a cosmic context. The poem immediately preceding this one in *Prabhatsangit* is called 'Endless Life'.

85. **Breasts** No. 2 and **The Kiss** (*Kadi o Komal*, Sharps and Flats): These poems undoubtedly reflect the consummation of the young poet's marriage and his delight in the sexual discovery of his adolescent wife. The period when he first got to know her intimately was probably in the post-rains of 1885 at Sholapur (Pal, vol. 3, pp. 19 & 64).

86-87. **Desire** (*Manasi*, She Who is in the Mind): Written on 20 Baishakh 1295, this poem undoubtedly remembers Kadambari who died in the month of Baishakh four years ago. I knew I had to translate the third person singular here as *she*.

87-89. **Death-dream** (*Manasi*): This poem, which may also be haunted by the memory of the dead Kadambari, was actually written on 17 Baishakh 1295, but was placed in *Manasi* after 'Desire', with two other poems, written on 13 and 15 Baishakh, in between. In the arrangement of poems in this part of *Manasi* there seems to have been a deliberate blurring of their chronological sequence. It does not serve any thematic purpose, but perhaps served a psychological need of the poet (Pal, vol. 3, p. 89). It is possible that Tagore was trying to blur the connection between some of the poems and Kadambari.

'the cosmic collapse' (stanza 12): I was very tempted to write 'the big crunch' or at least 'the cosmic crunch', but these proposals were firmly vetoed by members of my family, who thought that any introduction of the scientific jargon of our own times, and especially the use of the word *crunch,* would be inappropriate! Tagore's scenario is, of course, derived from the Puranic lore of his heritage. In Hindu mythology both creation and destruction are cyclic: see Zimmer for an elucidation of the relevant myths. Even the swan on whose back the poet rides in his death-dream is likely to be derived from the Hindu symbol of the cosmic gander (Zimmer, pp. 35 & 47-50). But the similarity of Tagore's language to what modern physicists tell us about the collapse of stars, black holes, the big crunch, etc. is striking.

Recently the critic Tapobrata Ghosh has taken me to task for not seeing that the image of the dying swan in this poem is likely to be derived ultimately from Plato's *Phaedo*, mediated, perhaps, by Shelley's *Epipsychidion* (*Rabindra-jijnasur Diary*, Bharabi, Calcutta 2009, pp. 121-126). He directs me to an essay by his late mentor, the noted Tagore exegete Jagadish Bhattacharya, in which the issue is mooted (Bhattacharya, *Rabindrakabitashatak*, tritiya dashak,

Kabi o Kabita Prakashan, Calcutta, 1983, 'Maranswapna', pp. 32-49). It is not possible to deal with every detail in this discourse within the space of a note, but a few salient points need to be made.

In his essay Prof. Bhattacharya says that Tagore's swan-image in this poem 'reminds him' of Shelley's *Epipsychidion*, after which he quotes five relevant lines. Let me quote them from my personal copy of Shelley's *Complete Poetical Works* (Oxford University Press, London, 1935): 'I am not thine: I am a part of thee.// Sweet Lamp! my moth-like Muse has burned its wings/ Or, like a dying swan who soars and sings,/ Young Love should teach Time, in his own gray style,/ All that thou art.' He also says that he has learnt from *The Platonism of Shelley* by James A. Notopoulos that Shelley got the image of the dying swan from Plato's *Phaedo*.

Shelley was of course very familiar with Plato's writings, reading them in the original Greek, and was deeply influenced by them. His translation of *The Symposium* is still being discussed. Likewise Tagore, by virtue of when and where he was born, was immersed in Western literature, and he read widely. He was familiar with Shelley's poetry right from his days as a teenager, and even translated a section of *Epipsychidion* while in his early twenties (Bhattacharya, *Kabimanasi*, Vol. 2, 2nd ed., Bharabi, Calcutta, 2000, pp. 263-5). It is also very likely that by the time he was writing 'Death-dream' he was reasonably familiar with some of the Platonic *Dialogues* in English translation. Some of his prose writings suggest that he had learnt something from the dialogic method. But I doubt if it makes much sense to claim that either Shelley or Tagore would be indebted *solely* to *Phaedo* for the image of the dying swan. The fact is that the myth of the swan that is mute in life but sings sweetly when dying was widespread throughout Europe from ancient times, and references to this myth are scattered throughout European literature. It can be found in Aesop and Ovid and Chaucer and Spenser. Tagore could have just as well picked it up from Shakespeare's *The Merchant of Venice* or *Othello*, or indeed from Tennyson's early poem 'The Dying Swan', which enjoyed a great vogue in the Victorian period. Indeed this poem was so popular even in the beginning of the twentieth century that it inspired the creation of the ballet *The Dying Swan* in 1905. Anna Pavlova knew Tennyson's poem and it was at her request that Michel Fokine, who had also read the poem, choreographed this solo ballet for her.

The swan in Tagore's 'Death-dream' dies, but does not sing. Any connection between that swan and the dying swan 'who soars and sings' in the lines from *Epipsychidion* quoted above, seems at best peripheral to me. To me the two poems are very different in spirit. Shelley refers to the fable of the dying swan's song *en passant* in a long, ebullient poem which is a highly animated discourse on love, especially in support of free love, and is directly addressed to Emilia Viviani. Tagore's poem does not address or mention any particular woman at all (though it may be haunted by the ghost of one), and its focus is very much on the central episode of the dream-experience, the dissolution of the universe, of which the death of the swan the poet is riding in his dream is only a part. There is also an emphasis on the actual fall of the swan, and as many of us can attest, and as analysts of dreams will surely know, the sensation of falling is a pretty common component of nightmares. What I take away from Tagore's poem is first the image of a cosmic flight, then the vision of cosmic annihilation, and at the end of the dream, the gentle restoration of what is simultaneously the earth's familiar reality and Maya in the cosmic perspective. That is how I read the poem, and have accordingly alerted Western readers (who will, in any case, be only too familiar with the myth of the dying swan who sings) to the Indian moorings that underpin the imagery of Tagore's poem and which may not be so obvious to them. The idea that the universe is periodically dissolved and regenerated is central to Hinduism, and these myths have their curious resonances in modern science. The poem is really an experience of the cosmic cycle in miniature. I have referred readers to Heinrich Zimmer, as he offers to the lay reader the most lucid (and poetic) exegeses known to me of the relevant Hindu myths. He comments that the myths and symbols of India are of a more archaic type than those in Greek literature. The poet's experience in 'Death-dream' has a remarkable affinity with the experience of the sage Markandeya in one of the Puranic stories, and readers are urged to read the story in Zimmer. Like Markandeya in the Puranic story, the poet literally falls out of existence as he knows it, into the waters of nothingness, and is brought back to the reality he knows. And that reality itself is dreamlike, like a dream inside the sleeping godhead, resting between his tasks of destruction and creation.

As for *Phaedo*, Tagore may well have read it by 1888 and been fascinated by it, especially as it is a discourse on death and the after-life, and the immortality of the soul (a concept with which Tagore would have been already very familiar from his Indian background and Upanishadic education); besides, it has a discussion on the lawfulness of suicide, and even shows us vividly how Socrates drank the poisoned drink and slowly succumbed to its effects. If it is true that Kadambari Devi had died from taking an overdose of opium, then such details might well have lingered in Tagore's mind. To some extent one can read Kadambari's death in the description of the swan's plunge to death in Tagore's poem. But I don't really recognise in Tagore's dying bird the dying swans of Socrates's discourse, who sing more sweetly than ever before because they know they are going to meet their master Apollo.

On the other hand, I do think that readers of Tagore's poem need to be aware of the archetype of the cosmic gander, to whose melody Markandeya listens in the Puranic story. This is the cosmic gander's song, as Zimmer articulates it (pp. 47-48): 'Many forms do I assume. And when the sun and moon have disappeared, I float and swim with slow movements on the boundless expanse of the waters. I am the Gander. I am the Lord. I bring forth the universe from my essence and I abide in the cycle of time that dissolves it.' This is connected to the philosophical core of the poem as I understand it. The generic Sanskrit word for 'gander', *hamsa*, if repeated as *hamsa, hamsa*, can be interpreted as *sa-'ham, sa-'ham*, meaning 'This is me' or 'I am He'. This is lore familiar to me from my childhood, but let Zimmer vocalise it (p. 50): 'I, the human individual, of limited consciousness, steeped in delusion, spellbound by Maya, actually and fundamentally am This, or He, namely, the Atman, the Self, the Highest Being, of unlimited consciousness and existence.'

The *hamsa* is regarded as a wise bird, who proverbially knows the distinction between milk and water, and a yogi of the highest order is known as a *parama-hamsa* or supreme *hamsa*. Tagore does use the word *hamsa* in his poetry, often in the context of migratory birds. It occurs in that great poem, no. 36 of *Balaka*, which I have translated in this collection. Another pertinent example would be song no. 148 of the Bengali *Gitanjali*, where the *hamsa* returning home to Lake Manas – near Mount Kailas in the Himalayas – becomes a metaphor for the poet's self-surrendering salutation to his Lord and the flight of his whole being 'to the shore of great death' (*maha-maran-paare*). The vernal flight of homing *raj-hamsas* (royal ganders, i.e., swans) to Kailas, where the snows have melted, is referred to in the poem 'The Victorious Woman', included in this collection. Another well-known use of the word *hamsa* occurs in the song '*Mon mor megher sangi*' (My mind is a companion of the clouds): there the poet's mind rides on (or flies with) the wings of a flock of *hamsas*. In all these examples we see the magical pull of the actual word *hamsa* dictating poetic meaning; we also see the great admiration that this poet feels for a bird's capacity for long-distance flight. It is this particular capacity that makes a bird's journey an appropriate metaphor for a spiritual adventure that dares to unlock the mysteries of the universe. I would draw the reader's attention to another great poem of Tagore's, translated in this collection as 'A Stressful Time', in which the bird, though not identified as a *hamsa*, is nevertheless making a supremely difficult crossing over a roaring sea.

The European archetype of the dying swan need not be excluded from the context of the poem 'Death-dream', for the imagery of a romantic poem operates, after all, like the aurora borealis, or a laser show, but then the Indian archetypes must surely not be excluded from the total picture either. Tapobrata Ghosh ridicules me for bringing in the gander of the Puranic story into my commentary, but the *hamsa* – 'gander', 'swan', call it what we will – is definitely a mighty Indian archetype; after all, Brahma, the god of creation, rides on one, and so does his consort, Saraswati, the goddess of learning and the arts. In some iconography she has twin *hamsas* by her. See the song 'The moon's laughter's dam has burst' in this collection, where I have translated a line as 'and Saraswati's swans have escaped'. A poet riding a swan in a cosmic flight is, at a certain level, almost an incarnation of Saraswati herself.

And we need not exclude from this laser display the image of the swan-maiden, the swan who can turn into a woman, and become a swan again. This legend is widespread and occurs in the *Arabian Nights* tale of Hasan of Basra. If we accept the swan-maiden as part of the laser display of images in 'Death-dream', then how does that affect our interpretation of the poem? Is the poet riding on a swan to meet Kadambari Devi in the land of the dead? Is the swan an embodiment of Kadambari herself, the Muse who has betrayed him by dying too soon? There is certainly an erotic tinge in the description of the ride in the fifth stanza of the poem. Eroticism is bolder in the description, in 'The Victorious Woman', of how the woman is caressing the she-swan's feathers. Readers are requested to compare the two passages.

After all such suggestions have been taken into account, the experience of a cataclysmic dissolution of the universe, and a gentle awakening from that nightmare, remain the philosophical core of the poem 'Death-dream'. Tagore's lifelong preoccupation with death, his perception of death and life as twins, were already well developed by 1888. In my opinion, 'Death-dream' is organically related to early poems such as 'Mahaswapna' (The Great Dream), 'Srishti Sthiti Pralay' (Creation, Preservation, Destruction, translated by William Radice in a shortened version), 'Ananta Jiban' (Endless Life) and 'Ananta Maran' (translated by me in the present collection as 'Endless Death'). All these early poems are from *Prabhatsangit* (1883). Anybody who reads 'Maha-swapna' (The Great Dream) with its climactic image of a cosmic dissolution will instantly see the thematic connection between it and 'Death-dream'. This connection, I believe, is more powerful than any tangential connection between 'Death-dream' on the one hand and Shelley's *Epipsychidion* and Plato's *Phaedo* on the other. I have a great admiration for Jagadish Bhattacharya's exegesis of the role of Kadambari Devi as an internalised Muse in Tagore's life, – he has installed, with appropriate ceremony, her statue where it rightfully belongs, – but with due respect, I think that any influence of those two texts of Shelley and Plato on the swan-image of this particular poem of Tagore's has been overstated. An essay by Prof. Taraknath Sen, who was one of my teachers at Presidency College, Calcutta, in the fifties, offers an appropriate caveat in such matters. 'Western influence on Tagore,' he says, 'is too often treated with Fluellen's logic: "There is a river in Macedon, and there is also more-over a river at Monmouth..." Parallels are cited between him and this or that western poet, and conclusions sought to be drawn accordingly. It is a common fallacy in criticism to take parallels for signs of indebtedness or influence. All that parallels really prove is the community of the poetic mind all the world over. Too much stress on parallels might lead to absurd conclusions.' (Sen, 'Western Influence on the Poetry of Tagore', in *A Centenary Volume: Rabindranath Tagore, 1861-1961*, Sahitya Akademi, New Delhi, 1961.) This essay remains worth reading; though it has a regrettable bias against the post-Tagore generation of modernist writers, it might answer some of the queries regarding Tagore's writings that might spring up in the minds of those who are reading the present discussion. Tagore was, of course, steeped in Western literature, but he was, at the same time, firmly embedded in the details of his country's literary, linguistic, artistic, and philosophical heritage, in its myths and symbols, folk traditions, and rural ways, just as he drew some of his strengths from his environment's tropical luxuriance. That quality of having deep roots in one's soil and yet maintaining a serious, ongoing interest in knowing and interacting with the bigger world, being capable of travelling abroad and remaining open to all meaningful foreign influences, of synthesising such influences with the home-grown elements through one's powers of imagination and creative energies: *that* precisely was what the Bengal Renaissance at its best was all about, a phenomenon from which some of us are still trying to draw inspiration to this day.

90-92. The Amatory Conversation of a Young Bengali Couple (*Manasi*): One would guess that in this hilarious poem, a remarkable piece of social satire in the context of its time, Tagore was to some extent drawing on his own experiences as the groom of a child-bride.

92-96. I Won't Let You Go (*Sonar Tari*, The Golden Boat): There's no doubt that the scenes of family life in this celebrated poem are derived from Tagore's own life. The little girl is modelled on his own eldest daughter, though in October 1892 she was actually six, not four.

After referring to the season as *hemanta* (autumn) in the second line of the poem, and mentioning specifically in the second stanza that Ashwin is gone and the Puja vacation has ended, Tagore slips into calling the season *sharat* (post-rains) twice later. The poem was written in mid-Kartik (end of October). The season of *sharat* ends formally with Ashwin and autumn proper begins with the month of Kartik. It is true that one season merges imperceptibly with the next one, and such an oscillation is quite natural in the context, but I have stuck to *autumn* throughout the poem to avoid possible confusion in the minds of readers not familiar with the tropical seasons.

'Golden moong beans': husked moong for making dal, not such an uncommon item in British shops nowadays.

'fine mustard oil': much prized as a cooking medium in Bengal and some other parts of the Indian subcontinent, as olive oil is in Mediterranean countries.

'blocks/ of date-palm molasses': made from the sap of date-palms, set and sold in block-form, eaten on its own as well as used as a sweetener in desserts.

'dried mango': *amchur,* which may be found as a powder even in some shops in Britain specialising in Indian groceries.

'mango cakes': *amsattva,* sun-dried mango pulp which can be cut into wedges and eaten as a sweet, in taste and texture resembling semi-dried apricots.

All the above food-references are in stanza 3. See the Glossary for *areca, betel leaves,* and *seer* in the same stanza.

97-103. **Earth** (*Sonar Tari*): 'mythic cow of plenty' (last section of the poem): a mythological cow of plenty yielding everything one could want. A letter written by Tagore from Shilaidaha on 9 December 1892 (included in *Chhinnapatra-bali*) contains many of the central ideas of this poem.

104. **On the Doctrine of Maya** (*Sonar Tari*): *Maya* is an important technical term in Indian philosophy, referring to the illusory nature of phenomena, as contrasted with the nature of ultimate reality. For insights into the positive aspects of this complex concept in myth and art, consult Zimmer, using the index, but the concept has also had a certain amount of negative influence on Indian thinking and life, encouraging apathy, inaction, and wrong action in human affairs. This is what Tagore is attacking here. See also the poem 'Renunciation' from *Chaitali.*

104. **Play** (*Sonar Tari*): This is Tagore's answer to the doctrine of maya. Maybe the world is an illusory play, but to join in the game with good humour is the only human option.

105-08. **Farewell to Heaven** (*Chitra,* She Who is Various): In this poem Tagore's rejection of mythical heavenly worlds and his firm commitment to the earth are put into the mouth of a hero who had earned a temporary sojourn in Indra's heaven, whose term in heaven is now over and who must now return to the earth. The hero may be modelled on Arjuna of the Sanskrit epic *Maha-bharata,* who spent five years in Indra's heaven, learning the martial arts from Indra himself and dance and music from the Gandharva Chitrasena. During this residence Arjuna was courted by the heavenly nymph and dancer Urvashi, whose advances he rejected, bringing a curse upon himself, whereby he had to spend one year as a eunuch in his later earthly life. That Tagore was ruminating these stories at this time is shown by the fact that the day before he wrote this poem he wrote an ode to Urvashi (pronounced *Urboshi* in Bengali), which precedes this poem in *Chitra.*

In the third stanza the poem refers to the practice of finding out whether a wish will come true or not by floating a lighted lamp on a river and watching its progress. A dot of powdered vermilion (cinnabar or red crystalline mercuric sulphide) indicates that the woman is married.

108-11. **The Victorious Woman** (*Chitra*): The inspiration for this poem came to Tagore from an episode in the Sanskrit prose classic of the seventh century, *Kadambari,* begun by Banabhatta, left unfinished at his death, and completed by his son Bhushanabhatta. Historians of literature have usually called this work a prose romance, attempting to distinguish it from a novel in the modern sense, but ironically the evolution of the novel in our times has blurred the distinction.

I would not hesitate to call *Kadambari* a seventh-century novel: story-within-story is now a common fictional technique and the spanning of an individual's successive lives through incarnations gives the same feel of time as the spanning of generations in a modern novel.

But Tagore's poem bears a rather interesting relation to his source of inspiration. The bathing woman is in a sense modelled on the Gandharva princess Mahashweta in *Kadambari*, who, coming to bathe in Lake Achchhoda with her mother and female friends on a glorious day of spring, falls in love with a young hermit named Pundarika, who also falls in love with her. But whereas in the Sanskrit story Mahashweta falls desperately in love, in Tagore's poem the bathing woman does not fall in love with anyone: instead, she seems to score a victory over the god of love himself. In the Sanskrit story no god of love appears in person; the woman and the man are simply vanquished by love. In Tagore's poem the mischievous god of love appears in person, ready to shoot his floral arrow at the woman's breast, but is then so overwhelmed by her that he lays all the tools of his trade at her feet as an admission of defeat. In this the poem is a completely new creation.

The twist Tagore gives to the story may owe something to the evolution of Mahashweta in *Kadambari*. Pundarika dies suddenly even as Mahashweta is rushing to meet him, and is carried off to the lunar regions by a celestial being who assures Mahashweta that she will be united to her beloved in a future time. Mahashweta begins her long wait by becoming a Shiva-worshipping female ascetic herself. In fact it is the ascetic Mahashweta that we meet first in the *Kadambari* story, the bathe in Achchhoda being a flashback account of the past given by her to Chandrapida. Tagore seems to have bathed his bathing woman with something of the ascetic Mahashweta's spiritual radiance and majesty. It is these qualities that ensure her victory over the god of love.

Tagore most probably derived the idea of the defeat of the god of love from the story of the destruction of the god of love by Shiva, on which Kalidasa (*circa* the 5th century A.D.) based his *Kumarasambhava*, a long narrative poem in several cantos and another of Tagore's firm favourites among the Sanskrit classics. Gods in Hindu mythology are periodically tormented by demons; during one such crisis caused by a powerful demon, it becomes necessary to wake Shiva out of deep meditation so that he can fall in love with and marry Parvati, for only a son of Shiva and Parvati can destroy that demon. The god of love is entrusted with this delicate task. In Kalidasa's poem he goes to the spot where Shiva is in meditation, and his friend the god of spring engineers a sudden season of spring. Taking a brief rest from intense meditation, Shiva receives Parvati, who has come to pay him homage. The god of love aims a powerful arrow. He does not even have to release it fully: the aiming is enough. Shiva notices that he is affected, glances around, spies the cause, and immensely annoyed, burns the poor love-god to ashes with the fire of the third eye on his forehead. (This is why one of the love-god's names is Ananga, one without a body.) Parvati embarks on an intense course of asceticism and meditation to win Shiva and succeeds. Needless to say, Ananga is also resurrected.

Tagore was fond of this story and a year and a half after writing 'The Victorious Woman', wrote two poems entitled 'Before the Burning of the Love-god' and 'After the Burning of the Love-god', both included in *Kalpana,* which show his obsession with the myth. He was specially intrigued by the suggestion implicit in the myth that by burning the god of erotic attraction, Shiva had dispersed his ashes throughout creation and thereby increased the dominion of eros over all.

In Tagore's imagination Parvati and Mahashweta in their ascetical aspects seem to have merged together to form a composite, who is the real model of his own victorious woman. She is victorious over the god of love because she does not need his help. She can win her beloved by means of her spiritual power, the power of her asceticism, not through the power of erotic attraction. The god of sexual love realises this when he gazes at her face and surrenders to the superior power she represents.

These and analogous ideas can be found in several other poems of *Chitra* and are recurrent throughout the corpus of Tagore's poetry. They receive additional strength from the facts of his personal life – indeed, they could be said to have been synthesised through the interaction of the facts of his personal life and the myths of his heritage – and become part of his total attitude to the female principle. The victorious woman is victorious not only over the god of love but also over the poet himself. She is victorious not by virtue of her sexual power over him but because of her power over his spirit. She is his Muse, internalised, *manasi* or 'of the mind', and can sometimes be identified with his *jiban-debata* or the deity of his life. She can inspire him even when she is dead or distant. At this stage in his life Kadambari was already a woman who had won such a victory over him. Much later, when he encountered a woman who was actually called Victoria, he gave her the name Vijaya (pronounced *Bijoya* in Bengali), which means roughly the same thing as the title of the poem we are discussing: 'Vijayini', pronounced *Bijoyini* in Bengali, meaning a victorious person, in the feminine gender. (Both words are derived from the Sanskrit root *ji*, to conquer, with the prefix *vi* which in this case intensifies the meaning.)

113. **Renunciation** (*Chaitali*, Chaitra Harvest): The title of this collection refers to winter crops which are harvested in late spring. A large number of poems in the collection were actually written in the month of Chaitra. Connect this poem with 'On the Doctrine of Maya' and 'Play' from *Sonar Tari*.

114-15. **The Worker** (*Chaitali*): A number of the *Chaitali* poems I have translated are clearly based on personal observation. This particular poem was based on a real experience of the poet in Shahjadpur several months before the date of composition. The servant was probably a Muslim named Momin Miya. The incident brought home to Tagore with a sudden shock how, beneath the relationship of master and servant, he shared with this man the common identity of a father. (*Rabindra-rachanabali*, vol. 5, Granthaparichay section; Kripalani, p. 177; Pal, vol. 4, p. 96.) The poem gains additional poignancy when one remembers the bereavements that fate was storing for Tagore.

116. **On the Nature of Love** (*Chaitali*): The idea of this poem first came to Tagore some months previous to the date of composition, when he was travelling in a steam-drawn tramcar in Calcutta in a dark evening (Pal, vol. 4, p. 97).

116-17. **Putu** (*Chaitali*): For a full appreciation of the mingling of 'gentle tears' and 'smiles' in this moving vignette, the English-speaking reader needs to know that Putu or Puturani (the first *u* is nasalised) is a homely pet name for a girl. The suffix *rani*, meaning 'queen', adds endearment, like the addition of *-y* or *-ie* to an English name. Imagine an English-speaking farm-worker wanting to bath a cow and calling: 'Come, Annie, come,' or 'Come, Kathy, come,' and you get close to the picture. Buffaloes like staying in muddy water to stay cool in hot weather. They are very important dairy animals in India, where the rural people are, of course, very close to their animals, thinking of each animal as an individual, a person. Connect with 'The Mediatrix' and 'The Companion', both from *Chaitali*.

118. **True Meditation** (*Chaitali*): The entire weight of a complex tradition sits on the image of the lotus here. The lotus is one of the most powerful symbols in both Hinduism and Buddhism. It also occupies an important place in iconography. See Zimmer; a glance at the index alone will give an idea of the complexity of the symbolism. 'Lotus' is there entered under 12 separate sub-headings; there is also a separate entry for 'Lotus Goddess' under several sub-headings and an entry for the epithet 'Lotus-in-Hand'.

119. **Hope Against Hope** (*Chaitali*): Connect this poem with the immediately preceding 'Drought', written on the same day, and the context will become clear.

120-21. The short, pithy poems from *Kanika* (Particles) are in the style of Sanskrit epigrammatic verses, with which Tagore was familiar.

121-27. **The Repayment** (*Katha*, Stories): Brian Houghton Hodgson was one of those remarkable scholar-administrators that Britain lent to the Indian subcontinent in the 19th century. He served for many years in Nepal in a diplomatic capacity, then lived on in Darjeeling for some more years, engaged in literary and scientific pursuits. During his long service in Nepal he collected a large number of Sanskrit Buddhist texts, which he subsequently distributed among six famous libraries of the world. A substantial collection went to the Asiatic Society of Bengal in Calcutta and supplied the materials for Rajendralal Mitra's classic work, *The Sanskrit Buddhist Literature of Nepal* (The Asiatic Society of Bengal, Calcutta, 1882), which was widely used as a source-book in both India and the West. Tagore used it as a source-book too. The book accompanied him on his travels and river-voyages, and the material for several poems of *Katha* was gleaned from here. It also provided him with the plots of some of his plays.

The story which is the source of 'The Repayment' is one of a group which tries to explain incidents in the life of the Buddha by means of references to his past incarnations. This particular story purports to explain why the Buddha left his wife Yashodhara. In the following extract from Mitra, taken from the 1971 reprint published by Sanskrit Pustak Bhandar, Calcutta, the spellings of names have been slightly edited to avoid the use of diacritical marks:

'There was in times of yore a horse-dealer at Takshashila, named Vajrasena; on his way to the fair at Varanasi, his horses were stolen, and he was severely wounded. As he slept in a deserted house in the suburbs of Varanasi, he was caught by policemen as a thief. He was ordered to the place of execution. But his manly beauty attracted the attention of Shyama, the first public woman in Varanasi. She grew enamoured of the man, and requested one of her handmaids to rescue the criminal at any hazard. By offering large sums of money, she succeeded in inducing the executioners to set Vajrasena free, and execute the orders of the king on another, a banker's son, who was an admirer of Shyama. The latter, not knowing his fate, approached the place of execution with victuals for the criminal, and was severed in two by the executioners.

'The woman was devotedly attached to Vajrasena. But her inhuman conduct to the banker's son made a deep impression on his mind. He could not

287

reconcile himself to the idea of being in love with the perpetrator of such a crime. On an occasion when they both set on a pluvial excursion, Vajrasena plied her with wine, and when she was almost senseless, smothered and drowned her. When he thought she was quite dead, he dragged her to the steps of the ghat and fled, leaving her in that helpless condition. Her mother, who was at hand, came to her rescue, and by great assiduity resuscitated her. Shyama's first measure, after recovery, was to find out a Bhikshuni of Takshashila, and to send through her a message to Vajrasena, inviting him to her loving embrace. Buddha was that Vajrasena, and Shyama, Yashodhara.'

The essential part of this gruesome tale reads quite like a plausible, realistic story, such as we might read in the newspapers even today, emerging from a criminal court case. The banker's son *is not persuaded* to offer himself as a sacrifice to please the woman he loves, but is quite simply murdered. Bribery and assassination secure the release of the condemned man. Tagore lifted the story out of its crude, sordid ambit, gave it a psychological twist, and turned it into a romantic-tragic narrative poem of considerable power and beauty. That Tagore was intrigued by the story is shown by the fact that he returned to it in his old age, making a musical play and then a dance-drama out of it in the last years of his life. In the dance-drama, *Shyama* (1939), the story reaches its height of psychological sophistication. Uttiya is not even *persuaded* to sacrifice himself: he offers to do so completely of his own accord. It is his idea. Shyama does accept his sacrifice, but also makes an unsuccessful last-minute attempt to save him. The inclusion of a few details ensures that even the Police Chief seems quite respectable. Bajrasen is arrested on reasonable grounds – because he refuses to open his case. And he refuses to do so because it contains a jewelled necklace brought by him from Subarna-dwip ('the golden island' of antiquity, usually identified with Sumatra), which he does not wish to surrender. When Uttiya pleads guilty to the charge of theft from the royal treasury, he shows the Police Chief a ring that Shyama had just given him as an ambivalent last gift, a royal ring which Shyama had herself had as a present from the king. This is accepted as evidence of his guilt. In these little subtle ways and with the help of powerful and moving songs, Tagore lifts the whole story onto a dizzy height of operatic tragedy (Tagore's dance-dramas incorporate both operatic and balletic elements) where a love-infatuated teenager's entirely spontaneous and voluntary act of self-sacrifice becomes the linchpin of action, miles removed from the original Buddhist story where the unsuspecting victim is persuaded to take food to the condemned man and is cut down by the executioners. *Shyama* is recognised by critics to be one of the highest of Tagore's artistic achievements, taking into consideration the many genres in which he worked, and 'The Repayment', also regarded as one of the most remarkable poems of the early years, is, as it were, its first incarnation.

See the notes on the lotus and the goddess Lakshmi in the Glossary and also the information on the symbolism of the lotus in the note on 'True Meditation' above to appreciate the ironies implicit in the third stanza.

The 'trident-peak' of the temple in the last stanza indicates that it is a Shiva temple, the trident being one of his weapons.

128-29. **The Realisation of Value** (*Katha*): Mitra's *The Sanskrit Buddhist Literature of Nepal* (see above) is also the source of this poem. In this case it is one of a group of stories illustrating miracles performed by the Buddha. In the following quotation from the 1971 edition, diacritical marks have been omitted and the punctuation has been emended in a few places:

'Before the advent of Buddha, Raja Prasenajit used to worship the Tirthikas, but after the appearance of that great preacher, he bowed to none but the great Lord. When the Lord was dwelling in the Jeta grove, a gardener of Sravasti brought a big lotus flower as a present for the king.

'A worshipper of the Tirthikas asked its price. At this time Anathapindada came and doubled its value. They bade against each other with emulous pride till the price rose to a hundredfold. Thereupon the gardener enquired about the whereabouts of Buddha, and hearing of his great power from Anathapinda-da, presented the flower to the Lord. Instantly the lotus swelled out to the size of a carriage wheel and stood over Buddha's head. The gardener, astonished at this, asked instruction in supreme knowledge. The Lord said to Ananda, "This man is to become a great Buddha, Padmodbhava by name." '

129-35. Dialogue between Karna and Kunti (*Kahini*, Tales): Translated from the text in the *Rabindra-rachanabali*, vol. 5, the older Visvabharati edition, this is a dramatic poem based on an episode in the *Mahabharata*. During the middle period of his life, Tagore was much preoccupied with claiming and reworking old stories from the *Mahabharata* or from Buddhist lore, offering reinterpretations which would resonate in his own times and act as bridges between tradition and modernity. He had been specially requested by his friend, the scientist Jagadishchandra Bose, to write a poem based on Karna's story. Tagore takes details from two contiguous sections of the 'Udyogaparva' of the *Mahabharata*, a dialogue between Krishna and Karna, and a dialogue between Karna and Kunti, to make a new composite story of an encounter between a fostered son and a long-lost natural mother, set against the back-drop of the preparations for the great war between the rival collateral houses of the Pandavas and the Kauravas. Kunti is the mother of the five Pandavas – the natural mother of the three elder brothers, Yudhisthira, Bhima, and Arjuna, and the stepmother of the two younger ones. Karna is Kunti's eldest child, born before her marriage, whom she had carefully packed and consigned to the mercy of a river, just as Moses had been consigned in the Jewish story. Karna was found and reared by foster-parents of the charioteer caste, eventu-ally becoming a warrior, a man noted for his generosity, and an ally of the Kauravas, led by Duryodhana. On the eve of the war of Kurukshetra there is an attempt to woo Karna over to the side of the Pandavas, first by Krishna, who is an ally of the Pandavas, then by Kunti. Karna refuses to change sides.

In the *Mahabharata*, Kunti meets her first-born son when he is finishing his late morning prayers by the Ganges. She waits in the scorching sun till he finishes his prayers at noon. Tagore transfers the meeting to the glow of twi-light deepening into a starlit night. The softer setting is more appropriate for Tagore's purpose of highlighting the human emotions. Also in the epic, Karna does not really learn about his birth for the first time from Kunti. Krishna has already told him the details before Kunti has had a chance to do so, and in any case, Karna seems to know the essential facts already, what Krishna says being merely a confirmation. Tagore, interested in making a different kind of audience impact, makes Karna hear about who his natural mother is from her own mouth, thus making the encounter much more meaningfully dramatic. At the same time, Tagore's Kunti, more of a Victorian aristocratic matron, is too embarrassed to reveal the actual details of how she had con-ceived Karna out of wedlock, whereas in the *Mahabharata*, both Krishna and

Kunti relate them to Karna in a matter-of-fact manner in keeping with the *mores* of the old epics. In the *Mahabharata*, Karna is much sterner with his mother, more outspoken, acerbic, and unambiguous in his condemnation of her actions, past and present, more sharply Hindu in his understanding of right action and caste ethics. He actually offers Kunti the consolation that he will not kill all her sons: he will either kill Arjuna or be killed by him, so that she will still remain the mother of five sons! He is, of course, eventually killed by Arjuna. Tagore's treatment is more psychological: Karna is humanised to suit the tastes of Tagore's own times. Tagore's Karna berates his mother indirectly, rhetorically, through questions, with a mixture of sentiment and irony. He wavers, is flooded with nostalgia and filial affection, then retreats to a noble resolve.

Jahnavi and Bhagirathi are names for the Ganges. Kripa is a martial instructor. In the transliterations of proper names within the poem I have given slight tilts towards the way they would be pronounced in Bengali. Thus I have written Adhirath, not Adhiratha; Bhim, not Bhima; Arjun, not Arjuna; Durjodhan and Judhisthir instead of Duryodhana and Yudhisthira; Pandab and Kaurab instead of Pandava and Kaurava. These details are in consonance with my practice in the rest of this book.

135-36. **A Stressful Time** (*Kalpana*, Imagination): In its MS. draft this poem had a different title, meaning 'On the Road to Heaven', the present title appearing when the poem was first published a year later in the magazine *Bharati* (Pal, vol. 4, p. 137). Interestingly, this new title, 'Duhsamay' (A Bad Time/ A Stressful Time) is also the title of a poem of *Chitra*, written just three years ago on 17 April 1894, which is likely to have some connection with the tenth anniversary of Kadambari Devi's death (Pal, vol. 4, p. 1). These facts may help us to understand the striking images of this poem. The bird, originally imagined as on its way to heaven, is now imagined as pursuing a strenuous flight over an ocean. The poet feels a strong identification with its plight. The difficult time is as much the bird's as the sympathising poet's. Does the bird embody both Kadambari's agony and the poet's grief? It would be hard to explain the intensity of the poem unless we assume some such anchorage for it in private grief. Compare this poem also with 'Death-dream' of *Manasi*, written on 28 April 1888, where the poet, dreaming that he is riding on the back of a swan, experiences the dissolution of the entire cosmos within himself. The similarity is striking. The fact that all these poems were written in the month of April, the month of Kadambari's death, seems to be a clue to the similarity of moods in them.

136-39. **Dream** (*Kalpana*): The background to this poem is Tagore's fascination with the period of the Sanskrit poet and dramatist Kalidasa (*circa* the 5th century A.D.: he is supposed to have lived some time between the middle of the 4th century and the end of the 5th). Kalidasa is thought to have pursued his literary career under the patronage of the Gupta emperors as one of the 'nine jewels' at the flourishing court of Ujjain. Elsewhere too Tagore has said that he wished he could have belonged to that time and that milieu. In this poetical fantasy, the details of the scenario are essentially derived from Kalidasa, especially the poem *Meghaduta*, a favourite of Tagore's, where an exile in the highlands of central India sends a message to his wife in Alaka in the far north by means of a wandering raincloud. The cloud is asked to make a slight detour to pass over Ujjain. Though the imagined woman of Tagore's poem lives in

Ujjain on the Shipra, she is also partly drawn in the model of the exile's wife in the Sanskrit poem, who lives in the city of Alaka. Accordingly there is an amalgam of details culled from the two sections of the Sanskrit poem, the *Purvamegha* and the *Uttaramegha*. Ujjain, Shipra, lodhra-pollen, dalliance-lotus, kunda-buds, kurubaks on the hair, evening service at the Shiva-temple, conchshell on the door, a young tree growing like a son by the door, pet doves or pigeons, pet peacock, incensed hair: all these minutiae are taken from the *Meghaduta*. But though the circumstantial details are Kalidasian, the human mood created is authentically Tagorean.

'dalliance-lotus' (stanza 2): a lotus held in the hand in dalliance, possibly used in flirtatious gestures like a hand-fan.

'conch-shell and wheel' (stanza 6): auspicious symbols, both associated with the god Vishnu. The *Meghaduta* mentions the conch-shell and the lotus (also associated with Vishnu). Some seem to think that those two symbols on the door in the *Meghaduta* may stand for the wealth of the householder, signifying a huge sum with many digits. Whatever the validity of that assumption, I am sure that in Tagore's poem the conch-shell and wheel are simply auspicious marks on the door and not an indication of the material affluence of the dreamwoman.

'pet doves' (stanza 7): The original word can mean either dove or pigeon, and doves and pigeons belong to the same family. This was an instance when I had to make a local decision to suit the sonic needs of the English poem. I wanted 'doves' so that I could have 'dovecot' in the next line and achieve some sort of assonance with 'golden rod' later.

'incensed hair' (stanza 8): hair perfumed by burning incense; 'tracery of sandal' (stanza 8): decorative patterns made with sandalwood paste to adorn and aromatise the skin.

For the flower-names and the other names in the poem see the Glossary.

In this translation I have taken more liberty than I usually take with regard to line-lengths and stanza-breaks vis-à-vis the original. A single line of the original is often broken into two lines in the English poem, and I have introduced extra stanza-breaks. I felt that a slightly different arrangement was necessary to make the English version effective both rhythmically and from the point of view of the pictures evoked.

139-40. **What the Scriptures Say** (*Kshanika*, She Who is Momentary): This poem is a rollicking rejection of the traditional concept of *vanaprastha* or retreat into the forest, the supposed third stage of life for the good Hindu. The four stages of life were more like an ideal to follow or a theoretical framework to live by than a mandatory code of conduct. They were: the stage of the celibate student, that of the married householder, that of the forest hermit, and lastly that of the wandering ascetic unattached to any earthly possessions or ties. In the third stage, supposed to start after the age of 50, a man was expected to hand over his family responsibilities to the next generation and retire with his wife into a forest hermitage, living a frugal and contemplative life in preparation for the final stage of total detachment. But, contends the poet, a sylvan retreat would surely be more appropriate in youth than in middle age! Note how the lack of privacy for young couples within the extended family strengthens his case.

142-43. Spiritual concerns predominate in the poems and songs of *Naibedya* (Offerings), which are said to have pleased Tagore's father so much that he paid for the publication of the collection. Dedicated to Debendranath Tagore, the book was accordingly first published in a handsome edition on expensive paper.

144. The poems of *Smaran* (Remembering) remember Tagore's wife, who died on 23 November 1902. In No. 14 he writes about the moving experience of discovering, among her things, some of his own letters which she had carefully preserved. Poem no. 5 was probably written in Calcutta in the fortnight after her death (Pal, vol. 5, p. 99).

145-47. The shadow of the dead Mrinalini also falls across many of the poems of *Shishu* (The Child). After the death of his wife, Tagore took his ailing second daughter Rani to the hills of Almora. Many of the poems in this collection were written there. The focus is often on the mother-child relationship, and the mood is usually a mingling of playfulness and pathos. It is as though Tagore is trying to tell his children that their mother has not really gone away. Seen in this context, a poem like 'Hide-and-Seek' becomes a comment on death, suggesting an oscillation between visibility and invisibility. The little boy proposes such a game of oscillation to tease his mother; could it be that a mother can also play such a game with her children? One can also make a connection between 'An Offer of Help' and poem no. 14 of *Smaran*: an extra dimension is added to this poem of *Shishu* when one remembers how Mrinalini cherished her husband's letters.

148. The two dates given after the title *Utsarga* (Dedications) need an explanation. All the poems of this book were first published in an edition of Tagore's poems in nine volumes edited by Mohitchandra Sen (1903-4). *Smaran* and *Shishu* were first published in book-form in this edition. *Utsarga* was not published as a separate collection till 1914. In Tagore's collected works *Utsarga* is always placed where it belongs chronologically, immediately after *Smaran* and *Shishu*, and I have followed that practice. (*Rabindra-rachanabali*, vol. 10, Granthaparichay section.)

149-50. **The Auspicious Moment** and **The Renunciation** (*Kheya*, The Ferry): MS. evidence indicates that these two poems were conceived of as one poem in two parts and were written on the same day (13 Srabon 1312). (MS. 110 (i) pp. 3-4, Rabindra Bhavana archives.)

150-54. The three poems from *Gitanjali* (Song-offerings) have been discussed in detail in the Preface to this edition. In poem no. 106 the phrase 'awesome vina' translates the word 'rudravina'. While the word may refer to a version of the musical instrument – there is indeed a musical instrument of this name – I wonder how many Bengalis reading this poem would interpret it in that sense. I think most of them would understand *rudra*, the first component of this compound word, to refer to a name of Shiva associated with his fierce aspect, and thence to mean, adjectivally, 'fierce, terrifying'. Thus the compound word can be interpreted as 'Rudra's vina' or 'fierce vina', suggesting an awesome music accompanying Shiva's dance of destruction, the destruction of the cosmos. I would also associate this word with the compound word 'agnivina' (fire-vina) which Tagore uses to open another of his songs, referring clearly to an imagined fiery music of the stars.

Also in this poem, *Om* is a sacred monosyllable which probably originated as a solemn way of saying 'Yes, so be it', rather like 'Amen'; it came to be regarded as an amalgamation of the three sounds, *a*, *u*, and *m*, signifying the gods Vishnu, Shiva, and Brahma (and standing for the functions of preservation, destruction, and regeneration), and was finally identified with the philosophical concept of the Absolute or Ultimate Reality (Brahman), worthy of the most solemn contemplation and meditation.

Further down in the same poem, the word 'mother-bird' perhaps deserves a comment. The original word is simply *janani*, one of the words for 'mother', but I felt that it would be worthwhile to bring over the underlying image, which is that of a mother-bird watching over her brood in a nest, staying awake through a difficult night. But that nest is *bipul* or vast, which tells us that it refers to the entire population of the land. This idea of the vast nest ties with Tagore's subsequent conceptualisation of the university he founded as a place where the world might become one nest. The mother-bird thus merges with the 'Mother' of the last stanza, the mothering spirit of the country, or the homeland imagined as a mother.

154-57. No. 6 of *Balaka* (A Flight of Wild Birds): This poem remembers Kadambari Devi and was probably inspired by an old photograph of hers. As the poem was written in Allahabad, 'this river' could refer to the confluence of the Ganga and the Yamuna by which that city is situated.

157-59. No. 36 of *Balaka*: Tagore has confirmed that a flight of wild birds he witnessed one evening brought home to him the mobility of all things, even when they were apparently still. He calls the birds wild ducks (*buno haans*). *Haans* is derived from *hamsa*, which has been discussed at length in the note on 'Death-dream'. This is a loose, non-specific description, and I do not think it is possible to identify them in any strict sense. What is clear is that they were migratory birds (*Rabindra-rachanabali*, vol. 12, Granthaparichay section). The image of a bird or birds in transit is a recurrent one in Tagore's poetry and is often charged with a great deal of symbolic significance. See, for instance, 'Death-dream' and 'A Stressful Time' in this collection.

159. No. 39 of *Balaka*: This poem was written for the approaching third centenary of the death of William Shakespeare in 1916. The devotion of English-educated Bengalis to Shakespeare was almost proverbial. 'The native generation who have been brought up at the Hindu College are perfectly mad about Shakespeare. What a triumph it is for him, dear creature!' (Emily Eden, *Letters from India*, 1872, vol. I, p. 186.) My own grandfather could recite whole scenes of Shakespeare from memory, earning for himself the epithet of 'Shakespeare Kushari', and the cult of Shakespeare was very much alive in my student days at Calcutta.

160-61. **The Last Establishment** (*Palataka*, She who is Fugitive): I would be tempted to make a connection between this poem and the death or at least the impending death of Tagore's eldest daughter Bela. Bela, the tiny heroine of 'I Won't Let You Go', died of tuberculosis (like her sister Rani) after protracted suffering on 16 May 1918, the year in which *Palataka* was published. This is the last poem of the book, the title of which means 'the fugitive one' in the feminine gender. Kripalani (p. 285) is of the opinion that the poems of *Palataka* 'bear unmistakable traces' of this bereavement, and Professor Sankha Ghosh agrees with me that a connection between Bela's death and 'The Last Establishment' is highly likely.

160. The other poem of *Palataka* which I have translated, **Getting Lost**, is also charged with a sense of loss. Is Bami, the little girl of this poem, a surrogate of Tagore's second daughter Rani, dead for some fifteen years?

161-64. The success of the poetic prose of the English *Gitanjali* encouraged Tagore to experiment with the possibility of similar composition in Bengali. The result was a group of "prose poems" which form the first section of the book *Lipika*, from which I have translated four examples. The title *Lipika* can be translated as 'Writings', with a suggestion, perhaps, of the diminutive dimension: 'Little Writings'. Extra spaces used in printing to indicate pauses are in keeping with the poet's intentions. Many bereavements have gone into the making of these fine poems which seem a distillation of the essence of grief.

I have wondered if **One Day** remembers the days Tagore spent with Jyotirindranath Tagore and Kadambari Devi at a villa in Telenipara, Chandernagore, 'the villa of the Banerjees' where he set to music several lyrics of the medieval Baishnab poet Vidyapati, including a celebrated one particularly charged with monsoon-melancholy which could well be the song he has in mind here. (See Pal, vol. 2, 1st edition, pp. 140-1, or 2nd edition, p. 107. See also Tagore's *Chhelebela* (*Rabindra-rachanabali*, vol. 26, pp. 623-34.)

In **The Question** the little boy is seven when his mother dies. Tagore's own youngest son was just a few days away from his sixth birthday when Mrinalini Devi died. Note also the terrace which figures in the second section of the poem. There was a terrace overlooking the room where Mrinalini Devi slept and died (Rathindranath Tagore, p. 52), and when she died Tagore spent the whole night on the terrace, 'walking up and down, having given strict orders that no one was to disturb him' (Kripalani, p. 203).

166. **Remembering** (*Shishu Bholanath*): This is another poem in which the accumulated sorrows of personal bereavements have been distilled into poetry. *Shishu Bholanath* can be translated as 'The Child Bholanath', 'Bholanath' being an epithet of Shiva, meaning 'the lord of the self-forgetful/absent-minded ones'. The title suggests the un-selfconscious nature of children.

167-68. **Gratitude** (*Purabi*): The collection is named after an evening *raga*. Written on 2 November 1924 on board the *Andes,* as Tagore was on his way to South America, this poem is haunted by the memory of a dead woman, someone with whom he seems to have had an intimate relationship ('On that day's kiss...'). Could she not be his wife, who had died on 23 November 1902? There is some similarity between the description of the opening lines and Rathindranath Tagore's description of his last meeting with his mother: 'The last time when I went to her bedside she could not speak, but on seeing me, tears silently rolled down her cheeks' (*On the Edges of Time*, p. 52). The phrase 'charged with your smothered vermilion' refers to the powdered vermilion (red crystalline mercuric sulphide) used on the forehead and hair-parting by a Bengali Hindu married woman as long as her husband is alive.

168-69. **The Apprehension** (*Purabi*): This poem was written at the villa Miralrio in San Isidro, a suburb of Buenos Aires, where Tagore, accompanied by his honorary secretary, Leonard Elmhirst, was staying as the guest of Victoria Ocampo, to recover from the effects of an influenza caught on board the *Andes.* Tagore had come to South America to visit Peru, where he had an invitation to attend the centenary of Peru's liberation from the imperial rule of Spain. But illness upset his plans, and he accepted the hospitality offered by Victoria

Ocampo, a 34-year-old Argentine woman who was an ardent admirer of his works in translation and who was beginning to make herself a name as an emerging writer. In the end Tagore stayed in Argentina for about two months and did not go to Peru at all. A triangular relationship developed between Tagore, Elmhirst, and Ocampo, which was fairly stormy during the San Isidro days, but settled into a mellowed long-distance friendship afterwards. Tagore dedicated the collection *Purabi* to Victoria, who eventually had a long and distinguished career as a writer, editor, and publisher, especially as the founder and director of the magazine *Sur* and of the publishing-house of the same name. She died only in 1979. For the story of the Tagore-Ocampo friendship and their influence on each other's work, the curious are referred to my study listed in the beginning of this Notes section. Tagore did a free English re-creation of this poem and after a great deal of hesitation and consultation with Elmhirst gave it to Ocampo. Those who are interested can find it in my book (p. 135).

Note the image of the anchoress and the association between love and penance/asceticism in the last stanza of the poem. Figures like Parvati and Mahashweta are lurking here. See the note on the poem 'The Victorious Woman' above.

169-70. The Skeleton (*Purabi*): This poem was written during a brief holiday which Tagore and Elmhirst had with Victoria Ocampo in Chapadmalal near Mar del Plata in Argentina. It was suggested by a bovine animal's skeleton lying on the grass, a common sight in the pampas, and possibly also in reaction to Charles Baudelaire's poem 'Une Charogne' from *Les Fleurs du Mal*, a book which Ocampo was trying to introduce to a somewhat reluctant Tagore. This poem could have been Tagore's answer to Baudelaire's vision of corruption and decay in that poem. Tagore did an English version of this poem as well for his hostess. For a full discussion of the episode and for Tagore's English version of the poem, see my book (pp. 163-66).

170-71. The Exchange (*Purabi*): Written on board the ship that took him away from Argentina towards Italy, this poem would seem to be about the encounter with Victoria Ocampo which Tagore had just had.

171-72. The Identity and **Disappearance** (*Mahua*): The history of how the poems of *Mahua* came to be written is interesting. Tagore's admirers wanted an anthology of his love poems suitable for presentation at weddings and wanted him to write a few new poems to go with the old ones. In no time at all the 67-year-old poet wrote a whole set of new love poems, which had to be issued as a new collection. Personally, I would connect a number of poems in this book, including the two translated by me, with his encounter with Victoria Ocampo. 'Mahua' is the name of a tree and its flowers from which an intoxicating drink is made. See the Glossary.

In 'The Identity', stanza 4, l. 1, the original of the word 'friend' is in the feminine gender. Unlike several other European languages, English has no corresponding word.

173-75. Kopai (*Punashcha*, Yet Again, or Postscript): In this collection Tagore made his second set of experiments with the possibility of prose poetry in Bengali – the first being in *Lipika* – this time daring to break up the lines, so that the line arrangement on the page looks like that of poetry. In 'Kopai', which is the first poem in the collection, he uses the river Kopai, which flows close to Santiniketan, as an analogy to his own experiments in a form that reconciles poetry and prose. In Bengali the word *chhanda* stands for both 'metre' and 'rhythm'; I have translated according to the context. Tagore seems to be implying that his prose poetry may not have formal metre, but it will have a rhythm of its own. What is interesting is his complete mastery over the new form: from the word 'go', as it were, he uses his new instrument with superb ease, continuing the style in several other subsequent collections with total confidence.

The indigo factory's ruined foundations in the second stanza take us back to the time when British planters planted large areas of land with indigo for the manufacture of dyes.

176-78. **Dwelling** (*Punashcha*): A letter to Pratima Devi, Tagore's daughter-in-law, written from Berlin two years ago on 18 August 1930, describing an imaginary studio by the River Mayurakshi, may be called the first draft of this poem (*Rabindra-rachanabali*, vol. 16, Granthaparichay section). See the entry on *Mayurakshi* in the Glossary to appreciate the aptness of the name in the context of the poem and especially the associations of the name in the last stanza.

178-79. **Memory** (*Punashcha*): The town remembered in this poem is most likely to be Ghazipur, now in Uttar Pradesh, where Tagore spent some time as a young man with his own nuclear family. Ghazipur is the location of three poems from *Manasi* translated in this volume. The phrase 'in the west country' refers to the region west of Bengal, generally to Bihar and the old United Provinces. The same town seems to be remembered in poem no. 4 of *Arogya*, which was written in Santiniketan on 31 January 1941. The names 'Bhajiya' and 'Girdhari' are appropriate for Hindi-speaking people.

183-85. **The Last Letter** (*Punashcha*): In a poem like this one cannot but see the shadow of Tagore's own bereavements. For instance, Tagore's second daughter was just two months away from her twelfth birthday when her mother died, and herself died nine months after her mother's death. 'Amli' is a shortened and familiar version of 'Amala'. The 'Agra shoes' (stanza 1) were presumably embroidered and with turned up toe-ends. See the Glossary for *Bethune School* and the place-names.

186-90. **Camellia** (*Punashcha*): Tagore had very probably seen the camellia plant in the Indian hills (see the entry on it in the Glossary), but the idea of using it in a poem could have occurred to him via Verdi's *La Traviata*, a performance of which he attended at La Scala in Milan in 1925 on his way back from Argentina. The libretto of that opera was based on a play entitled *La Dame aux Camélias*, and Tagore may well have read about it in his theatre programme.

190-91. **A Person** (*Punashcha*): 'Dhoti in wrestler-style' (stanza 1): i.e. with the folds tucked front-to-back between the legs. The dhoti is the unstitched drapery worn by men, the male equivalent of the sari.

'merchants from Kabul' (last stanza): travelling traders from Afghanistan who also acted as moneylenders. One such man is the hero of one of Tagore's short stories.

191-92. **Writing a Letter** (*Punashcha*): In the last stanza the obligation to serve a meal to her husband's young nephew shows the young woman's duties within the extended family.

192-93. **No. 1** of *Shesh Saptak* (The Last Octave): It is quite possible that this poem, written in mid-November 1932, remembers Tagore's wife, who died on 23 November 1902. Note that the word *saptak* in the title, though meaning, strictly speaking, a set of seven notes, has to be translated 'octave' in English. The *saptak* of Indian music is effectively the octave of Western music; it is just that the eighth note of the octave is not taken into account in the Indian term.

193-94. **No. 2** of *Shesh Saptak*: The eighth line of the second stanza is an attempt to render one single word of the original, *meed*, which is a technical term of Indian music. I thought that to do justice to the musical metaphor it was better to translate the word in this way than to introduce it physically into the text, for the word by itself would not be comprehensible without a gloss and the metaphor would therefore be stillborn.

194-95. **No. 3** of *Shesh Saptak*: See the entries on *Valmiki* and *Tamasa* in the Glossary to appreciate the comparison in the first stanza. From Valmiki the poem moves on to the memory of a dear one who is dead.

195-97. **No. 9** of *Shesh Saptak*: The phrase 'seven seas' in the first stanza is an exact translation of the original phrase, which is an idiomatic expression signifying great distances.

199-200. **No. 13** of *Shesh Saptak*: This poem is a play of metaphors from the philosophical songs of the itinerant Baul singers of Bengal. The Bauls are a fascinating religious-philosophical sect special to Bengal, incorporating both Hindu and Muslim (especially Persian Sufi) elements. The word *baul* literally means 'mad, crazy'. The Bauls are essentially rebels: against caste, dogma, and all kinds of convention. In their songs they like to probe deep and go to the heart of the matter. Their contribution to the religious and social thinking of Bengal and to the region's folk poetry, music, and dance is considerable. They like to give the impression that they are simple and unsophisticated, but in reality their conceptual finesse is quite remarkable. Concepts like 'the unfamiliar bird' or 'the uncatchable' are characteristic Baul concepts. Tagore was himself a notable collector of Baul songs and was deeply influenced by them. The district of Birbhum has always had many Bauls and they still congregate in large numbers during certain fairs. Modern Bauls have composed many new songs, – exciting, innovative, clever, – using images drawn from contemporary life. Baul buskers can often be heard twanging their instruments and singing in their characteristic shrill and passionate style (not unlike the *cante jondo* or 'deep song' of Spanish gypsies) on long-distance buses and railway trains. The curious might like to look at *The Mirror of the Sky*, an anthology of Baul songs translated by Deben Bhattacharya (Allen & Unwin, London, 1969).

200-01. **No. 22** of *Shesh Saptak*: The expression 'earth-ridge-bound' in stanza 5 refers to the earthen ridges which are built by Indian farmers to act as boundaries between fields. One can walk on them.

202-03. **No. 27** of *Shesh Saptak*: 'The green-forest-enamelled valley's/ cup of blue sky' (stanza 2): the image of the blue sky as a cup from which one can drink light is a recurrent one in Tagore. He says elsewhere: 'I love the sky and light so cordially! The sky is my cup-bearer, holding a transparent cup of blue crystal upside down, and the golden light, mingling with my blood like wine, is making me equal to the gods' (letter written from Shahjadpur, 2 July 1895,

Chhinnapatrabali, p. 312, my translation). Compare with No. 7 of *Patraput* ('I have accepted in my body and mind/ the juice of creation's fountain dripping from skies') and No. 8 of the same collection where the flowers of the wild plant of unknown name, nicknamed 'Peyali', are 'like crafted cups of a violet hue/ for drinking the light'.

203-04. **No. 29 of *Shesh Saptak***: 'image-immersion rituals' (stanza 1): in a number of Hindu festivals clay images of deities are made annually. At the end of the festivals the images are ceremonially cast into rivers or lakes.

'contest between bards' (stanza 2): referring to the tradition of contests where poets and singers tested their skills in oral composition and improvisation. The two contending parties would engage in a dialogue which they would make up as they went along.

'peacock-neck-coloured' (stanza 4): the original word *dhupchhaya* literally means a mingling of sunshine and shade, from which the connotation of 'peacock-neck-coloured' has evolved. In textile weaving the term is applied specifically to certain colour combinations in the warp and woof of a fabric.

205-07. **No. 31 of *Shesh Saptak***: This poem, put in the mouth of a widower, seems to spring from the inmost depths of Tagore's loneliness. The domestic incident at the centre of the poem could well be from his own married life.

210. **The Indifferent One** (*Bithika*, The Avenue): Personally, I think that in this poem and in poem no. 11 of *Patraput* Tagore is writing in veiled terms about his relationship with Victoria Ocampo.

211-13. **No. 5 of *Patraput***: The title of this collection means a plate or a cone-shaped container made from leaves. The Vedic words saying that this earth's dust is honeyed (stanza 4) are from the *Rigveda*. The 'red-dyed feet' (stanza 5) would have been coloured with a lac dye, used to both adorn the feet and keep the skin from getting chapped. For Bauls (last stanza), see the note on poem no. 13 of *Shesh Saptak* above. For other items, including the *nut tree* (stanza 8), see the Glossary.

214-16. **No. 7 of *Patraput***: Note the word 'juice' used three times in stanza 5. In the original it is the important word *ras*. Its first meaning is 'juice', but a technical term of Indian aesthetics has developed from that, connoting aesthetic enjoyment – in a highly refined state, passing into ecstasy or bliss.

In stanza 6, the phrase 'ascents and descents' renders a technical term of Indian music, *murchhana*.

The last stanza of the original poem harbours some intriguing poetic ambiguities, which heighten the sense of haze and nocturnal mystery. The trees silhouetted in the night's light seem to be siblings sitting together *as well as* their whimsical brushwork. Or is the night's light also a sibling of the trees, the night landscape being also their joint whimsical composition?

Lines 15 and 16 of the last stanza could be literally translated as follows: 'It was as if I had gone off to a neighbouring planet of the earth,/ one can see it through a telescope.' Line 16 is surprisingly vague and loose in the original. What is the 'it' that can be seen through a telescope? Is the poet watching a neighbouring planet from the earth, through a telescope, or physically transported to another planet which is normally only known through a telescope, or watching the earth through a telescope from another planet? Interestingly, what the poet is getting at, that what was quite familiar has suddenly acquired a distance, an unfamiliarity – a common idea in Tagore – remains roughly the same in each case. The way I have translated line 16 seemed the most natural way to say it in English; it blocks the possibility of interpreting it in the second of the three ways mentioned above, but leaves the two other suggestions intact.

216-17. **No. 8 of** *Patraput*: The flower Tagore writes about in this poem has not been definitively identified. It has been suggested that it could be the morning-glory, *Ipomoea pulchella*, Roth., Convolvulaceae. The name 'Peyali' is made up from the word *peyala*, meaning 'cup'. See the note on song no. 20 below.

217-19. **No. 11 of** *Patraput*: See the note on 'The Indifferent One' (*Bithika*) above.

219-20. **Dream** (*Shyamali*): The title of this collection, which means 'she who is dark', 'the dark one' (feminine gender), has a connection with an earthen cottage of that name which Tagore had built for himself in Santiniketan and where he lived for a brief period. The house still exists. The first quotation in this poem, which is repeated in the last stanza, is from a song by the 16th-century Bengali Baishnab poet Jnandas (pronounced *Gyandas*, with a hard *g*), in which Radha relates to a female friend a dream-encounter with Krishna. The second quotation is from a song by another Bengali Baishnab poet of the same period, Lochandas, in which Krishna asks a friend the identity of a girl he saw bathing at the ghat and who then went her way, wringing her wet blue sari and his heart with it. The girl was, of course, Radha.

221. **The Lost Mind** (*Shyamali*): The boundary-ridges in stanza 3 refer to earthen ridges built by farmers as boundaries between fields.

222-24. **Tamarind Flower** (*Shyamali*): There seems to be an error in Tagore's reference to Chitrarath in this poem; see the entry on Chitrarath in the Glossary.

229-31. **A Sudden Encounter** (*Shyamali*): stanza 2, l. 2: see the entry on *pomegranate blossoms* in the Glossary and the note on song no. 37 below.

231. **No. 5 of** *Prantik* (Marginal): All but three poems of *Prantik* were written while Tagore was convalescing from a sudden bout of illness. On 10 September 1937, at Santiniketan, he suddenly lost consciousness and remained in a coma for nearly 48 hours. The condition was later diagnosed as erysipelas, the infection being located behind one of his ears. 'Beneath the stupor of coma, the seemingly suspended consciousness must have been active underground, for the experience of the borderland where he hovered between life and death survived very vividly, and was described by the poet in a series of poems...' (Kripalani, p. 414).

231-32. **No. 14 of** *Prantik*: This earlier poem was included in *Prantik* for obvious thematic reasons. I am afraid I have had to add an extra line to this poem in order to accommodate, in the language of poetry, all the ideas packed with extraordinary tightness in the last three lines of the original, so that what was a sonnet has become a fifteen-liner. I tried and tried to do it in 14 lines, but found that to keep to 14 lines either some unit of thought would have to be omitted, or poetry would have to be sacrificed. In the end I decided that the only way to do justice to the original was to add an extra line in translation.

232. **No. 18 of** *Prantik*: This is the last poem of *Prantik*, showing Tagore's acute awareness of the conflict that was about to engulf Europe.

232-37. **The Dark Girl** and **Green Mangoes** (*Akashpradip*, The Sky-Lamp): These may be called twin poems, both charged with the memory of Kadambari Devi. In his memoirs, *Jibansmriti* (1912), Tagore has recalled the excitement that was generated in his boyish heart by the arrival of a new bride in the family, the first bride to arrive in the Tagore household during his childhood. That young bride was Kadambari Devi. And as he has also reminisced in his later years, he did indeed get a ring from her as a present once, which he lost while bathing in the Ganges at Ghazipur (*Rabindra-rachanabali*, vol. 23, Granthaparichay section). The title of the collection refers to the custom of lighting a lamp for the spirits of ancestors and for the gods on the top of a bamboo pole each evening of the month of Kartik.

237-39. The title *Nabajatak*, meaning 'the newborn', signals that the poet is defiant of approaching death . He still thinks of himself as an entity that is an ongoing project, engaged in constant self-renewal. 'Bhairab' and 'Multan' in the poem **Romantic** are names of musical *ragas*.

239. For the meaning of the title *Sanai* (pronounced *Shanai*), see *shanai* in the Glossary.

241-43. The poems of *Rogashajyay* (On the Sick-bed) and *Arogya* (Convalescence) were written, or rather composed and then dictated to others, in the shadow of Tagore's last illness. On 26 September 1940 he suddenly became ill while holidaying in Kalimpong and was brought to Calcutta for treatment on the 29th. After he improved a little, he was brought back to his beloved Santiniketan.

242-43. No. 9 of *Arogya*: In this poem theatrical images merge with those of dance and mythology. The compound word used in the original for 'actors and actresses' is *nata-nati*, which can also mean 'dancers, male and female'. The concepts were fairly interchangeable in India in ancient times, *natas* and *natis* being performing artists who were skilled in the four arts of singing, dancing, instrumental music, and acting. What I have translated as 'the king of the theatre' in the last line is *nataraj*, a term which could be glossed as 'the king of actors/dancers' and is an epithet of Shiva as the cosmic dancer, the lord of dance. In the context of the poem the word suggests a supreme theatre-director, choreographer, and ballet-master, a Director-God lonely in his theatre's deserted green-room.

243. No. 28 of *Janmadine* (On the Birthday, i.e., On My Birthday): Most poems of this collection, including this one, are also from the period of the poet's last illness, though the collection includes a number of poems from the months preceding it. From his days of river voyages the river is a constant source of imagery in Tagore, but in this poem the very geography of the delta of Bengal, formed by the rivers Ganga and Brahmaputra, and often called *nadimatrik* or river-mothered, has been commandeered for the purpose of poetry.

244. No. 5 of *Shesh Lekha* (Last Writings): This collection, published posthumously with a foreword by Tagore's son, gathered in the last poems. Rathindranath has informed us that some of the poems were written down by his father himself; others were dictated and then corrected (*Rabindra-rachanabali*, vol. 26, Granthaparichay section). This particular poem is about an armchair which Tagore had used in Argentina while convalescing there and which Victoria Ocampo had insisted on giving him as a present on his departure from that

country. It would not go through the door of the ship's cabin, so the impetuous Ocampo persuaded the captain to get a workman to remove the door from its hinges so that the chair could be put in. The process had to be repeated to get the chair out. The chair accompanied Tagore to Italy and from there to India and is preserved in the Rabindra Bhavana at Santiniketan. Tagore liked sitting on it in the last days. Tagore and Ocampo exchanged some jokes about this chair in their correspondence. Tagore claimed that the 'lyrical meaning' of the poem 'L'Invitation au Voyage' by Baudelaire, which Ocampo had tried to read with him without success (Tagore had mischievously given Baudelaire the name of 'furniture poet') had at last been revealed to him by means of this armchair. Ocampo wrote back: 'So, at last, you understood Baudelaire through my armchair!...I hope that you may understand, through that same piece of furniture, what the lyrical meaning of my devotion is! I hope, at least, *part* of its meaning shall be revealed to you! The part a confortable [*sic*] seat can reveal ...(Helas! it is only a small part)...' (Dyson, pp. 384-85 and p. 394). The possible connection between this chair and some recurrent images in Tagore's visual art is also discussed in my book (pp. 322-27).

245. No. 11 of *Shesh Lekha*: The use of the river-name Rupnarayan is pregnant with meaning. Rupnarayan is a river flowing through West Bengal that falls into the Hooghly near its mouth. A few miles upstream from the point where it joins the Hooghly stands the town of Tamluk, the Tamralipti of ancient times and once a flourishing maritime port. The river here is now a fairly long way away from the sea, but it is still accessible to tides and is at such times dangerous to navigate. Near the junction of the Rupnarayan and the Hooghly the famous James and Mary sands were the scene of many boatwrecks in the near past. The name Rupnarayan is a compound formed of two words, *rup*, meaning appearance, manifest form, beauty etc., and *narayan*, which is one of the names of Vishnu. The whole can be glossed as 'this ever-changing world of manifest forms, which is God, this life, this visible reality which is sacred'. Thus the river, both by virtue of its geographical identity and its philosophical-sounding name, becomes symbolic. Waking up on its bank is enlightenment, knowing what the world really is. It is no dream, as navigating this tidal river is no joke. As this river meets the sea, so life meets death. The proximity of danger reveals our own identity to us. In line 6 the word 'countenance' translates *rup*, a conscious echo of the river-name. On the bank of Rupnarayan the poet sees his own *rup* written in the script of blood. Self-knowledge has come to him through repeated suffering. Truth is hard, as this river is hard to sail on. But the poet has never flinched from it, and the sea, which is death, is very near.

246-47. No. 15 of *Shesh Lekha*: This is Tagore's last poem, dictated in the early hours of the morning before being carried to the operation-table. Unlike No. 14, which he first dictated and afterwards corrected, he never had a chance to revise or correct this poem. He did not recover from the after-effects of the operation and died a week later. Note that this last statement is addressed to a cosmic feminine principle, an enchantress-mother, to submit to whose wiles is to gain lasting peace. Compare it with poems like 'Hope Against Hope' of *Chaitali* and nos. 89 and 90 of *Naibedya*.

264. Song No. 28: Fields of mustard need no comment as such, for mustard is grown in Britain too, but it would probably help readers to know that mus-

tard occupies an important place in the Indian kitchen and hence in cultivation. Not only are mustard-seeds used both whole and in ground form, but also in certain parts of the Indian subcontinent, such as Bengal and Kashmir, the pungently aromatic oil expressed from mustard-seeds is the preferred medium of cooking. In such areas large tracts of land are devoted to the cultivation of the mustard-plant and are quite a sight to see when the fields are in flower. Tagore has himself written elsewhere about his fascination for mustard-fields and his attachment to the fragrance of mustard-flowers. I translate two brief extracts below:

'Midday; by the house of the milkmen in front of me the blossoms in a mustard-field are like fire...' (Letter written from Potisar, 29 November 1895, *Chhinnapatrabali*, p. 340.)

'This fragrance of the mustard-field enchants me so much...it is as if the deep happy memory of the satisfied love and absolute peace of some distant time is associated with that smell of mustard-flowers.' (Letter written en route to Shahjadpur, 11 December 1895, *Chhinnapatrabali*, p. 346.)

Shortly after translating this song, I myself happened to travel in Kashmir in the month of April, when the whole valley seemed to be a witness to the truth of Tagore's song.

268. **Song No. 35**: The swinging of Krishna and Radha in the forest, often depicted in Indian miniature art and celebrated as a monsoon festival, could be regarded as the general backdrop to a lyric like this. In addition, there could well be the personal memory of a particular pictorial scene behind it. Tagore has reminisced how in a villa in Chandernagore, overlooking the Ganges, where he spent some idyllic months as a young man in the company of Jyotirindranath and Kadambari (not 'the villa of the Banerjees' at Telenipara referred to once before, but another one called 'Moran Sahib's villa' to which they moved) one of the stained glass windows in the lounge depicted a couple swinging by themselves in a swing suspended from a leafy tree in a secluded bower dappled with light and shadows (Tagore, *Jibansmriti*, quoted and discussed in Pal, vol. 2, 1st edition, p. 153, or vol. 2, 2nd edition, pp. 116-17). The picture of the swing is remembered by Tagore in *Jibansmriti* (*Rabindra-rachanabali*, vol. 17, pp. 391-92).

269. **Song No. 37**: See the entries on *ashok* and *polash* in the Glossary. I have not commented on Tagore's references to the red colour elsewhere, but as the second stanza of this song is such a paean in praise of red, a comment would not be out of place here. There is good reason to believe that Tagore suffered from a form of red-green blindness known as protanopia, of genetic origin, in which red is lost to vision. Statements he made during his lifetime, the evidence given by certain contemporaries, and his use of colours in his paintings would point in that direction. Travelling in Italy, for instance, he could not respond very much to fields of red poppies in flower, which almost engulfed the countryside like a spreading fire, but he used to get immense pleasure from looking at various shades of blue and violet. See R.W. Pickford and J. Bose, 'Colour Vision and Aesthetic Problems in Pictures by Rabindranath Tagore', *British Journal of Aesthetics*, vol. 27, no. 1, Winter 1987. It is well known that blue and violet were his favourite colours. He was very attached to the flower-clusters of the *Petrea volubilis*, L., Verbenaceae, giving it the name *nilmonilata* (blue-jewel-creeper). Note his love of blue and violet in poem no. 27 of *Shesh Saptak*, poem no. 8 of *Patraput*, song no. 28 etc. He was once asked why he

liked the polash so much, in that case. He replied that it was because the polash was not just red, but had a lot of yellow mixed in it, and there was also a contrast with the dark green, nearly black colour (of the calyx); he also pointed to the beautiful shape of the flower (Nirmalkumari Mahalanobis, *Baishe Srabon* (Mitra o Ghosh, Calcutta, 3rd impression, 1966), pp. 47-48).

Immediately after completing the translation project which led to the present book, I went on to undertake an interdisciplinary project, in collaboration with other research colleagues, on looking carefully at Tagore's use of colours in his writings and visual art. This investigation resulted in the following book: Dyson, Adhikary et al., *Ronger Rabindranath* (Ananda, Calcutta, 1997). Subsequently I wrote an article in English summarising our main findings, entitled 'Rabindranath Tagore and His World of Colours', which was published in July 2001 in the web magazine *Parabaas* (www.parabaas.com/rabindranath/articles/pKetaki2.html). A paper adapted from this article was presented by me at an international Tagore conference at the University of Toronto in November 2005 and is available in *Rabindranath Tagore: Reclaiming a Cultural Icon*, edited by Kathleen and Joseph O'Connell (Visva-Bharati, Calcutta, 2009).

In poem no. 106 of *Gitanjali*, translated for the present edition, the phrase 'suffering's red glare' is a characteristic Tagore colour image. There is an ambiguity in his literary use of the colour red, which occasionally has traditional festive associations, but more often has a negative connotation, connected with death, darkness, violence, suffering, shame, embarrassment, humiliation etc.

271. **Song No. 39:** The second stanza of this song uses two technical terms of classical Indian music, *meed* and *murchhana*; I have translated the ideas instead of introducing the terms, so that the images can have direct impact on the reader.

Glossary

Achchhod: literally, 'that which has transparent waters', the name of a lake in the seventh-century Sanskrit work of fiction, *Kadambari*. See the note on 'The Victorious Woman' in the Notes section.

Aghran/Agrahayan: the eighth month of the Bengali calendar and the second month of autumn, mid-November to mid-December.

Ajay: a river that rises from the Rajmahal Hills of Bihar, flows through West Bengal, and falls into the Bhagirathi.

amloki: a beautiful deciduous tree with feathery foliage and sour-astringent fruit which is valued medicinally and also used as a condiment, the *Emblica officinalis*, Gaertn., Euphorbiaceae, the same as *Phyllanthus emblica*, L., of the same family.

areca: Bengali *supari*, the tall, slender, elegant, feather-leaved areca palm, *Areca catechu*, L., Arecaceae (Palmae). Its nuts, resembling nutmegs, are sliced and eaten, sometimes with betel leaves. The word *areca* is ultimately of South Indian origin.

Arjun: Arjuna in Sanskrit, a celebrated character in the epic *Mahabharata*, one of the five Pandava brothers. For the reference in 'Tamarind Flower', see the entry on *Chitrarath* below.

Ashadh: the third month of the Bengali calendar and the first month of the rainy season, mid-June to mid-July.

ashok: an evergreen tree with a dense crown of dark green leaves and clusters of lightly scented flowers which are at first orange and then turn scarlet. The young leaves of the ashok tree have a pretty reddish tinge and its flowers are one of the major beauties of springtime. Its current botanical name has been given to me as *Saraca asoka*, (Roxb.) de Wilde, Caesalpiniaceae, but the curious are likely to find it often referred to as *Saraca indica*, L., of the same family, subsumed in the larger order of Leguminosae. Its earliest Latin name was *Jonesia asoka*, Roxb., after Sir William Jones.

ash-sheora: a shrub the twigs of which are used to brush the teeth, the *Glycosmis pentaphylla*, (Retz.) DC., Rutaceae, which would seem to be the same as *Glycosmis pentaphylla*, Corr., and *Glycosmis Retzii* of the same family.

Ashwin: the sixth month of the Bengali calendar and the second month of the post-rains, mid-September to mid-October.

Badrinath: a town in Uttar Pradesh, high up in the Himalayas, close to peaks of the same name, and a famous centre of pilgrimage.

Baishakh: the first month of the Bengali calendar and the first month of summer, mid-April to mid-May.

banana: the fruit of the banana tree is familiar to everybody in Britain, but those who have not travelled to the tropics will not know what the tree looks like. Strictly speaking, the *Musa sapientum*, L., Musaceae, is not a tree but a herbaceous plant with a trunk that is a cylinder of encircling leaf stalks pressed close together (Thomas H. Everett, *Living Trees of the World* (Thames and Hudson, London, 1969), p. 87). Sanskrit poets often likened a woman's shapely thigh to the trunk of a banana tree. From the top of this distinctive trunk emerge large flapping rectangular leaves of a soft yellowish green colour. The predominant impression the banana tree makes is of leafiness and greenness. 'Young-banana-leaf-green' is an expressive Bengali way of naming a certain shade of green. The large leaves are used as disposable plates. At night moonlight on the flapping leaves can make the tree look like a veiled woman beckoning, and this resemblance is a fruitful source of ghost stories.

Bankipore: an important town in Bihar, close to Patna.

banyan: Bengali *bot*, the *Ficus benghalensis*, L., Moraceae, the spreading branches of which send down shoots which take root and become additional trunks. Spreading itself in this manner, one tree can eventually cover a very large area. The shady banyan tree plays an important part in Indian village life. The curious are likely to find the name of this tree more often than not entered under the broad family name of Urticaceae. The word *banyan* came to English from Gujarati, via Portuguese, and is ultimately of Sanskrit origin; the name was first given by Europeans to a particular tree of this species growing near Gombroon (modern Bandar Abbas) on the Persian Gulf, under which *banyans* or Hindu (presumably Gujarati) traders had settled and built a small temple.

Baruna: a river bordering Benares that joins the Ganges. The name of the city, properly Varanasi, derives from the two rivers, Varuna (or Varana) and Asi, which enclose the principal part of the city and fall into the Ganges.

Baruni: a river of this name exists in eastern Bengal (Bangladesh) at latitude 24.35N, longitude 90.58E, and I have traced it in a 1927 Government of India Survey map. Did Tagore choose this name in the poem 'Impossible' to evoke the magic of his youthful days in the riverine landscape of eastern Bengal, when he lived in houseboats and went up and down the rivers? The name has a strong association with water itself, meaning the daughter of Barun (Skr. Varuna), who in later mythology is the god of the oceans, a kind of Indian Neptune. Baruni or Varuni rose from the waters at the time of the churning of the oceans and is the presiding deity of wine. There is also an association, through the sound of the name, with the mythological river Baitarani (Skr. Vaitarani) which encircles the underworld, an Indian Styx.

Baul: See the note on poem no. 13 of *Shesh Saptak* in the Notes section.

bel: a small climbing shrub of the jasmine family, usually clipped down to a low height in gardens, with fragrant white flowers, the *Jasminum sambac*, (L.) W. Ait., Oleaceae.

Benares: the celebrated sacred city of the Hindus on the Ganges in Uttar Pradesh. See the note on Baruna above.

betel leaves: leaves of the *Piper betle*, L., Piperaceae, sweetish and pungent at the same time, which are rolled, for chewing, into little triangular packets with areca nuts and other ingredients inside them. The word *betel* is ultimately of Sanskrit origin and has journeyed to English via Malayalam and Portuguese; the Bengali word commonly used is *paan*.

Bethune School: initially known as the Victoria Girls' School, was founded in Calcutta in 1849 by the British administrator J.E.D. Bethune. Targeted at the daughters of the Hindu upper classes, it was the first public institution for the education of girls which was not under the control of Christian missionaries. After Bethune's death in 1851, it was maintained for five years by Lord Dalhousie, the Governor-General of British India, from his private purse, after which it was taken over by the government. It had to struggle to establish itself; Ishwarchandra Vidyasagar, the noted activist for female emancipation, was involved in its management for many years. By the closing decades of the 19th century Bethune School and its collegiate extension, Bethune College, had become trail-blazers in female education in Calcutta.

Bhadra: the fifth month of the Bengali calendar and the first month of the post-monsoon season, mid-August to mid-September.

bigha: a unit of land measurement, approximately a third of an acre.

black drongo: the *phinga* or *phinge*, a common bird of the Bengali country-side, belonging to the Dicruridae family, brisk and busy, with a long forked tail which it dangles as it perches on a tree or a telegraph wire. It sometimes sits on the hump of a grazing cow or buffalo, from where it swoops on insects dislodged from the grass by the movements of the feeding animal. Black drongos are valued in farms because of their depredations on insects.

boinchi: a low compact spiny shrub that bears berries. When ripe, the berries are dark purple – nearly black – in colour and sweet in taste. The Latin name given to me is *Flacourtia indica*, (Burm. f.) Merr., Flacourtiaceae. I have also seen it called *Flacourtia sepiaria*, Roxb., Bixineae, with variants *Flacourtia ramontchi* and *Flacourtia cataphracta*.

bokul: an evergreen tree with a dense crown and small, fragrant, star-shaped flowers, *Mimusops elengi*, L., Sapotaceae.

cajan: Bengali *arhar*, a variety of pulse that is made into dal, *Cajanus cajan*, (L.) Millsp., Fabaceae, identical with *Cajanus indicus*, Spreng., Leguminosae.

camellia: a shrub belonging to the tea family, *Camellia japonica*, L., Theaceae, bearing showy flowers.

casuarina: Bengali *jhau*, the tall straight-stemmed *Casuarina equisetifolia*, Forst., Casuarinaceae, with jointed near-leafless branches that look like huge horse-tails and rustle in the wind. 'Its so-called leaves are really jointed branches bearing a whorl of minute scale-leaves' (Satyendra Kumar Basu & Rammohan Dutta, *Trees of Santiniketan* (Visvabharati, 1957), p. 50).

Chaitra: the twelfth month of the Bengali calendar and the second spring month, mid-March to mid-April.

chakravaka: literally, the bird 'with the speech of wheels', so called because of its screeching cry, known in colloquial Bengali in the shortened form of *chakha* (male) and *chakhi* (female), which are the actual words used in the original of Song no. 6 translated in this volume (beginning 'Sunshine and shadows play hide-and-seek today'). This bird has a strong symbolic meaning in Indian bird-lore. The male and the female of the species are supposed to spend the night apart, calling to each other from opposite banks of a river, thus representing the faithful couple doomed to stay apart. Known as the Brahminy Duck in old Anglo-Indian terminology, the bird is identified in *Hobson-Jobson* as the *Casarca rutila* or 'Ruddy Shieldrake': 'constantly seen on the sandy shores of the Gangetic rivers in single pairs, the pair almost always at some distance apart' (Col. Henry Yule and A. C. Burnell, *Hobson-Jobson*, Routledge & Kegan Paul, 1969, p. 112).

chalta: the *Dillenia indica*, L., Dilleniaceae, an evergreen tree bearing large white scented flowers and globose fruits which consist mainly of the enlarged sepals which are hard outside and fleshy inside. The fruit is made into sweet and sour dishes.

chameli: a flowering creeper of the jasmine family. The Latin name given to me is *Jasminum grandiflorum*, L., Oleaceae.

champa/champak: an evergreen tree bearing very fragrant yellow-orange flowers with longish petals, *Michelia champaca*, L., Magnoliaceae.

Chandi: one of the many names of the Mother Goddess. She is the same as Durga or Kali.

Chariot Festival: the annual festival, held in the monsoon month of Ashadh, in which the god Jagannath ('Lord of the World', an aspect of Vishnu) is carried in procession on a grand chariot pulled by devotees. The festival is accompanied by a country fair in which children are well catered for and where there are toy chariots on sale. It is from this festival, especially the one held in Puri, Orissa, where the principal temple of Jagannath is situated, that the English word *juggernaut* is ultimately derived.

Chitrarath: Tagore seems to have made a mistake in his reference to Chitrarath in 'Tamarind Flower'. A Gandharva of this name (Sanskrit Chitraratha) does exist in the *Mahabharata*, but far from being a vanquisher of Arjuna, he was in fact vanquished *by* him. His chariot too was burnt by Arjuna. Because of the prayer of his distressed wife Kumbhinasi and at the intercession of Yudhisthira, the eldest of the Pandava brothers, Chitraratha was afterwards released by Arjuna, became a friend of his, and there was an exchange of gifts between them. It seems that Tagore has mixed up two Gandharvas, because there is another Gandharva in the *Mahabharata* named Chitrasena, a courtier of Indra and a teacher of music and dance in Indra's heaven, who fits the reference partially, but again, not totally, because Chitrasena was never a vanquisher of Arjuna either. Chitrasena was a friend of Arjuna during the latter's sojourn in Indra's heaven and taught him dance and music. He actually vanquished Duryodhana, the head of the Kaurava brothers, but released him at Yudhisthira's request after being nearly overcome in battle by Arjuna.

coconut: remember that the tree that bears coconuts, the *cocos nucifera*, L., Arecaceae, is a tall and elegant palm, often with a leaning trunk, crowned by long dark-green pinnate leaves that seem to comb the air as it blows through them. A group of rustling coconut trees contributes greatly to the beauty of the landscape in which it occurs. In commercial terms the tree is the world's most valuable palm and produces numerous products from ropes to oil. Every part of the tree is used. It is certainly very important in India's economy.

Darjeeling: a hill resort and important town, 7000 ft. above sea-level, in the north of West Bengal. The British regarded it as 'the most important sanatorium of Bengal' (*Handbook for Travellers in India, Burma and Ceylon* (John Murray, London, 13th edition, 1929), p. 486). Both Everest and Kanchenjunga are visible from here. Teas grown in the tea gardens of the Darjeeling district are regarded by connoisseurs as 'the champagne' of Indian teas.

date tree: is likely to be the wild variety, *Phoenix sylvestris*, Roxb., Arecaceae, a native of India, valued specially as a source of molasses and toddy, rather than the *Phoenix dactylifera*, valued for its fruit. Remember that in either case it is a palm tree with its characteristic shape.

Dehra Dun: an important hill town in the state of Uttar Pradesh. In the British days Dehra Dun enjoyed a great reputation as a hill resort and had a large resident population of retired people, both British and Indian (Murray's *Handbook for Travellers in India, Burma and Ceylon*, cited above, p. 422).

deodar: literally, 'the timber of the gods', a tall long-lived native of the western Himalayan region, the *Cedrus deodara*, (Roxb.) Loud., Pinaceae, not to be confused with the *Polyalthia longifolia*, Benth. & Hook. f., Anonaceae, which is a native of Ceylon and Tanjore, which has been given the name 'deodar', and which is often planted as an ornamental tree in avenues. There are deodars of this latter variety in the Santiniketan campus, but in poem no. 36 of *Balaka* Tagore is referring to the Himalayan deodar of Kashmir.

dolonchampa: the *Hedychium coronarium*, Koen., Zingiberaceae, a plant growing from ginger-like rhizomes; the stalks bear crowns of flowers with an exquisite fragrance, usually white with a yellowish tinge at the centre, though other colours are also known. This is the flower currently called the dolonchampa in Santiniketan; it is, however, possible that Tagore was thinking of a different flower, perhaps a variety of the champa/champak.

Durvasa: a sage famous in legend for his bad temper and readiness to pronounce curses. He curses Shakuntala, the heroine of Kalidasa's celebrated play *Abhijnanashakuntala*.

ektara: a one-stringed instrument used by Bauls and other folk musicians.

fan palm: the tall palmyra or *Borassus flabellifer*, L., Arecaceae (Palmae), valued for its fruit, leaves, timber, and sap. The large fan-shaped leaves have many uses, including in the manufacture of hand-fans, sun-hats etc. This is the tree (Beng. *tal*) from the name of which the word *toddy* is ultimately derived, it being one of the trees the fermented sap of which is turned into an intoxicating drink (*tadi*).

frangipani: Bengali *golokchampa*, the *Plumeria acutifolia*, Poir., Apocynaceae, a deciduous tree with thick branches full of milk, bearing fragrant funnel-shaped flowers, white with yellow centres, in compound cymes. There is also a variety bearing pure white flowers, *Plumeria tuberculata*, and a variety bearing red flowers, *Plumeria rubra*, in the same family. These trees came to India from the New World.

Gandharva: an order of demi-gods who are the celestial musicians of Indra's heaven. For the reference in 'Tamarind Flower', see the entry on Chitrarath above.

Ganga: the Indian name for the Ganges. (*Ganges* is the Greek version of the name.)

ghat: steps which give access to a river or water-tank, where people congregate for washing or fetching water, or where boats can be moored.

guava: the tasty fruits of the *Psidium guajava*, L., Myrtaceae, Bengali *peyara*, are still very rare on supermarket shelves in Britain, but guava jelly can sometimes be seen. The tree was introduced to India from tropical America.

heloncho: a variety of edible bitter greens that grow near water, *Enhydra fluctuans*, Lour., Asteraceae, used as a vegetable. The family name may be subsumed in the larger order Compositae.

henna: Bengali *hena* or *mehedi*, the *Lawsonia inermis*, L., Lythraceae, the same as *Lawsonia alba*, Lam., Lythraceae, a pretty shrub with fragrant greenish white flowers, often used for hedges. Its shoots and leaves have long been used in oriental cosmetic preparations to dye the skin and hair. Nowadays one can see the name of this plant on labels of shampoo bottles in the West as well. Both Eng. *henna* and Beng. *hena* are ultimately derived from Arabic.

hibiscus: the red-flowering variety of the Bengali *joba*, *Hibiscus rosa-sinensis*, L., Malvaceae, is the commonest, the white-flowering variety being rarer. Many varieties and hybrids are cultivated. I have read a description of the white hibiscus of Hawaii, a slightly different species, but I do not know if it is cultivated in India and doubt if Tagore was referring to its flower in 'Camellia'. A reference to a white variety of the *Hibiscus rosa-sinensis*, very common in India, is much more likely.

Howrah Station: the railway station at Howrah, a town facing Calcutta on the west bank of the Hooghly, used for westward journeys from Calcutta, including to Bombay, Delhi, and Madras.

Indra: the mythological king of the gods.

jaam: a large evergreen tree with a dense crown and shiny leaves, yielding juicy fruits which are dark purple, nearly black in colour. The fruits look like black grapes or olives, have stones in the centre as olives do, and have a strong, sweet-astringent taste. Its current botanical name, I am told, is *Syzygium cumini*, (L.) Skeels, Myrtaceae; in most old authors it is called *Eugenia jambolana*, Lamk., Myrtaceae.

jack: the *Artocarpus heterophyllus*, Lamk., Moraceae, the same as *Artocarpus integrifolia*, L., Urticaceae, a large evergreen tree bearing huge edible fruits which have a potent smell when ripe and which are also cooked as vegetables when green. The jack fruit is described thus in Basu & Dutta, p. 49: 'a globose or cylindrical aggregate formed by a large number of flowers growing together, mostly sterile but many with seeds; 12–30 by 6–12 in. hanging on short stalks from the trunk and larger branches, the rind with conical protuberances, each representing a single flower'. It is apparently the largest known fruit in the world: specimens weighing 90 pounds have been recorded (Everett, p. 133). When a large fruit is opened, several people can make a meal of it. The timber is used for furniture. The word *jack* is ultimately from Sanskrit, via Malayalam and Portuguese. The Bengali word commonly used is *kantal* or *kanthal*, also of Sanskrit origin.

Jamuna: or Yamuna, or the Jumna of the old maps, one of the important rivers of northern India, which rises from the Himalayas, flows past Delhi and Agra, and meets the Ganga at Allahabad, an important place of pilgrimage. The Jamuna also flows past Vrindavan and Mathura, two places strongly associated with Krishna.

jarul: the *Lagerstroemia speciosa*, (L.) Pers., Lythraceae, identical with *Lagerstroemia flos-reginae*, Retz., Lythraceae, a deciduous tree with 'Large handsome mauve flowers in terminal erect panicles' (Basu & Dutta, p. 28). The timber is highly prized.

jasmine: I have always translated the Bengali *juthi* or *jui*, the *Jasminum auriculatum*, Vahl., Oleaceae, as the jasmine, as it comes closest to the jasmine of English gardens. To avoid confusion, other members of the jasmine family retain their Bengali names in the texts.

jujube: Bengali *kul*, the spiny tree *Zizyphus mauritiana*, Lam., Rhamnaceae, in older sources called *Zizyphus jujuba*, Lam., Rhamnaceae, bearing tasty drupes which are eaten raw when ripe and also made into pickles and chutneys. The taste of the ripe fruit resembles that of ripe gooseberries.

jungle crow: larger than the common house crow, uniformly glossy jet-black in colour, with a heavier bill and a deeper, hoarser cawing. It normally lives in the countryside, avoiding urban areas, but sometimes hangs around the out-skirts of human habitations in search of food.

Jyaishtha: the second month of the Bengali calendar and the second summer month, mid-May to mid-June.

kadamba: a tree bearing strongly scented yellow-orange ball-shaped flowers which are really composed of numerous small florets 'united by their confluent calyx tubes' (Basu & Dutta, p. 30). The tree flowers in the rainy season. The fruit is edible. Its current botanical name was given to me as *Anthocephalus chinensis*, (Lamk.) A. Rich. ex Walp., Rubiaceae, but the curious are likely to encounter it under a variety of other names, such as *Anthocephalus indicus*, A. Rich., Rubiaceae, *Anthocephalus cadamba*, Miq., Rubiaceae (as in Basu & Dutta, from where I have just quoted), or even *Nauclea cadamba* (Monier-Williams).

Kailas: a mountain to the north of the Himalayan range, in Tibet, to the north of Lake Manas. It is the dwelling-place of the god Kubera and also one of the favourite residences of the great god Shiva.

kajari chants: a genre of folk songs associated with the rainy season.

kanchon: the *Bauhinia purpurea*, L., Caesalpiniaceae, an almost evergreen tree with large fragrant purple flowers, or the *Bauhinia variegata*, L., of the same family, which is deciduous, bearing white, red, or purple flowers. I was also given the name *Bauhinia acuminata*, L., of the same family.

kantalichampa: a small scandent shrub with dark green leaves and very fragrant flowers of a pale yellow or pale green colour. Its current Latin name was given to me as *Artabotrys hexapetalus*, (L.f.) Bhandari, Anonaceae. In earlier sources it is called *Artabotrys odoratissimus*.

kantha: a hand-sewn wrap made from old clothes. Re-cycling old cotton pieces by layering them and sewing them into wraps used to be one of the traditional domestic crafts of Bengal, and much ingenuity of women's needlework was lavished on them. The kantha is humble but can be pretty. It is not necessarily an image of poverty. In 'The Old House' it is its patched state that indicates the wearer's indigence.

Kartik: the seventh month of the Bengali calendar and the first autumn month, mid-October to mid-November.

ketaki: a shrub belonging to the screwpine family, with very spiny long leaves and strongly scented flowers of elongated shape (like heads of sweetcorn) that blossom in the rainy season. In legend it appears to have been a flower that was cursed by Shiva (S. Bhattacharya, *Chiranjib Banowshadhi* (Ananda Publishers, Calcutta), vol. 5). Its powerful aroma is known to have a drugging effect on snakes, which like coiling round it, and its essential oil is used in Indian perfumery and confectionery. In most old sources its botanical name is given as *Pandanus odoratissimus*, but I was told that it could be identified with *Pandanus foetidus*, Roxb., Pandanaceae. To the sensitive noses of botanical taxonomists *odoratissimus* may verge on *foetidus*, but on behalf of a flower celebrated for its fragrance in Indian poetry, and on behalf of those who, like myself, are named after it, I would like to register my protest against this new name! Bhattacharya, whom I have just cited, gives its new name as *Pandanus tectorius*, which does not sound so bad!

Khoka: meaning 'little boy', is also a common pet name for a boy. In 'Hide-and-Seek' it is clearly a name in the first stanza, but in the second and third stanzas it could be translated either way, especially as there is no capitalisation in the Bengali alphabet to stamp a word indisputably as a proper name.

kochu greens: *Colocasia esculenta*, (L.) Schott., Araceae, probably the same as *Alocasia indica*, Schott., Araceae, delicious as a vegetable. Although it is called 'greens' in an honorific sense, it is really the esculent stems, not the large leaves, that are cooked and eaten, just as one does with rhubarb.

koel: Bengali *kokil, koyel*, belongs to the cuckoo family and is one of the most indefatigable singers of the Indian spring. Its high-pitched, insistent song, increasing in intensity as it goes on, is very different from that of the cuckoo which comes to Britain in the spring.

kolmi: a variety of edible greens that grow near water, *Ipomoea aquatica*, Forsk., Convolvulaceae, the same as *Ipomoea reptans*, Poir., of the same family, delicious when cooked as a vegetable.

Kopai: the name of a small river of Birbhum district, West Bengal, which flows near Santiniketan.

koromcha: the *Carissa carandas*, L., Apocynaceae, bearing fruit which look somewhat like cherries and are pleasantly tartish in taste.

kunda: a scandent shrub of the jasmine family, with white fragrant flowers in dense cymes, *Jasminum multiflorum*, (Burm.f.) Andr., Oleaceae, the same as *Jasminum pubescens*, Willd., Oleaceae.

kurchi: the *Holarrhena antidysenterica*, Wall., Apocynaceae, a deciduous tree bearing creamy white flowers 'in many-flowered corymbose cymes' (Basu & Dutta, p. 39). Its bark has been used in the treatment of dysentery.

kurubak: the reference in 'Dream' (*Kalpana*) is taken by Tagore straight from Kalidasa, but it is not so easy to establish the exact identity of this flower in Kalidasa. According to the *Sanskrit-English Dictionary* of Monier-Williams, it could be either a red amaranth or a red variety of *Barleria cristata*, L., Acanthaceae.

kush-grass: a variety of grass used in religious rituals and famous for its sharp points. The Latin name given to me is *Desmostachya bipinnata*, Stapf, Poaceae. Monier-Williams identifies it with *Poa cynosuroides*.

Lakshmi: the goddess of grace, beauty, luck, and prosperity, the consort of Vishnu who is the second deity of the Hindu trinity and one of the most powerful gods of Hinduism.

lemon-grass: a fragrant tropical grass yielding an aromatic oil, the *Cymbopogon nardus*, (L.) Rendle, Poaceae. Stalks of this grass are used in the cookery of S.E. Asia.

lime flowers: the fragrant flowers of the *Citrus medica*, L., Rutaceae.

lodhra: the *Symplocos racemosa*, Roxb., Symplocaceae. Flowers in the winter. The fine pollen of the fragrant white flowers was used by women as a powder for the face.

lotus: the Indian lotus, *Nelumbo nucifera,* Gaertn., Nymphaeaceae, is unlikely to be the same as the plant the fruit of which, according to Homer, induced a state of dreamy torpor and which is celebrated in Tennyson's poem 'The Lotos-eaters'. The Indian lotus belongs to the same family as the humble water-lily, but as a many-petalled thing of beauty emerging from water or slime, it occupies a special place of honour and has a tremendous symbolic significance to the Indian mind. It is a powerful symbol in both Hinduism and Buddhism. See the note on the poem 'True Meditation' (*Chaitali*) in the Notes section.

madar: properly *palte madar* in Bengali, the *Erythrina variegata,* L., Fabaceae, also called *Erythrina indica* in older sources, a deciduous tree which, in the flowering season, sports dense erect spikes of bright scarlet flowers at the tip of leafless branches.

madhabi: a climber with sweet-scented flowers in abundant racemes. The Latin name most commonly given for it is *Hiptage madablota,* Gaertn., Malpighiaceae, but I was given the name *Hiptage benghalensis.*

Magh: the tenth month of the Bengali calendar and the second winter month, mid-January to mid-February.

magpie robin: Bengali *doyel,* famous for its sweet song in the breeding season.

Mahabharat: the great Sanskrit epic, the *Mahabharata,* supposed to be the longest poem in the world. In 'Hide-and-Seek' it would be a Bengali version, most probably Kashidas's, which the little boy's mother would be reading, which is why I have spelt the name without the final *a,* in keeping with Bengali pronunciation.

mahaneem: an evergreen shady tree belonging to the same family as the neem, with sweet-scented lilac flowers. Bunches of fruit remain on the tree for a long time. The Latin name given to me is *Melia azadirachta,* A. Juss., Meliaceae. I have also seen it called *Melia azedarach.*

Mahashweta: a character in the Sanskrit work of prose fiction, *Kadambari*; see the note on the poem 'The Victorious Woman' in the Notes section. To appreciate the statement in 'Tamarind Flowers' that the kurchi branch, in its 'prayerful striving for flowers...has become a Mahashweta', remember that the flowers of the *kurchi* (q.v.) are creamy white, that the name 'Maha-shweta' means 'the very white one' (fem. gender), and that Mahashweta became an ascetic while waiting to be re-united with her beloved.

mahua: a deciduous tree with sweet-smelling cream-coloured flowers and edible fruit, the *Madhuca latifolia,* (Koen.) Mac., Sapotaceae, or *Madhuca indica,* Gmel., Sapotaceae, or *Bassia latifolia,* Roxb., Sapotaceae (all three names refer to the same tree). Mahua wine is a favourite drink of Santhals and other tribal people. One also hears local stories of bears getting intoxicated after eating the fruit, which is a favourite food of many wild creatures. One of Tagore's collections of love-poems, from which two poems have been translated in this book, is named after this tree/flower. A valuable oil is expressed from the seeds.

malati: a climbing shrub with fragrant white flowers, *Aganosma dichotoma,* (Roth.) K. Schum., Apocynaceae, identical with *Aganosma caryophyllata,* G. Don, Apocynaceae.

Malavika: the name of the heroine of Kalidasa's play *Malavikagnimitra,* hence used by Tagore to evoke the image of a charming and sophisticated woman of Kalidasa's time.

312

Mallar: a generic name in Indian classical music for a group of *ragas* pertaining to the rainy season. In 'One Day' Tagore is probably referring specifically to Raga Megha-mallar.

Mandakini: the river Ganges in its mythological aspect, when it flows through the heavenly world.

mandar: often identified with the *palte madar* with its brilliant scarlet blossoms (see *madar* above), but in the poem 'Farewell to Heaven' the reference is clearly to the mythological *mandar*, which is a celestial tree growing in the pleasure-garden of the gods. By the logic of its very being such a tree and its flowers cannot be found on this earth.

mango: mangoes, usually flown from Kenya, are now not uncommon in British supermarkets, but this king of Indian fruits deserves a note. The word *mango* is ultimately from Tamil. The common Bengali word is *aam*, from Skr. *amra*. The tree, the *Mangifera indica*, L., Anacardiaceae, is an evergreen with a dense rounded crown of dark-green leathery leaves. The strong, heady scent of its flowers is one of the characteristic odours of the Indian spring and is often referred to in Tagore's poetry and songs. The fruit, when ripe, has a large stone in the centre, and is sweet, fleshy, and juicy, the nearest European equivalent in taste being a really ripe peach. The green fruit is used in pickles, chutneys, and other condiments. Numerous varieties of the mango are cultivated in India. Some of the best reach the West in canned form. The cashew-nut tree belongs to the same family as the mango.

Manu's codes: The lawbook attributed to Manu was probably put together in its final form in the 2nd or 3rd century A.D. (A.L. Basham, *The Wonder that was India*, 3rd revised edition (Sidgwick & Jackson, London, 1969), p. 113). It codified Hindu orthodoxy.

masha: a unit of weight used by jewellers. It can also refer to a unit of weight used by apothecaries, in which case it is smaller.

maya: an important philosophical concept; see the note on the poem 'On the Doctrine of Maya' (*Sonar Tari*) in the Notes section.

Mayurakshi: a river that rises from the Rajmahal Hills of Bihar, flows through the Santhal Parganas district and into West Bengal. Pronounced *Moyurakkhi* in Bengali, the name means 'peacock-eyed', in the feminine gender. Hence in the poem 'Dwelling' the name itself is magical, evoking a world of beauty and romance.

Menaka: a celestial nymph and dancer at Indra's court.

muchukunda: an evergreen tree bearing yellowish white sweet-scented flowers, the *Pterospermum acerifolium*, Willd., Sterculiaceae, identical with *Pterospermum suberifolium*, Lam., of the same family.

myrobalan: Bengali *horitoki*, a large deciduous tree, the *Terminalia chebula*, Retz., Combretaceae, the astringent fruit of which is used medicinally.

Nandan: the heavenly garden of Indra, pleasing in all seasons.

neem: the *Azadirachta indica*, A. Juss., Meliaceae, a beautiful, virtually ever-green tree with sweet-smelling white flowers which is much valued in the Indian pharmacopoeia for the antiseptic properties of its products. Its twigs are used to brush the teeth; its bitter-tasting leaves are cooked and eaten, and are also used as insect-repellents; its essential oil is used in the manufacture of soap and toothpaste. Birds and bees love the honey of the flowers, and birds also love the small yellow fruits, which tend to fall off soon after ripening.

nut tree: In poem no. 5 of *Patraput* and 'The Dark Girl' of *Akashpradip* this is likely to be the *Terminalia catappa*, L., Combretaceae, a tall handsome spreading tree with horizontal, whorled branches. Its leaves turn coppery red before falling. The kernels of the fruit are edible.

oleander: the Bengali *karabi*, a poisonous shrub with whippy branches and fragrant white or reddish flowers, *Nerium indicum*, Mill., Apocynaceae, identical with *Nerium odorum*, Sol., of the same family. The red variety received its apotheosis as a symbol in Tagore's play *Raktakarabi*. Not to be confused with what is sometimes called the yellow oleander, Bengali *kolke-phul*, the *Thevetia peruviana* or *Thevetia nereifolia* of the same family, bearing yellow flowers.

Padma: the name given to the main branch of the Ganga in eastern Bengal, now Bangladesh.

palmyra: the same as *fan palm* (q.v.).

parijat: like *mandar*, often identified with the *Erythrina variegata*, L., Fabaceae, but in Song No. 36 it is without a doubt a celestial flower of mythology which cannot be found on this earth. Any association with the scarlet flower of the *Erythrina variegata* must really be ruled out here, because Tagore is making parijat pollen serve as a metaphor for moonlight. As in the previous stanza, where sandalwood paste serves the same purpose, Tagore wants to evoke a pale golden colour.

passiflora: Bengali *jhumka-lata* or *jhumko-lata*, a flowering shrub climbing by tendrils. The Latin name I was given for it is *Passiflora incarnata*, L., Passifloraceae.

peepul: the *Ficus religiosa*, L., Moraceae. Resembles some species of the poplar, especially the aspen, like which its leaves quiver constantly in the breeze. The shade of this tree is most attractive in the hot season. Its seeds, blown by the wind or dropped by birds in the cracks of brickwork or masonry, can be very destructive to buildings. The Buddha is said to have attained his enlightenment under one of these trees. The word *peepul* came to English from Hindi and is ultimately from Sanskrit. The word *pippal* does exist in the Bengali wordstock, but Bengali usually prefers another name for the tree, *ashwattha* or *ashath*, also of Sanskrit origin.

Phagun/Phalgun: the eleventh month of the Bengali calendar and the first spring month, mid-February to mid-March.

polash: the *Butea monosperma*, Kuntze, Fabaceae, earlier known as the *Butea frondosa*, Roxb., Papilionaceae, a deciduous tree which is a treat for the eye in springtime, bearing on its leafless branches a profusion of shapely flame-coloured or yellow flowers set off by velvety dark-green calyces. Many polash trees grow in and around Santiniketan, and the flower, used as an adornment by Santhal women and much used in the Santiniketan spring festival, was one of Tagore's favourite flowers. The tree yields a red resin and is an important host of the lac insect, the source of a valuable red dye. The flowers yield a dye too.

pomegranate blossoms: the fruit of the *Punica granatum*, L., Punicaceae, will be more familiar to most readers than the red blossoms which are lovely.

Poush: the ninth month of the Bengali calendar and the first winter month, mid-December to mid-January.

Puja: any ceremony of religious worship, but if otherwise unqualified, in Bengal referring to the festival of Durga, the Mother Goddess, which takes place in the month of Ashwin and lasts several days.

Radhika: the same as Radha, the beloved of Krishna, an incarnation of the god Vishnu. Those who have seen examples of Indian miniature painting should be familiar with representations of Radha and Krishna. The story of their love is a common ingredient in many Indian art-forms, including medieval Bengali poetry. It would feature in the traditional open-air plays of Bengal known as *jatras,* in which female parts were taken by boys, as in the Elizabethan theatre.

Rajbangshi: the name of a rural community of tribal origin in northern Bengal.

rattan: the *Calamus rotang,* L., Arecaceae, the pliable stems of which are used for making baskets, trays etc.

red sandal: the red heartwood of the *Adenanthera pavonina,* L., Mimosaceae, called *raktachandan* (i.e. red sandal) in Bengali, yields a red dye, but the true *raktachandan* or red sandal/sanders comes from the wood of the *Pterocarpus santalinus,* L., Leguminosae, which grows in South India.

rongon: the white variety of this dense shrub is the *Ixora arborea,* Roxb. ex Sm., Rubiaceae; there is also the *Ixora coccinea,* L., Rubiaceae, a variety which bears brilliant scarlet or yellow blossoms and is much liked by gardeners.

Rupnarayan: see the note on poem no. 11 of *Shesh Lekha* in the Notes section.

sal: pronounced *shaal* in Bengali, the *Shorea robusta,* Gaertn., Dipterocarpaceae, a large tree valued for its timber and resin. Its leaves are used to make disposable plates and conical containers for outdoor eating.

sandal: the fragrant wood of the *Santalum album,* L., Santalaceae, is rubbed with a little water against a mortar to make a paste, which is applied to the skin to aromatise, cool, and decorate it. The wood is highly prized for the manufacture of *objets d'art* and the essential oil is used in perfumes and soaps. The word *sandal* is really the same as Bengali *chandan* and came to English from Sanskrit via medieval Latin.

san-hemp: the *Crotalaria juncea,* L., Fabaceae, cultivated for its valuable fibre. Its yellow flowers make a pretty sight.

Santhal: the name of an important tribal people of India whose largest concentration is to be found in the states of Bihar, West Bengal, Jharkhand and Orissa. They used to give their name to an entire district of Bihar and they are also numerous in the Birbhum district of West Bengal, where Santiniketan is situated. They are noted for their songs and dances, their various home-made brews, a marked aesthetic sense, and a festive spirit.

Santhal Parganas: a district named after the Santhals (see the entry above), which used to be a part of Bihar, but is currently a part of the new state of Jharkhand, which has been carved out of the southern part of Bihar.

saptaparna: also known in Bengali as *chhatim,* a large evergreen tree, the *Alstonia* scholaris, (L.) R. Br., Apocynaceae, with distinctive leaves in whorls and strongly scented greenish white flowers in many-flowered cymes. The name *saptaparna* implies that the leaves are in whorls of 7, but the number can vary. The pollen of the flowers can cause hay-fever and other allergies in those who are susceptible to such problems. People at Santiniketan have a special affection for this tree, as it played a role in the foundation of the place as a Tagore family country-house. The story is that Tagore's father, on his way to a friend's country estate, got off the train at Bolpur and proceeded in a palanquin till he came to an open plain, where he sat down under a pair of chhatim trees for his evening meditation. He was so delighted with the spot that soon thereafter he bought the land, built a house, and laid out a garden, naming the place Santiniketan (see Kripalani, op. cit. in the Notes section, p. 48). It was here that Tagore later founded a school and, later still, a university. A leaf of this tree is given to each graduate at the convocation of the university.

Sarang: a group of *ragas* pertaining to the middle of the day, from noon to 4 p.m., serious and contemplative in mood, suggesting the heat of the sun. In 'The Nap' it may well be the Vrindavani Sarang, much played at weddings. In the context of the poem, it is being played in the bride's house on the day after the wedding day and will be touched with pathos, as the bride will soon leave her parents' home for her husband's home.

Saraswati: the goddess of learning and the arts. She is white, holds a vina, and rides a swan.

seer: a unit of weight which varied in different parts of India and also a measure of capacity for fluids. I remember milk being sold in seers in my childhood; four *powas* made a seer. Nowadays in cities milk is sold in litres. As a unit of weight the kilogram has replaced the seer.

serpent-maidens: fabulous creatures belonging to myths and fairy tales. *Nagas* and their females, *naginis*, are important snake-spirits or genii in Hindu mythology. They dwell in rich underwater palaces and guard aquatic treasures. In the context of the poem 'The Boy', the suggestion is more of creatures from children's fairy tales than of full-blown mythological figures. The maidens the boy imagines will be of the order of supernatural princesses. They may be half-human, half-serpentine, and will naturally be ambivalent in nature – alluring but dangerous.

Shachi: the wife of Indra.

shaddock: also known as the pomelo or pompelmoose, a small tree bearing fragrant blossoms and fruit resembling the grapefruit, but much larger in size. The English name *shaddock* is derived from the name of a Capt. Shaddock who is supposed to have introduced the fruit to the West Indies. The Bengali name, *batabi lebu*, i.e., citrus of Batavia, indicates that the fruit was probably brought to Bengal from the East Indies. Its botanical name in most old sources is *Citrus decumana*, L., Rutaceae. I understand that its current name is – very appropriately – *Citrus maxima*.

Shahana Ragini: the mood of this nocturnal *raga* would be more serious than that of Sindhu Kafi, suggesting love mixed with a sense of pathos.

shajina: a small tree bearing panicles of sweet-smelling flowers that develop into pendulous seed-pods. Leaves, flowers, and pods are all edible. Its current Latin name is *Moringa oleifera*, Lamk., Moringaceae. Not so long ago it was known as *Moringa pterygosperma*, Gaertn. f., Moringaceae.

shanai: a wind instrument which may be called the Indian oboe, often played at weddings and other celebrations.

Shaon: a soft version of the month-name *Srabon* (q.v.).

Shipra: a river flowing by Ujjain (q.v.).

shirish: a large deciduous tree with a broad crown, topped with spreading limbs, bearing fragrant flowers which are white with green-tipped filaments, the *Albizzia lebbek*, Benth., Mimosaceae. In the winter months the pods hang from completely leafless branches.

shishu: a large deciduous tree yielding valuable timber, the *Dalbergia sissoo*, Roxb., Fabaceae. Its withered flowers hang from the branches for a long time and the dry seed-pods rustle characteristically in the wind.

shiuli: the sweet scent of the flowers of this small deciduous tree, the *Nyctanthes arbor-tristis*, L., Oleaceae, is associated in the Bengali mind with the post-rains season and the Puja holidays. The star-shaped white flowers with orange tubes blossom at night and in the morning can be seen carpeting the ground beneath. Shiuli flowers are a perfect emblem of the transience of beauty. The orange stalks yield a dye.

Shiva: the third deity of the Hindu trinity of gods and one of the most important gods of Hinduism, with many roles and aspects. He is the Destroyer, the Supreme Ascetic and meditative Yogi with matted locks, as well as the consort of the Hindu Mother Goddess (variously known as Parvati, Durga, Kali etc.). He is often worshipped in the form of a phallic symbol, and many Westerners will be familiar with bronze statuettes of this god depicted as the Cosmic Dancer. The trident is one of his war-weapons.

shulpo greens: or *shulfa*, from *shatapushpa*, should probably be identified with an umbelliferous annual plant valued medicinally and cultivated for its seeds, *Anethum sowa*, the aromatic leaves of which are used in pickles and chutneys, but the term could also refer to what is called wild shulfa, *Fumaria indica*, Pugsley, Fumariaceae (S. Bhattacharya, *Chiranjib Banowshadhi*, vol. 3, Ananda, Calcutta, 1978).

Sindhu Kafi: the mood of this nocturnal *raga* would be a little light-hearted, with suggestions of nostalgia and romantic pain.

sitar: Hardly needing any introduction to Western readers nowadays, this stringed instrument is descended from the vina. It is possible that there was some Persian influence on its development. The name itself is of Persian origin (*setar*).

Srabon: the fourth month of the Bengali calendar and the second month of the rainy season, mid-July to mid-August.

Sumeru: often identified with various trans-Himalayan mountains or highlands, but effectively a fabulous mountain which could be called the Olympus of Hindu mythology. Zimmer explains it as the central peak of the world, the main pin or vertical axis of the universe (Zimmer, op. cit. Notes section, p. 52). As a modern geographical term, the name refers to the North Pole, and in many contemporary Bengali compound words it is the equivalent of 'arctic'.

tamal: the one thing that is certain about this tree is that it has a dark bark, whence its name, and Tagore's references to it are usually to evoke a scene and a mood, echoic, reminiscent of Kalidasa. Should we identify it with the *Xanthochymus pictorius* of Monier-Williams's *Sanskrit-English Dictionary*, or is it perhaps the *Diospyros tomentosa*, Roxb., Ebenaceae, as has also been suggested?

tamarind: the *Tamarindus indica*, L., Caesalpiniaceae, a large beautiful tree with a dense round crown of feathery foliage, valued for its timber and acid fruit. The English name *tamarind* is of Arabic origin meaning 'the date of India'. The Bengali name *tentul* is of Sanskrit origin. The tamarind is not famous for its flowers, yet its racemes of fragrant pale yellow flowers streaked with red are lovely. The flowers develop into brown pods inside which the seeds are embedded in the soft brown acid pulp which is widely used in cookery, not only in India but also in the preparation of certain well-known bottled relishes in the British market, such as HP sauce and Worcestershire sauce.

Tamasa: Geographically, there are several rivers in India bearing this name. What matters is that on the border of one of these the poet Valmiki (q.v.) is said to have uttered his first lines of poetry.

Taxila: or Takshashila, an ancient and powerful city of the Punjab, the site of which is now in Pakistan.

Terai: The word *torai* in Bengali primarily means any damp land at the base of a mountain. In the context of geography it can also refer specifically to the belt of marshy and jungly land lying between the Himalayan foothills and the plains. Because of the absence of capitalisation in the Bengali script there is nothing except the context to indicate the precise meaning. In poem no. 27 of *Shesh Saptak* both meanings would fit the context. I have chosen to translate it as I have for the sake of convenience. The name 'Terai' has been used in English in the context of geographical descriptions for two centuries.

tuberose: the *Polianthes tuberosa*, L., Amaryllidaceae, a small plant growing from a tuberous root, with very fragrant white funnel-shaped flowers that shed their fragrance at night (hence the Bengali name *rajanigandha*, 'night-fragrant').

Ujjain: properly Ujjayini, now in the state of Madhya Pradesh, has been an important city from very ancient times and is also one of the sacred cities of India. It was specially meaningful to Tagore because of its association with Kalidasa, who describes it in his *Meghaduta*.

Urbashi: a celestial nymph and dancer at Indra's court, whose advances to the hero Arjun were rejected by him.

Valmiki: the supposed author of the Sanskrit epic *Ramayana*. The *Ramayana* itself relates how Valmiki, after bathing in the Tamasa, was wandering in the bordering woods when a hunter shot dead the male of a pair of mating birds. The female began to lament the death of her partner. Profoundly upset and moved, Valmiki uttered a curse on the hunter. Having done so, he was astonished at what he had done and slowly realised that he had uttered two lines in formal metre. In Indian tradition this is the birth of poetry, of genuinely human poetical composition, as different from verses which are divine revelations. In poem no. 3 of *Shesh Saptak*, the shaddock tree's astonishment at its own self-renewal is compared to Valmiki's primal astonishment at his own poetic creation.

vetiver: the roots of a fragrant grass, the *Andropogon muricatus*, Retz., Gramineae, which are made into mattings or screens called tatties and placed in door and window openings during hot dry weather, where they are kept constantly wet so that the air indoors becomes cool and aromatised. This grass seems to have a host of other Latin names. The current one could well be *Vetiveria zizanioides*: I saw it in a recent issue of the *New Scientist*. The word *vetiver* is ultimately from Tamil and came to English through French. The Bengali word, *khaskhas* (Anglo-Indian *cuscus*), is of Persian origin.

vina: Described to me by a practising Indian musician as 'the mother-instrument of the Indian stringed instruments', the vina belongs to the lute family and is still used. It has a very sweet tone and usually has two resonating gourds, one at each end.

water-lily: refers to a tropical variety, Bengali *nal*, most probably the *Nymphaea nouchali*, Burm. f., Nymphaeaceae.

Ketaki Kushari Dyson was born in Calcutta in 1940 and studied English literature at Calcutta and Oxford, obtaining firsts from both universities. She also holds a doctorate from Oxford. She settled in Britain after her marriage to an Englishman, but did not give up writing in her first language and her links with the literary life of her native Bengal. She writes in both Bengali and English and belongs to that small minority of poets who write poetry in two languages. Poet, novelist, playwright, essayist, translator, scholar, and critic, and well-known for her skill in mixing the genres, she is the author of more than thirty titles in her two languages, including ten full-length poetry collections, and is regarded as an outstanding Bengali writer of her generation. She received the Bhubanmohini Dasi Medal of the University of Calcutta for eminent contribution to contemporary Bengali letters (1986), the Ananda Award twice (in 1986, and again in 1997 in conjunction with a co-author), and in 2009 was felicitated by the TV channel Star Ananda for being the Best Bengali of the Year in Literature. She led an interdisciplinary research project on the effects of Tagore's protanopic colour vision on his writings and visual art, leading to a major scholarly publication (Dyson, Adhikary et al., *Ronger Rabindranath*, Ananda, Calcutta, 1997).

Her English publications include two acclaimed scholarly books, *A Various Universe: A Study of the Journals and Memoirs of British Men and Women in the Indian Subcontinent, 1765-1856* (Oxford University Press, Delhi, 1978, second edition 2002, Oxford India paperbacks, 2006), and *In Your Blossoming Flower-Garden: Rabindranath Tagore and Victoria Ocampo* (Sahitya Akademi, Delhi, 1988, reprinted 1996). Her *Selected Poems of Buddhadeva Bose* was published by Oxford University Press, Delhi, in 2003. Her edition *I Won't Let You Go: Selected Poems* by Rabindranath Tagore was first published by Bloodaxe Books in 1991 and reissued in an expanded second edition in 2010, and is a Poetry Book Society Recommended Translation.

She was for a period a Research Associate at Oxford's Centre for Cross-Cultural Research on Women, for which she co-edited *Bilingual Women: Anthropological Approaches to Second-Language Use* (Berg, Oxford/Providence, 1994).

For a full list of her published books, visit her website at: http://www.virgiliolibro.com/kkd

320